Best wishes

Jim Bremner

FLYING FREE

Jim Bremner

Bloomington, IN   Milton Keynes, UK

AuthorHouse™
1663 Liberty Drive, Suite 200
Bloomington, IN 47403
www.authorhouse.com
Phone: 1-800-839-8640

AuthorHouse™ *UK Ltd.*
500 Avebury Boulevard
Central Milton Keynes, MK9 2BE
www.authorhouse.co.uk
Phone: 08001974150

© 2007 Jim Bremner. All rights reserved.

No part of this book may be reproduced, stored in a retrieval system, or transmitted by any means without the written permission of the author.

First published by AuthorHouse 8/6/2007

ISBN: 978-1-4259-9855-4 (sc)
ISBN: 978-1-4259-9856-1 (hc)

Printed in the United States of America
Bloomington, Indiana

This book is printed on acid-free paper.

Foreword

"I remember one particular day when the trench floor was just a mess of thick, clinging mud but we'd laid our trench capes on top of the mud and along with the rest of our kit, we were lying in the sun. It was the first day in a week when it hadn't rained and it was an opportunity for all of us to try to dry everything. The sky, a clear cloudless blue, was magnificent and the silence was intense. Suddenly three pigeons, liberated by one of our officers, flew along the trench. Desperately the birds flapped their wings and tried to gain height. Enviously all of us in the trenches watched those pigeons. Unlike us, they were free. As they gained height and climbed into the sky, to all the troops, they were symbols of freedom and hope. Two of the birds, still trying to gain height, veered to the left and circled. The third bird veered right and sped off behind our lines. All of us, including the Germans, cheered. We all knew that fastened to the birds' legs was a message giving the co-ordinates of the German big guns. It didn't matter to any of us, the front line troops on both sides didn't care; we were so well dug in that even the big guns couldn't get at us.

The German snipers were slow. Like us, they must have been enjoying the sunshine but then shots rang out. The two pigeons still circling turned into balls of feathers and fell back to earth behind the enemy lines. The third bird, now just a dot in the sky, flew on and we all cheered. How we wished that, like that bird, we could fly back to our homes and our waiting families. That one bird had what you must look for in a good racing pigeon. It was capable of thinking for itself, it didn't follow the others, and it knew where it was going and went for it."

Chapter One

No one knew where Blanco came from. One day, unannounced, he arrived on the gardens and started to build his loft. No one objected no one could. The gardens were for public use and the council owned the land. Anyone, providing they paid a small rent to the council, could occupy a garden area, build a loft and keep pigeons.

The garden areas had been created on the site of the old Banwell quarry. The site looked out over the valley of the River Tyne and provided spectacular views up and down the river. Previously the quarry had been used as a rubbish tip then when it was full of rubbish; it had been covered with cinders from the local, coal-burning, power station. Finally, to landscape and flatten the area it had been topped off with topsoil. The finished area was unfit for building houses on but was good enough for allotments and pigeon lofts. Individual, smaller garden areas had been marked out and to make them secure they had been sectioned off and enclosed with high wooden fences.

Anyone renting a garden and building a loft did not have to join the pigeon club. However, if they wished to race their pigeons, club membership was necessary. The club organised and ran the pigeon races and managed the gardens. The lofts and their owners were strongly independent but friendly, sporting rivalry existed between them. When a person joined the club, automatically, they became a member of the Homing Union. The Great Britain Homing Union was the governing body of all pigeon racing in Great Britain. No pigeon could be entered into a race unless it was wearing an official union metal ring. In addition, the details on the metal ring should have been registered in the name of the person owning the bird. All the pigeon fanciers with lofts on the Banwell site were members of the club.

In nineteen eighteen, when the garden areas were created, the council had split the whole site into two definite areas. The bottom half, with a gate leading off Elwick Road, was allocated for allotments and was to be used only for growing vegetables and flowers. The top half with a gate leading off the West Road was specifically for the pigeon fanciers and their lofts. The two areas had been positively divided by one high, unbroken, wooden fence, which ran right across the site, and there was no way through it. This barrier had proved inconvenient for the pigeon men who lived off Elwick road and for the gardeners who lived off the West Road. However, one weekend, mysteriously, a gate had appeared in the fence. The gate had been installed in a very professional way and it was obvious that whoever had done the job must have been a qualified joiner. No one complained and no one told the council, both parties on the gardens were happy with the two access routes.

At this time, my granda was one of the founder members of the Banwell Pigeon Club. On returning from France and the trenches of the First World War, he had built one of the first lofts on the reclaimed tip. As he was a qualified joiner, it had not been a difficult task and the loft had taken shape constructed with tongued and grooved floor boarding. This type of wooden flooring was being used in most of the quality houses being built in the Newcastle area and granda was working on them. My granda was an honest man so I never thought that the wood was stolen. Years later, he told me that most of the wood was off-cuts and I am sure he must have had permission to remove it.

Over the following years, the original loft had changed very little. In nineteen fifty, assisted by my father, granda had extended the loft and added a young bird section. Despite the loft's age the original wooden structure was still sound and in very good condition. This was due mainly to granda's original building skills and his regular maintenance. Every year, religiously, following the racing season the wooden exterior received a coat of paint. Then the interior walls were scraped clean, disinfected, and a coat of whitewash was applied. As dampness encouraged parasites and germs, the floors in the loft were never scrubbed or washed. Granda always said that the dreaded canker germ, and other parasites, made their homes in the wooden floors and used them as launching pads to attack the birds. The thought of some dreadful worm like creatures living in the floors of the loft waiting and planning their attacks on the birds always horrified me. At least once a day we scraped clean the floors and sprinkled sharp sand on them. Sometimes we added slaked lime, this granda said, killed all known parasites. However, I can still remember a time when he really thought we had the canker germ living in the floors and, panicking, he spent the entire day scorching the wooden floors with a paraffin blowlamp.

Blanco's arrival created a lot of interest. Of course, Blanco was not the stranger's real name; shortly after his arrival, he was given the nickname. The first day he was on the gardens someone noticed he had one good eye and one false eye. Most of the other pigeon men were domino players and instantly, and rather unkindly, they christened him 'One Blank.' Of course, Blanco knew none of this. However, the most unusual, striking thing about him was his appearance. His unusual clothing did nothing at all to inspire confidence in his ability to build a loft. He was dressed in a long raincoat fully buttoned to the neck, and underneath he wore white trousers. On his feet, he wore white sandshoes. The sandshoes were immaculately clean and white and it was obvious that every night he must have cleaned them. His clothes created great humour amongst the other pigeon men. The ex soldiers amongst them, who in the past, had used the phrase 'blanco' to clean the white parts of their uniforms swore that he was 'blancoing' his sandshoes.

"Something to do with Spain," Mattie Walker had explained.

Once the other men heard this, the name 'One Blank' was changed to 'Blanco'. However, apart from his clothing Blanco was still an impressive figure. He was over six feet tall, which automatically gained him some respect. Whenever he was within hearing distance, his height served to deter the garden comedians from cracking jokes about him.

When Blanco arrived, it wasn't only his appearance that created a lot of interest and humour. He started building his loft using old scraps of wood, which he had obviously found lying on the local rubbish dump or around the gardens. His actual building skills left a lot to be desired and his pieces of wood were assembled in a most haphazard way. His endeavours created a lot of smug humour amongst the other loft owners. Most of the other lofts on the gardens had been built using old flooring timber or old wooden doors. However, whatever material had been used the owners had worked hard to maintain a certain professional standard of workmanship. All of the lofts had been built to roughly the same basic design, rectangular wooden boxes with wooden dowelling at the windows and sloping roofs. In addition built out in front, there was always a wooden platform or gantry. However, despite their similarity they had all been painted and customised to give each one its own individual identity. Some club members had even painted slogans on the front doors of their lofts. The one I remember, mainly because it shocked me was 'FLY OR DIE'. This was painted in dripping red paint, which looked like blood, on the two front doors of Roger Black's loft. Roger or 'Rat Face' as everyone called him was a weasel of a man and I being only nine years old was frightened of him.

On his arrival and during his building work Blanco appeared oblivious to the men's discussions and jokes about him. Quietly and contentedly, he started and continued with his loft building work. He used old nails that he had collected and, using his one and only hammer, straightened out. Everyone knew he wasn't English; his accent gave it away and only added to the other men's amusement. Someone said they recognised the accent and he was from Russia or maybe Poland or even Spain. Blanco did not encourage conversation so, very quickly; everyone grew bored and left him alone. No one thought to ask him where he was from or to offer him help.

It was nineteen fifty-six when Blanco arrived on the gardens and for a number of weeks, with great interest, my grandfather Sammy Baker watched his building endeavours. Then, I think, mostly out of sympathy and a desire to retain a certain professional standard of workmanship on the gardens he stepped in to help. At first Blanco, appearing to be a very independent person flatly refused his help. Whether this was through lack of trust or just stubbornness was difficult to decide. However, professional pride would not allow my granda, now a foreman joiner, to stand by and allow a ram-shackled pigeon loft to be built on his beloved gardens. First, in an attempted to gain Blanco's confidence, he left a half-full bag of nails outside the gate to Blanco's garden. The next day he left a stack of long, floor boarding off-cuts leaning against the fence. For three days, the nails and the wood remained there untouched. None of the other pigeon men dared to touch the gifts. They all knew and respected my granda. They all knew that the small man with the moustache had a terrible temper and if pushed could also use his fists.

For three days, the nails and the wood remained untouched outside Blanco's loft then they disappeared. However, even with these new materials, Blanco continued to build his loft in his own chaotic way. It was blatantly obvious to everyone on the gardens that during the first decent storm his work would be demolished. Eventually, granda, unable to accept the frustration of seeing Blanco waste his time, stepped in. The council storage yard was just along Elwick Road not far from the gardens. Granda knew the foreman and for five shillings, he agreed to leave the gate open. One Saturday afternoon, after work, my granda, my uncle and my father raided the council yard and along with any old pieces of wood they could find, they took all the old doors that were waiting to be burned.

They made three journeys to the council yard and each time they carried their haul back to the gardens. There they stacked everything outside Blanco's garden and then granda raided his own shed. This wooden shed standing at the bottom of our pigeon garden, for us children, was an Aladdin's cave. However, we were forbidden to play in it. Granda stored wood and fittings in the shed. He told us it was all unwanted, and left over items, from the many jobs he had worked on. On the few occasions when he left the shed door open and we managed to sneak inside, the drawers full of hinges, screws, and nails fascinated us.

Sometimes when we were inside the wind would blow and worryingly, the roof trusses would groan with the weight of the long planks of wood stored up there.

When granda opened his shed and actually gave away, some of his treasured wood, it was a real sign that he was frustrated by Blanco's efforts. Nevertheless, on that Saturday afternoon when they returned from the council yard, the three men set to work and knocked down Blanco's pieces of wood. They worked hard all afternoon then, using granda's wood, they created a framework for a properly constructed pigeon loft. Their efforts did not go unnoticed and very shortly, standing on the small hill in front of the pigeon lofts, a crowd of curious pigeon fanciers gathered. Over many years, the dumping of pigeon droppings had created the small hill. This waste had been scraped, from all of the lofts on the gardens. It was the unofficial club dumping area and really was just a manure heap. Every day the pigeon men scraped and cleaned the floors of their lofts. Then they spread dry sand on the floor, this absorbed any water from the droppings and made it easier to scrape and pick up. The sand also acted to cut down the risk of parasites. Of course, all this cleaning generated a large amount of pigeon muck, which was difficult to dispose of and the hill had provided the answer.

The hill, whilst not the healthiest place to stand did provide an elevated position enabling the spectators to look over the fence into Blanco's garden. They joked and made comments but even this did not deter the three men from their endeavours. By seven o'clock that night small brick pillars, cemented into the ground, supported a sturdy wooden frame. The old doors lay stacked alongside the framework ready to be nailed or screwed into position, and the whole structure stood magnificently in the fading daylight. By the time they had finished the spectators had long gone. The draw of the local pub and the creeping cold of night had thinned their interest. They had all left shaking their heads saying,

"Nee one helped me build my loft, Sammy Baker's going soft. That Blanco's conning him, he's getting a loft built for nothing."

Sammy Baker was my granda and he wasn't going soft. For some reason Blanco's efforts had touched him. The man's independence and hard work had impressed him. Sammy Baker was the same type of man, strongly independent and determined. On the gardens, the Blanco story became a legend and I heard it many times over the following years.

Being only nine years old and much more interested in trying to ride my father's old bike I, of course, was oblivious to all of these happenings. My world was very safe. I had good parents who never argued and I idolised my grandparents. Sammy my granda could do no wrong and when I was with him, I felt secure and safe. The gardens to me were a place of safety, enjoyment, excitement and adventure. I knew every member of the club; most of them were friendly and they knew me. I felt part of something I felt important and secure. The Baker family were respected, not only for their building abilities but also for their knowledge of pigeons. I was happy just going to the gardens, watching the pigeons and being part of it.

Of all the days of the week Sunday morning was the busiest time for the pigeon fanciers. Everyone opened their lofts and allowed their pigeons to fly and exercise. The club had a happy feeling. There were thirty members and whilst some lofts won more races than others did, the racing was fairly even. Probably throughout the racing season, from one or other of the race points, every loft had a bird in the first three places. Of course, every one of the members was an expert, or thought they were, and this created some friendly, competitive banter. Success really depended on commitment, experience and knowledge of the birds. We were one of the lofts that did win more races than the others did. However, the competition was always fair and the races were looked upon as good, friendly sport. At the end of the season, the prize money was shared out quite evenly across the club.

It was early February when granda built the framework for Blanco's loft and the rest of the pigeon men were getting ready to pair up their birds to start their breeding programmes. The Sunday morning after granda had built the framework, all the club members watched eagerly as Blanco walked up the path leading from Elwick road to the gardens. As he approached his garden, he must have seen the new framework but he showed no signs of emotion. Slowly he inspected the new structure and, to test its stability and strength, he shook it. Then seeming satisfied he set to work nailing the doors onto the framework. Someone shouted over.

"Very canny Blanco eh?"

Blanco never answered he just continued nailing the doors to the frame.

Granda did not look for thanks and in a funny way, I think he respected Blanco even more for not showing any emotion. That Sunday morning passed very slowly. The pigeon men exercised their birds, cleaned out their lofts then fed and watered the birds. In-between all of these tasks they chatted and commented on each other's pigeons. Blanco, unconcerned, continued covering the framework only stopping at lunchtime to eat a sandwich.

Sunday lunch in the Baker household was an institution. On the menu was roast beef, Yorkshire pudding, mashed and roast potatoes and vegetables. Thick, rich gravy always topped off the meal and at two o'clock, the whole family met at my grandparent's house to enjoy it. As usual granda, looking forward to his Sunday dinner and having fed his birds and locked up his loft was heading home. As he passed Blanco's garden a hand touched him on the shoulder. Granda would never have told Blanco that he had built the framework; he hadn't done it for praise. He told me years later that he had only wanted things to be done properly.

It was Blanco's hand that stopped him and, "thank you Mister Baker," was all Blanco said.

Then he held out his hand towards granda. Granda said nothing, just nodded and shook the offered hand, that Sunday afternoon a new friendship was formed. Over the next few days, the friendship developed until Blanco, now fully assisted by granda, finished his pigeon loft. Over the next months, that friendship flourished and developed even further.

Chapter Two

My contact with Blanco was very limited; I only visited the pigeon gardens at weekends and Blanco whilst interesting me also frightened me. His size, silence, raincoat and pot eye made him a very fascinating but frightening figure. His sandshoes and raincoat amused me but his ability to produce a penny from behind my ear really annoyed me. It was clever but childish and I was too old for that type of thing. Nevertheless, he was very quick and I could never see where the penny came from, or went to.

When Blanco finished building his loft, the next item on his agenda was to stock it. Granda was reluctant to give or sell to anyone, any of his pigeons, including Blanco. He had bred and developed his own stock of pigeons and they all originated from his own controlled bloodstock. He had worked hard for over thirty years breeding the birds. He had watched them fly then paired together only the very best fastest pigeons to create his own unique bloodstream. To sell or give away birds meant racing against your own bloodstock. However, Blanco appeared to have no money and my granda had a big heart. For two days he and my father studied the birds and the breeding records then, eventually, they decided which birds they could safely give away. Finally and reluctantly, they caught and placed in a basket two old blue hen birds, an old blue chequered cock bird and a blue cock bird.

I watched them catch these pigeons and longed to be able to handle the pigeons the way they did. Quietly they cornered the bird they wanted to catch. Then when they were ready quickly, a hand would shoot out and the bird was caught. Gently they cupped the bird between their hands then transferred it to one hand with the bird's feet between their fingers. They smoothed out the breast feathers and felt the bird's breastbone. They spread out the wing and tail feathers and counted each feather. From this, they could tell how far the bird was through the moult and how healthy it was. They opened the bird's beak and stared down its throat into its crop. They knew every bird and when they had finished inspecting the feathers, they held the birds up and looked deep in to their eyes. There were many theories for judging the fitness and health of pigeons. My granda had read many books but relied upon the eye method. He could tell many things about the health of a bird by just looking at the iris or the rings in its eyes and even the eye colouring was important. During these inspections, the birds were not frightened and did not struggle; in fact, they seemed to enjoy the individual attention. The four birds they had decided to give to Blanco were old and probably only had a couple of good breeding seasons left in them. They had won nothing and were not part of granda's favourite, elite racing team.

Blanco had actually started to stock his loft and had some pigeons, skemmies. No one knew where he had got them from. They had no rings and probably someone had caught them on the church roof and sold them to Blanco. These skemmies were feral pigeons, rats with wings some of the fanciers called them. They carried pests and disease and were far removed from the thoroughbred racing birds, which lived in our loft. Everyone knew that on the first occasion when Blanco let them out they would return to the church clock and the small amount of money he had paid for them would be wasted. Blanco was delighted when granda gave him our birds. However, granda insisted that he must keep our birds separated from his skemmies. One day after granda had given him our birds; Blanco surprised everyone when he arrived on the gardens with six ringed pigeons in reasonable condition. Four of the pigeons looked good and we thought they would make two good breeding pairs. All four of the pigeons were blue in colour. A whisper went round the gardens that they were 'Belgium Blues.' For some reason the Belgium breeders seemed to be breeding exceptionally good racing pigeons and predominantly the colour of their birds were blue. Belgium Blues were only talked about in whispers they were the new mystical racing pigeons. Anyone selling eggs from Belgium Blues was sought after and could make quite a profit.

"Belgium Blues," granda laughed when some of the members whispered the secret to him. "Where do you think Blanco would get the money to travel to Belgium and buy four pigeons?" he said.

The other two pigeons a cock and a hen bird were white fantails. These pigeons, bred mainly to provide decorative birds for gardens or parks, were useless for racing. They could hardly fly and just managed to flutter around on the front gantry of Blanco's loft. This caused great humour on the gardens.

"Blanco thinks this is bloody Buckingham Palace, those birds lower the tone on the gardens," one of the members complained to granda.

Granda smiled and replied.

"There are no rules about what types of pigeons are bred on the gardens."

However, later back at his house I heard him and my father having a good laugh about the birds.

"Belgium blues, fantails whatever next," he chuckled.

Granda, my father and I were the only fanciers allowed into Blanco's loft, so no one could check the ring numbers on his six new pigeons. Consequently no one knew where they'd come from. I didn't visit Blanco's loft very often, only on the odd occasion when my father or granda were visiting him would I accompany them. It was on one of these visits that I noticed Blanco's hands. I was in his garden and was watching him handle the two-fantail pigeons. His hands were soft and clean, his fingernails were white and filed and he handled the birds expertly. As he held the birds, he talked to them, not in English but in a soft, quiet, soothing voice. The birds responded by laying still and quiet in his hands. When, to allow them to fly back to their perches, he opened his hands they were reluctant to leave and still lay, as if hypnotized, in his palms. My father and granda's hands were hard and calloused; their nails bitten down and dirty. They handled their birds expertly but when they opened their hands, the birds immediately flew off flapping their wings. The confidence and trust that the birds obviously had in Blanco was impressive.

The pigeon club had thirty members and granda was the secretary of the club, a job that he took very seriously. The club had combine with another twenty clubs in the Newcastle area to create the Federation, and granda was also secretary of the Federation. The Federation organised the races and the transportation of the birds, belonging to members of its clubs, to the various race points. Granda kept all the race records, organised the races, prizes and maintained all the paperwork for the club members. He was a man with great integrity and would never discuss a member's details with anyone else. The lack of information about Blanco and his birds frustrated many of the members and regularly they pumped granda for information. The club was like a family and men met, talked, and got to know each other. Blanco was the misfit, the mystery man; he never mixed or talked unnecessarily to anyone. The only garden he visited was granda's and even here he spoke very little and never discussed his job or his family. However, the unusual friendship that had sprung up between the two men appeared to be creating jealously on the gardens and other members were beginning to murmur behind granda's back.

A number of the pigeon club members were out of work and were always short of money. Quite often, these men on the strength of their season's winnings would try to borrow money from granda. However, granda would never oblige by paying out. He always said that before the end of the racing season he definitely would not pay out any prize money. All prizes and prize money were presented at the presentation night. This event was held in November, it was a big occasion for granda and at the Co-op dance hall in Newcastle, he organised a special presentation function. It was his night and it was the only time when he used his position as secretary to his advantage. He always invited a local councillor to present the prizes and before the presentations, he always sat next to him or her at the dinner table. All members were encouraged to bring their families to the function and a number did. However, most of the members turned up just to collect their money and they would sit patiently throughout the meal and the speeches waiting for the prizes to be presented. Prizes for the races were usually cups or plaques always accompanied by a certificate. These certificates were usually placed in the lofts or sheds of the members in prominent positions.

The cups and certificates were sought after and treasured, but the real prize was the money. The prize money was accrued over the year by collecting member's subs, selling number draw cards, raffles and sponsorship. Each member had to buy a certain amount of the number draw cards and each member had his own regular customers. The cards were sold all over the west end of Newcastle. The weekly prizes of five and three pounds with half-crown spot prizes created quite an interest in the area. Granda also encouraged local companies to sponsor races. 'Bradford's' the local corn merchants sponsored a couple of races. They also presented a cup and gave a donation to the club. In return, most of the members bought their corn and other needs from them. Small donations came from other local businesses and usually these businesses benefited in other ways from the members. The local pub 'The Magpie' sponsored a race and also gave a donation.

All of the members worked hard during the year collecting money. Surprisingly, probably because granda knew how much each member had to collect each week there was no dishonesty. Of course, each member knew that the more there was in the club funds, the bigger the prize money would be. The first three birds in each race received prize money. However, when the fancier entered his bird into a race he would also place a bet on it, or nominate it. These nominations were for three pennies, sixpence, one shilling and a halfcrown. A winning bird, if nominated, would win all the money in that particular pool of money. Fanciers would normally nominate all their birds in the three-penny pool then they would be very selective about the bigger nominations. The system worked well and it was unusual for a member to nominate a bird in all pools unless, of course, he was sure it was going to win. The system tended to share out the nomination money across the gardens. This was a good thing, as most of the men did not have a lot of money to spend. All of this money along with the prize money was held until the presentation night. Overall, the prize money was good and a member with two or three wins with his pigeons nominated could expect a reasonably large pay out.

For our family the presentation night was a big night and my granny, father, mother, uncle and aunty were all expected to attend. However, granda's policy of not subbing members before the presentation night did create friction. Members would come to him and say they needed the extra money for their families. Granda was no fool and he knew that if he did sub the men the money would be wasted on drink and the presentation night often proved him right. On the night as soon as the members received their envelopes containing their prize money the beer would flow, men would pay off debts and lend other men money. Many of them would buy Sammy Baker a whisky and respectfully place it on the table in front of him.

"Good season Sammy, great night," they would say.

These were the same men who, during the year, had referred to granda as 'that mean old buggar'.

"They all have short memories," granda would say as he sipped at his collection of whiskeys.

Quite often, by closing time, on the presentation night some of the members would have managed to spend all of their prize money.

One man who was constantly asking for a sub was rat faced Roger. Roger Black really was a weasel of a man and actually did have a face like a rat. His nickname had come very easily and openly everyone called him Rat Face. It always surprised me that he never seemed to mind. He was the only member of the club I disliked and I tried to avoid him. One Saturday afternoon, a few days after Blanco had brought his new pigeons onto the gardens Rat Face caught me. I had just opened the main gate to get into the gardens and Rat Face was just about to leave the gardens when he grabbed me and pinned me against the fence. I was carrying sandwiches from my granny for granda and I had seen Rat Face coming down the path and, as usual, I tried to ignore him. However, just as I was passing through the gate he grabbed me by the shoulders and pushed me hard against the fence.

"Where's Blanco getting them pigeons from?" he snarled into my face.

He smelt strongly of beer and sweat and I was terrified. I panicked and kicked out and fortunately, my foot connected with Rat Face's shin; he jumped back and released his grip on me. I turned and raced off grasping the sandwiches and shaking. It was the first time I had ever been threatened on the gardens and the whole experience was new and frightening.

Granda met me at the gate to his garden.
"What's wrong son?" he said putting his arm around me.
"Nothing," I replied trying to stop shaking.
I had decided not to tell granda about my encounter with Rat Face, I knew he would go looking for him and probably a fight would ensue.
"I slipped in the mud at the gate," I said.
My excuse satisfied granda and he took his sandwiches. My father was cleaning out the loft and later, as they ate the sandwiches, I listened as they talked.
"Don't take it to heart dad," I heard father say, "Rat Face is always skint and he's been drinking. If you had subbed him he'd have pissed it against the wall by tonight."
I knew what he meant and it was obvious to me that granda had just refused Rat Face a sub. Obviously when he had met me, he'd been looking for someone to take his frustration out on and I had been the handiest person. However, his reference to Blanco's pigeons troubled me and I wondered why he wanted to know where Blanco had got his stock pigeons from. The Rat Face incident stayed in my mind and I avoided him as much as possible.

Having finished his loft and obtained some pigeons, Blanco along with all the other club members started his breeding programme. He paired the birds together and because they were still not trained to return to his loft, he kept them locked in. He had taken my granda's advice and got rid of the unrung skemmy pigeons. A number of the pigeon fanciers on the gardens killed, cooked and ate the pigeons that they did not want and I think Blanco did the same with the skemmies. Our family could never bring ourselves to eat our pigeons. I think we grew too close to them, or perhaps because my father and granda were in work we could afford other meats. When, because of old age or injury we had to kill a bird we would ask another club member to kill it. Blanco quickly slipped into this role of exterminator. He had an ability to pick up a pigeon and with one movement of his thumb kill it. Quite often you didn't realise the deed had been done until the motionless bird was hanging from his hand. On the few occasions when Blanco did kill pigeons for us, he always took the dead pigeons away. We never asked him what he did with them but we all knew that they would be part of his evening meal.

Springtime was always an exciting time. Everyone had paired their pigeons up for breeding and the eggs were hatching. New life and hope was being introduced onto the gardens. Most of the breeding pairs produced two eggs and usually, they successfully reared two young pigeons. If extra eggs were laid then granda would control the numbers by removing these eggs. Occasionally if one of his best hens laid three eggs, he would allow a nest of three young birds to be raised. However, we were always aware of the strength it took out of the parent birds in raising these 'youngins'. We were always aware that these were racing pigeons, not pets, and we had to prepare the parent birds for the forthcoming racing season. This control of numbers ensured that the parent birds could cope with feeding and looking after the youngins. It also ensured that the young birds were always well raised. I loved to watch as the young birds, inside the eggs, started to chip their way out. At first a small hole chipped in the eggshell would appear. Then slowly the hole would be enlarged until eventually the shell split and the young bird, exhausted, would make its first appearance into the world. When this happened, the featherless, naked, blue-eyed pieces of skin with huge beaks that emerged from the eggs fascinated and horrified me. When they waved their flaps of skin, which very soon would become their wings, they looked like miniature space creatures. Their beaks, which were as big as their heads, were always open, and constantly they looked for food. Previously, in the nest pans, the parent birds had built a rough nest with pieces of straw and now they took it in turns to sit on it and cover the young birds. They would feed the youngsters by regurgitating their food into their crops. Then they would open their beaks and the young birds would stick their beaks and heads down into the crop of the parent bird. A bizarre pumping ritual would then begin, it frightened me; the young birds always appeared to be choking the parent birds.

As soon as possible, usually after three or four days the ritual of ringing the birds would be carried out. Granda as secretary of the club would issue all club members with the small metal rings. The identification rings had been sent, to granda, from the Homing Union. They kept the records of each ring number so that any bird that had strayed, or got lost and was found could be traced back to its owner. No fancier could race or show a bird, which had been given or sold to him, unless the ring number had been transferred to his name in the records of the union. When the rings had been installed on the young pigeons' legs, granda would visit all the lofts, on the gardens, and record the ring numbers. This early ringing was the only time when the young bird's feet were small enough to allow the metal rings to be pushed over them and onto their legs. Any later and the birds feet, mainly the rear toe or claw, would be too well developed to allow the ring to be fitted. Without these rings the pigeons could not compete in any of the races, so all members should have taken the process very seriously. Really, there was no need for granda to visit the lofts; he already had a record of all the ring numbers. However, traditionally he would go around all the club members' lofts just to see how the young birds were developing. The club members did not object, granda was a trusted person and on these visits, he didn't just note the ring numbers, he also gave out advice and passed on any news. I think the members always enjoyed his visit. Pigeon fanciers are very proud of their birds and granda did have a wealth of knowledge and experience and was always willing to pass this on. I think they looked forward to this private, free, confidential consultation.

In our loft, ringing was a sacred ritual. Granda would slowly push his hand under the parent birds and ease them off the nest pans. The parent birds, in a vain attempt to protect their youngsters, would respond by flapping their wings. This wasn't just a random flapping; it was aimed blows at granda's hand. However, this never put him off and he would talk soothingly to the birds.

"Now then don't be silly, I'm not going to hurt them," he'd say.

When he withdrew his hand, it would always emerge from the nest pan gently cradling a now fluffy, plump youngster. I would watch fascinated as he eased the ring onto the young pigeon's leg. He would straighten the three main claws and push the ring over them. Then he would press the rear claw back, straight in line with the bird's leg. This to me looked terribly painful, but granda always assured me that the bird's feet weren't fully developed and they could not feel it. I was never quite convinced.

During this ritual, my father holding the pigeon ledger in his hands would stand beside granda. Granda would call out the number on the ring and dad would enter the number alongside the records of the pair of parent pigeons. It was difficult at this early age to sex and give a positive description of the colouring of the young pigeons. Later when their feathers had developed and granda could sex the youngsters he would go back through the records and update them.

At the beginning of the breeding season, the pairing of the pigeons was not a hitty-missy affair. A number of the breeding pairs had been together for years. These birds had, previously, produced good, fast, fit youngsters and were used as stock birds. Other pairings were experimental, an attempt to improve the quality of the bloodstock and the quality of the birds. Through the ledger, granda could trace the family trees of all his pigeons. He was immensely proud of his records and in his selection of pairings; he would try to avoid all types of in breeding. The young bird ringing was always a landmark in the life of the loft and there was always a feeling of great satisfaction when it was completed.

"A good kit of youngins," granda would say proudly and my father would nod in agreement.

Occasionally one of the club members would leave the ringing too late. Granda would get annoyed with these men because they always came to him pleading for him to do something. My granda's knowledge of pigeons was extensive and, carrying a jar of Vaseline, he would go along to their loft. He would cover the young pigeon's leg with Vaseline then gently he would force the ring onto the bird's leg. His concern was always for the bird and usually, without damaging the pigeon's rear claw; he would succeed in getting the ring onto the leg. He did this because he knew that if he didn't help the pigeon was useless to its owner. Moreover, if the owner tried to ring the bird himself he'd either damage the bird's leg or dislocate the bird's rear claw.

Over the following days, the little birds' body fluff disappeared and they developed feather quills, then feathers would appear. The nest pans would now be brimming with balls of feathered, opened beaked, squealing, young birds and lots and lots and lots of droppings. Continuously the young birds squealed for food and as soon as they had been fed, they ejected it from their rear ends. Now the parent birds, sitting on the nest pans, had to spread their wings to completely cover the youngsters. Next, the young birds would start to explore, they'd escape from the nest pans and take over the nest boxes. Relentlessly they would demand food and would virtually attack their parents whenever they returned to the nest boxes. Moreover, as fast, as the food went in to the youngins, it came out of the other end and the boxes were always full of piles of droppings and now required cleaning twice a day. It was always a busy and exciting time for the pigeon men. It was a time of new life and new hope. However, it was also a time of worry and hard work. These young birds were new pigeons expected to fly for the honour of the loft and everyone hoped that this year they had bred the best, the channel bird, or the sprint bird that would be a winner.

Chapter Three

Thanks to granda, Blanco was able to start breeding his pigeons at the same time as the other pigeon fanciers. Together they had finished one section of the loft and granda had lent him nest pans and helped him build breeding boxes. If a fancier wanted to race his young birds on the year of their birth, it was important that he started breeding as soon as possible. However, he had to be careful not to start breeding too early. Frost and cold could seriously damage the young pigeons or overstretch the parent birds. The condition of the parent birds was also always under scrutiny. They had to be fit enough to start racing in April and they needed sufficient recovery time from feeding their youngins to recover for their races. Granda always tried to work on pairing the birds sixty days before the first old bird race. This he said gave them plenty time to produce healthy youngins and for the parent birds to recover for the racing season.

Blanco had four breeding pairs, the two pairs of pigeons from granda and the two other blue pairs, which we now knew had come from Scotland. We had noticed that granda was unusually keen to help Blanco with his ringing. He had even bought a new exercise book and given it to

Blanco to enable him to start recording his breeding records. Standing in Blanco's loft, he'd shown him how we recorded all the numbers and details of our parent birds. Then to start him off he'd set out and filled in the details for the pairs of birds we had given him. His eagerness was explained when Blanco read out the ring numbers of the other parent birds.

"Scotsmen Blanco?" granda had asked casually as he had recorded the parent birds ring numbers.

"Yes," Blanco had replied "I a got a them off one of the lorry drivers from work."

This was granda's opportunity and he'd jumped at it.

"Where do you work?" he'd asked nonchalantly.

"It's a Spillers Flour Mill," Blanco had replied.

So there it was no real mystery, Blanco worked at the big flourmill on the banks of the river Tyne. It had never been a secret just no one had asked him. I think granda was quite relieved at having found out where Blanco worked. Legitimate employment, in granda's opinion, made him an honest person and granda liked things to be straightforward. One night during tea at my granny's I remember him talking to my father and saying.

"See Blanco's a flour grader, I knew he was alright. The white trousers and sandshoes, they're all part of his working overalls nothing unusual about them."

Because of the relief in his voice, I remembered the conversation; it meant that his new friend was genuine. I also remember my father saying that it explained where Blanco had got his unrung pigeons; the flourmill was absolutely covered in skemmies

There were unwritten rules on the gardens and one was you did not ask questions about a man's private life. As long as he obeyed the rules of the gardens, and the club, he was accepted. Everyone knew that there were wife beaters, drunks, rogues and many good, hard working men enjoying keeping pigeons on the gardens. However, as long as no bad habits were brought onto the gardens everyone was accepted. In addition, there was an unwritten but accepted hierarchy in the club and granda through his knowledge, honesty and willingness to help anyone was at the head of it. Nearly every member had a nickname and granda's was The Colonel.

He knew it but did not respond to it, nor did any of us ever refer to him by that name and the men on the gardens never called him Colonel to his face. However, deep down I think he was quite proud of the name and the kind of status it gave to him. The men certainly respected him and I think the respect came from his honesty and the work he did for the club. As secretary of the club, he kept all the records and because of his willingness, he collected the men's subs and the money from the numbers draw. The treasurer Pincher Martin never objected and he would take the money off granda and put it into the bank.

The pigeon-racing season always commenced mid April and continued until the second or third Saturday in September. The race points had been established over the years. In the early days on Saturday mornings, friendly stationmasters had agreed to take the baskets of pigeons off the trains and at a set time liberate the birds. Of course, this system still left the club with the problem of getting the pigeons to the railway station, bicycles, handcarts and any other mode of transport had been used. The club had progressed from using the rail system and had combined with the other clubs in the Newcastle area to create the Federation. This joining together of the clubs had enabled them to buy lorry transporters. Now these vehicles full of baskets of pigeons, and accompanied by official conveyors, drove to the race points on a Friday night and liberated the birds on the Saturday morning. The Banwell club always raced from the South of England to the North.

For the old birds the Federation organised ten or eleven races from within England and from France, four our five races across the channel. Then for the young birds, eight or nine races were organised from within England. The young birds were birds hatched during the current year and for the first race, they would only be three or four months old. The old bird races commenced with a race from a distance of about sixty miles. The distances then gradually increased during the season until the channel races. These channel races were usually from distances varying from about four to five hundred and fifty miles from the lofts.

Similarly, the young birds commenced racing from a distance of about sixty miles, which was steadily increased over the weeks to a distance of about two hundred miles. All of the races to the Banwell club were from the same direction, which was known as the South-East-Route. The winners of all the races were the pigeons that flew at the greatest speed or as the pigeon men called it the highest velocity. Of course, each loft located on the gardens and lofts at other clubs were different distances from the actual race points. The distances involved, on the gardens, were not great but yards mattered and to overcome this anomaly each loft had been carefully pinpointed on an ordnance survey map and the map then sent off to the National Homing Union Headquarters. There the Union determined the longitude and latitude of each loft and calculated the exact distance from the race point to the loft. This exactness enabled them to calculate the velocities at which the birds, returning from a race, had flown. The racing season for the old birds started mid April and as the first race drew near the levels of interest and enthusiasm, amongst the members, greatly increased. Every member hoped that this season he would be a winner.

This time of year was also the time that heralded the start of the silly season for the young birds. After 18 days, they had all developed feathers and this enabled them to flap around and eventually flutter around the loft. After 21 days, they had been weaned from their parents and could pick up corn, feed and look after themselves. At this point, the young birds were separated from their parents and transferred into the young bird section of the loft. Granda then started their training. He would put them into baskets and place the baskets on top of his woodshed at the bottom of the garden. The shed was directly in front of the loft and for two days there they stayed just looking at the loft. This was supposed to familiarise them with the look of the loft and hopefully on their first flights they would identify it as their home. However, like all youngsters they were always headstrong and when eventually they were allowed to fly free from the loft, they would fly for hours. We tried to start training the young birds to fly from the loft on a quiet day when they would not team up with other young pigeons from other lofts. Quietly we'd open the loft doors and gently encourage the young birds out onto the gantry. Then by placing corn on the roof of the shed, we would encourage them to fly from the gantry to the roof. Then, once again using corn, we would encourage them to fly back to the gantry. Slowly they would feel their wings and eventually they'd take off and circle the loft. Then patiently we'd rattle the corn tin and try to coax the birds back to the loft.

The first flight of these young birds was a remarkable sight. The birds, as yet, had not co-ordinated the use of their wings and their tail feathers and chaotically they dived and swooped around the gardens. It was always a trying time and quite often all over the gardens young birds would drop into other fancier's lofts. However, after a few days the birds could identify their lofts and they would respond to granda's calling and drop onto our gantry. During this training time our garden gate was always locked shut. Someone entering the garden could easily have scared the birds and if this happened, they would be shocked and reluctant to return. We would then have to spend hours trying to coax them back or go round other lofts collecting them. After a week, the young birds had mastered the use of their wings and developed confidence in their flying. At this stage they would fly for hours, quite often they would be that high in the sky that they were just dots. Occasionally they would join up with other birds from the gardens and, worryingly for us, disappear for hours. However, apart from this it was a pleasure to behold the birds enjoying life and flying free.

When the young birds were removed from their parents, the old birds were allowed to mate and pair up again. However, this time the eggs were not allowed to hatch or if they did the youngsters weren't allowed to survive. Usually the eggs were removed and replaced with pot eggs, which the birds accepted. Alternatively, the original eggs were left out in the cold night air stopping the growth of any chicks inside. During the early races, a round of eggs or youngsters might well be used as an incentive for the parent birds to return to the loft as quickly as possible.

To create an incentive for the pigeons to return home quickly the pigeon men, although they would not admit to it, experimented with different types of methods. Jealousy, widowhood and young bird removal were all words and methods used but only spoken about in hushed voices. Just as they would not discuss what they were feeding the pigeons, no one would admit to using incentives. These things were secret. Once the racing season started, no one could enter a fancier's loft without an invitation and usually these weren't forthcoming. An invitation into a loft during the racing season was looked upon as a privilege and a compliment. If for some reason you were lucky enough to receive an invitation, then during your visit, you noted everything. I think it was expected of you. The lay out of the nesting boxes, whether the cock and hen birds were separated, the location of the young birds and whether the hens were sitting eggs all of these things could be used to create an incentive for the birds to return home. The loft owner would expect you to be interested and would have removed anything he didn't want you to see.

Leading up to the first race granda had 'pipe openers' for the pigeons, this was his name for his training flights or 'chucks'. He was now a foreman joiner with a local building firm and knew all the lorry drivers. Granda didn't smoke but a packet of cigarettes would change hands between him and a driver. For this, the driver would collect a basket of pigeons from the garden and put them on his lorry. Then starting a short distance from the loft ten, fifteen-miles the driver would release the birds and they would fly home. These training flights would be repeated time and time again, the distance from the loft increasing on each occasion. These were always exciting times. Granda would be up at six o'clock in the morning to clean the loft and to catch and basket the birds. During his lunch break, he would rush back to the loft to check which birds had returned and what condition they were in. Then at five o'clock, after work, he would return to exercise, feed and water the birds then clean out the loft.

The management and organisation on the gardens was very thorough and I thought very democratic. However, every man was expected to contribute to the running of the club. Committees had been established for everything, race basketing committee, clock committee, garden committee and the actual committee for the running of the club. Blanco's ability to handle pigeons had not gone unnoticed by granda, and before the racing season started Blanco's name appeared on the notice board as a nomination for the basketing committee. Granda proposed him so no one voted against him. The basketing committee's responsibilities were quite simple. On the Friday night before each race, each club member brought their pigeons in their own baskets to the clubhouse. There they handed in their baskets with a note of their nominations and their fees. Dixie Dean, the chairman of the club and the basketing committee, recorded their nominations in the ledger, collected the money and passed it onto Pincher Martin who was the treasurer of the club. The basketing committee members removed the pigeons from the baskets, recorded the ring numbers, placed a rubber race ring on the pigeon's leg and placed the pigeons into larger club race baskets. Cocks and hen birds were placed in separate race baskets then the baskets were sealed. The next time these baskets would be opened would be at the start of the race. No members were allowed to race basket their own birds. All the birds were precious to their owners, an ability to handle the birds gently and confidently was necessary, and Blanco fitted the bill admirably.

Whilst all of the members of the club were men, one woman was prominent on the gardens. Beryl Morris was the wife of one of the older members. Jack Morris owned and ran a furniture shop in Newcastle and he didn't have much time to look after his birds. Beryl was younger than he was and dressed more as a teenager and, whilst her husband was registered as the club member, Beryl ran the loft. Granda frowned upon her but being a gentleman he always treated her with respect. The other club members loved her. They would drool as Beryl with her hair backcombed into a beehive, wearing her tight skirt and top, balancing on her high-heeled shoes swayed down the garden path carrying a basket full of pigeons. Usually she didn't have to carry her basket far as someone always stopped her and carried it for her. Beryl could get anything done for nothing. Most of the gardens had small vegetable plots in front of the lofts and if Beryl needed vegetables, she just had to ask. If at any time, her vegetable plot needed attention a number of men would volunteer to give her a hand.

I remember when Beryl once asked my father to refit the loft doors for her and he captured me to labour for him. Why he volunteered to do the job I'll never know but I remember that I was sworn to secrecy. My granda never knew, my mother was never told and the half-crown I received for my toil ensured my silence. When the doors were fitted I do remember his haste to get tidied up, then he pushed me out of the garden and told me to go home. His abruptness hurt me especially as I had laboured hard; I had held the doors in place, whilst he refitted the hinges. That night at home, as I watched our black and white television he was very quiet and I knew he was watching me. Little did I know that, that day would come back to haunt the whole of my family. In later years, my suspicions about that day would be aroused but at that time, I respected my father and could never have contemplated him doing anything that would have upset my mother. However, after that day, Beryl always had a special word for me and I did find the smell of her perfume and the way she chewed her gum very attractive.

Chapter Four

That first year, because he'd bred off his old birds and was just starting to loft train them, Blanco didn't compete in any of the old bird races. Because he had paired the birds up and put them straight down on eggs, he'd kept the old birds locked in the loft. He had not had time to train the old pigeons to return to his loft and his racing hopes were on his young birds. On old bird race days, when we were racing, Blanco would come to our loft and watch the birds returning home. On these race days, it was difficult to know who was the most excited granda or Blanco. The first race of the season was from Selby, which was about ninety miles from Newcastle. It was a short race and usually all the pigeons returned very quickly.

Selby was a good sprint race and granda had some fine sprint pigeons. He knew all of his pigeons and their capabilities and he knew when they were fit to race. He kept records of when they were paired together so that none of his hen pigeons ever went to a race when they were due to lay eggs. He would be disgusted when the race baskets were returned from the transporters and eggs had been laid.

"Bloody amateurs, don't even know when their birds are egg bound," he'd mumble in disgust.

The pigeons did the flying. However, when they returned home it was up to the loft keeper to trap the bird, remove the rubber race ring from its leg and place the ring into a small metal thimble. The thimble was then put into the timing clock, the handle on the side of the clock was pushed down or 'struck', and the time was recorded. Confidence in trapping the bird and clocking it in was most important on these short races. Normally a number of birds would return to the gardens together and the speed at which they were clocked in could decide the winner of a race. Clocks were treasured possessions and were probably the most expensive items in the lofts.

On the Friday nights before the races, the clock committee would collect all the clocks. Then just before six o'clock, they would assemble, in the living room, at granda's house. The club paid money towards granda's telephone bill and at six o'clock; he'd ring 'Tim'.

"On the third stoke it will be six o'clock precisely." The monotonous, recorded voice would say through the Bakelite earpiece of the telephone and granda would count it down. Really the counting was unnecessary as the solid pips could be heard in the hushed room. At this point even my grandmother stopped fussing and stood perfectly still. I remember being in the room and holding my breath just in case, someone missed granda's instructions.

"One, two, three, go," granda would count down in time with the pips.

On his signal "go," the six-man committee would all press down on the striking levers of the clocks and the room would be filled with the solid clunk of the levers. The lever, drove a needle through a circular paper disc fitted inside the clock and punctured the disc. The disc was graduated with the time and the puncture mark indicated whether the clock was running fast, slow or on time. As soon as the first six had been struck, the second six would be struck then the third and in under a minute all the clocks would have been struck. Each of the clocks was then checked to confirm that they were still running and were on time then they would be sealed. Occasionally one clock would have stopped or broken down. If the clock committee couldn't get it going it was a disaster for the owner; it was now up to him to arrange to clock in on someone else's clock. Of course, this would slow down the procedure when their pigeon arrived home and other men were not keen to have someone else using their clock. Granda had two clocks and always struck his second clock as a reserve. He had saved many a club member by lending him the clock.

My grandmother enjoyed the Friday night clock committee. She would fuss around giving the men cups of tea and biscuits, granda would say,
"For goodness sake woman get out of the way, you'll spill tea on the clocks."
This never deterred her; Friday night clock checks were her times to catch up on any gossip. Discreetly as she handed out tea, she pumped the men for information on their wives and families. On Sunday when the whole family assembled for Sunday lunch, she would pass on the information to my mother and my auntie. Usually, looking at my brother and me and lowering her voice, she would say,
"She's expecting again you know. Got seven already, he doesn't work, where's the money coming from, I don't know. I don't even think she knows what's causing it."
It was a Sunday afternoon ritual and the three women would go through all of the news as the three men fell asleep in front of the fire.

I will always remember that sunny Saturday afternoon of the first Selby race in nineteen fifty-six. I believe it was on that day that the bad feelings on the gardens started. When the pigeons were due home, I was always banished to the small shed at the side of the garden well out of sight of any returning pigeons. The shed faced South East and enjoyed a good view down the Tyne Valley and, when I looked out through the shed window, I could see any returning birds. At that time, the rules of the club did not stop anyone letting their pigeons out on a race day. However, the unwritten rule was that only a few pigeons would be allowed out on the gantries at the front of the lofts. Granda had three old pigeons, his favourites, which he allowed to parade around on the gantry. These were the elders of the loft and granda's pets. They would sit on his shoulder or his trilby hat and take corn out of his mouth. The two cock birds, fanning their tails and blowing up their crops, would rant around on the gantry, trying hard to impress the old hen bird. She would ignore them but if she ever squatted down for one of the cocks to tread her granda would jump off his bench seat.

"Dirty beggars," he'd mumble as he kicked out at them.

He never hit them and quite often, I think they did it just to upset him.

This race was the first occasion when Blanco joined me in the shed and the two of us stood staring out of the window. Blanco was too tall for the shed, and to gain a clear view he had to stoop. As he leaned forward to look out of the window, he placed his arm around my shoulders. His touch made me freeze and I shrugged him off. I didn't look at him and he didn't look at me but thankfully, he removed his arm. The shed had always been my domain, my sanctuary, and a place of safety. Occasionally my brother shared it with me but usually I had it to myself. Now I felt confused and vulnerable. Had Blanco just been trying to be friendly? or was there something suspicious about his actions? One thing I did know was that in the future I would avoid being alone with him.

The lofts on the gardens were laid out in three rows, one behind another with ten lofts in each row. The path leading from the West Road ran down the east side of the gardens. We were in the front row, eight lofts from the east end of the gardens. Pincher Martin's loft was at the very east end of the front row and usually he was the first to spot any returning pigeons. Pincher Martin was also one of the founding members of the club. He'd flown pigeons on the gardens for over thirty years. His bloodstock was good and he had some fine racing pigeons. Usually Pincher had pigeons in the first ten from most of the races. Pincher also prided himself on being able to identify every pigeon on the gardens, and much to everyone's annoyance, on race days; he usually spotted the first returning birds. Irritatingly, he would call out the colour of the pigeon and to whom he thought it belonged. Usually he was right but his first sighting of the pigeon, and his identification, always seemed to take the edge off the fanciers identifying their own birds.

That Saturday afternoon as usual Pincher was the first to see the pigeon.

"One on its own, gannin like a train," he called out.

Suddenly everyone was alert; all eyes strained South East staring down the valley.

"Over the church," Pincher shouted.

All eyes now centred on the old church steeple. Sure enough, a small black speck had just passed the church and was fast approaching the gardens.

"Little blue hen, looks like Sammy's," Pincher continued.

The words were electric; Blanco and I pressed our noses against the shed window. Corn tin in hand granda jumped up onto the gantry and stared at the fast approaching pigeon then suddenly he burst into life.

"Aye it's the little blue hen," he said and called out "How-way pet, how-way."

Granda now moved along the gantry rattling the corn tin and kicked out at the droppers, causing them to flutter, to attract the little blue hen's attention.

"Two more over the church," Pincher was off again.

Granda never looked; his eyes were fixed on his little blue hen.

"How-way pet, come on, come on," he called.

The bird was now travelling along the front of the lofts. She had pulled her wings in tight to her body and it was obvious she was heading for our loft. She was four lofts away, granda, with a big smile on his face, was standing well clear of our loft doors just waiting for her to turn sharp right and shoot through the doors into the loft.

Rat Face's loft was also on the front row, three gardens down from ours, and just as the blue hen was approaching his loft the doors flew open and a full loft of pigeons were chased out. My granda standing on the gantry froze speechless, twenty or thirty pigeons flew out of Rat Face's loft and overwhelmed the blue hen. She veered off and, with the newly released pigeons, was forced to circle. Blanco glanced down at me it was obvious that he was confused and didn't know what was happening. I had a lump in my throat. I knew the two other returning race pigeons would now beat granda's hen and I glanced in his direction. His face had changed and the urgency had gone, now granda called out sympathetically to the bird.

"Come on pet, come on."

The blue hen circled twice with Rat Face's pigeons then she clapped her wings together and dropped straight into the loft. Granda followed her in, caught her, slipped off the rubber race ring, placed it in the metal thimble, placed the thimble in the clock and struck the clock. He worked in silence never saying a word. Blanco and I had now left the shed and watched as granda checked the clock. Still he never spoke; there was nothing to be said. Having checked that the blue hen was alright and the clock was running he closed the loft doors, locked them, and marched down the garden. Not knowing what he was going to do we followed. Outside the garden gate, granda turned left and marched along the path in front of the lofts and, silently, we followed him.

Everyone on the gardens had seen what had happened and the atmosphere was tense. Unusually for a race day, the gardens were now silent. Men, trying to see what was going on, strained their necks to look over their fences. Blanco and I didn't follow granda into Rat Face's garden. Granda pushed open the garden gate and entered. We stopped at the gate, held it open and watched as granda marched up the garden path. Rat Face stood defiantly on his gantry starring as granda approached him.

"Sorry Sammy never saw."

He never finished the sentence; my grandfather had climbed the two steps onto the gantry and now he hit him straight in the mouth. I had never seen adults fighting before and I had never seen such a punch; it was straight and carried all of granda's strength and fury. Rat Face crumpled and clutching his face fell down on to the gantry; I could see blood seeping through his fingers. Granda turned, climbed down from the gantry, and walked past us and out of the gate. He never spoke just marched down the path leading off the gardens and solemnly Blanco and I trailed behind him. At the gate to the gardens Blanco turned left and walked off along Elwick road. He never said anything; I turned right and followed my grandfather.

My grandparents lived very near the gardens probably about half a mile away and I followed my granda at a respectful distance. I knew he wanted to be on his own and besides I had nothing to say to him. I trailed behind him until we reached the house. Then when he opened the front door and went in to the kitchen, I slipped in behind him and went straight in to the living room. It was very unusual for us to return so soon on a race day.

"What's wrong? What's happened?" granny demanded.

Granda said nothing, just ignored her and passed through the kitchen making his way to the green house, which was at the bottom of the back garden.

"What's happened?" my grandmother demanded of me.

"Granda punched Rat Face," I stuttered.

"He did what? I've never heard anything like it, grown men acting like children," she said as she bustled out of the house towards the greenhouse.

I watched through the back window of the living room as my granny, now in the greenhouse, laid the law down to granda. I couldn't hear what was being said but could guess. As she spoke, she was wiping her hands on her pinny and he was slowly, unemotionally inspecting the tomato plants. It was obvious when my granny had had her say as she stood arms folded in front of her waiting for a response. She was disappointed granda, not saying a word, continued pricking out the suckers from the tomato plant stems. Eventually granny gave up and shaking her head returned to the kitchen. I grabbed the dog and its lead and hurried out of the front door. I knew that without a response from granda, she would be looking for someone to take it out on and I was the only other person in the house.

The old Yorkshire terrier didn't want to go for a walk and, to get clear of the house; I had to pull it along the street. My father had been working that Saturday afternoon and I knew as soon as he'd finished he would go to the pigeon garden. I, dragging 'Tiny' the Yorkshire terrier behind me, retraced my steps back to the entrance to the gardens. Dogs weren't allowed on the gardens so I stood at the gate and waited. I had decided to tell father what had happened, before the other pigeon men confronted him, so I waited until I saw him.

It was unusual for any of our family to be involved in a fight and my father listened intently to my story. He told me to wait at the gate and made his way onto the gardens. I sat on the kerb and waited; a couple of the pigeon men leaving the gardens ruffled my hair and made comments about the colonel's boxing second. I wasn't impressed and ignored them. Father eventually returned and we made our way back to my grandparent's house. Granda was in the living room sitting in his usual chair. Father ushered the dog and me into the kitchen granny was there. She said nothing just placed a glass of dandelion and burdock in front of me and we waited in silence for my father.

Later as we walked home, my father told me what had happened. He said he had re-opened the loft and let the rest of the birds, returning from the race, in. Then he'd taken the clock along to the clubhouse and the little blue hen would be third, Donkey Smith had won the race and Mattie Walker was second. In the clubhouse, Rat Face and a number of his cronies had confronted him. Rat Face's nose was still bleeding and I was pleased to hear that. However, he was demanding that my grandfather apologised to him or he was going to the police to report him for assault. He was also going to report granda to the Federation to try and get him banned from racing pigeons. I didn't really understand. I had never seen a real fight between two adults before and the one punch knockout had greatly impressed me. I thought my granda had done an excellent job of punching Rat Face. As for him wanting an apology, granda was secretary of the club and The Federation. He was well in with all the officials and to me he appeared to be untouchable. The situation didn't really worry me but father seemed concerned.

Chapter Five

During the following weekdays, I didn't go to the gardens and I knew nothing of the arguments that were taking place. On Friday nights, I usually spent my time cleaning and dubbening my football boots, getting them ready for the Saturday morning school game. Unusually that Friday night my father came home early from work and insisted that I accompany him to the gardens. He had been looking for my elder brother but he'd not yet returned from school. He was three years older than I was and I knew he was with some of the girls from his class. I couldn't see the attraction but not wanting to cause trouble pleaded ignorance as to his whereabouts.

As soon as father had finished his tea, we were off, he walking at a tremendous pace and me scurrying along behind him trying to keep up.
"Son all I want you to do is watch the loft, you call me if anyone comes near. Your granda and I have to go to a meeting."
He shouted the words over his shoulder as we raced along the West Road towards the gardens. I was delighted but slightly apprehensive. To be given such responsibility meant I was being accepted as an adult, it

was the first time that it had happened and it was unusual, it meant that something important was going on.

At the gardens, the atmosphere was different, groups of men stood on the corners of each row of lofts. Some groups nodded and waved at father. However, other groups turned their backs and deliberately ignored him. We had entered the gardens through the gate off the West Road and to get to our loft had to walk down past the clubhouse. Ten years earlier granda, helped by some of the other club members, had built the clubhouse and like everything else he had done he had made a good job of it. The clubhouse stood at the end of the second row of lofts on the other side of the path. Outside screwed to the wooden wall was the notice board. This was a fine wooden case with a glass front; it usually contained race results, scribbled messages for club members and details of missing pigeons. Tonight the case contained only one large notice. The notice was printed and I knew granda had printed it on his screen printer. The words were large and jumped out at me.

EXTRAORDINARY GENERAL MEETING
FRIDAY NIGHT 7 O'CLOCK
ALL MEMBERS MUST ATTEND.

```
Item 1    Selby race
Item 2.   Droppers.
```

It was signed in bold letters at the bottom by granda.

Sammy Baker
Secretary

I read it and felt quite proud. My father passed it without even glancing at it but I stopped to read it. Without even looking back, he shouted angrily at me,

"Come on."

The tone of his voice warned me not to hang about and I raced after him. For the first time on the gardens, I felt uncomfortable. The familiar easy feeling, I usually experienced, was gone and I was glad to reach the gate to our garden and the safety of our loft. A number of men were already in the garden and Blanco stood out amongst them. His size meant he towered above the others. He was the only one that acknowledged me and much to my annoyance, as if I was a child, he patted me on the head. Father's arrival was the signal for everyone to leave.

"Remember what I told you," he said.

He looked at me and I knew something serious was happening. It was the only thing he said to me then he turned and followed granda and the other men out through the gate.

I was left alone and suddenly I was quite afraid, it was a new sensation. Quickly I scrambled onto the loft gantry but the railings were too high and I couldn't see anything. I hung onto the railings and pulling myself up peered over the top. I was just in time to see the group of men led by my granda disappearing around the corner going towards the clubhouse. I could also hear raised voices as all the other members of the club converged on the clubhouse. Then it went quiet, it was obvious to me that they had all entered the clubhouse and the door had been shut. I lowered myself down from the railings back onto the gantry. The responsibility of being loft manager hung heavy on my shoulders and I searched around looking for anything untoward. However, everything seemed fine. Once again I pulled myself up the railings only this time I climbed onto the railings and then onto the roof of the loft. This was something I would never have down if granda or my father had been there.

From the roof of the loft, I had a clear view of all the gardens. I was amazed they were totally deserted. I looked up into the sky and once again was amazed, the sky was empty, not one pigeon was flying. This was unique; usually someone was training young birds or exercising old birds. However, tonight all the lofts were locked shut and the gardens were silent. Cautiously I climbed down from the roof and went to the garden gate; I opened it and peered outside. Except for clumps of overgrown grass, swaying in the breeze nothing was moving. The silence was deafening it was too much for me and curiosity took hold of me. Now curiosity had the better of me and I felt like one of the cowboys off the Saturday matinee. With my back to the fencing, I slid along the front of the gardens past all the lofts. At the end of the fencing on the front row, very slowly, I peered around the corner and looked up the path towards the clubhouse. It was deserted. Slowly, holding my breath and on my toes, I crept up the path to the clubhouse. As I approached, the sound of raised voices coming from inside the clubhouse grew louder. Amongst them, I could hear the familiar voice of granda.

"If you'll all shut up, I'll tell you what happened."

His voice was raised but positive and authoritative.

"Let the Colonel speak," I heard someone shout.

I was surprised that someone had actually used the nickname in granda's presence.

Now curiosity certainly had the better of me and I had to see what was happening. Silently I skirted around the wooden building. To pass under the windows of the clubhouse I had to bend over but eventually at the side, underneath one of the windows, I found a comfortable place to sit. I lowered myself onto the grass and pressed my ear against the wall. Silence had returned to the clubhouse and even through the wall I could feel the tension from within.

"Now I'm surprised and disappointed that any of you would ever think that I would deliberately punch another club member."

It was granda speaking and even though I couldn't see him I felt quite proud of him.

"I'm sure that on Saturday afternoon you all saw what happened," he continued, "Roger here chased his birds out just as my little blue hen was heading for the loft."

I had to think who Roger was then I realised that he was talking about Rat Face.

"Now, you'll all know the disappointment you feel when something like that happens. You all know that I would have won that race and the bird was fully nominated. There was a lot of money riding on that pigeon. However, I knew that Roger would never deliberately sabotage my pigeon."

"Crap," someone shouted.

"Now then, now then, there's no need for that type of language this is a civilised meeting," I heard granda reply and I listened intently as he continued.

"I knew Roger would never have deliberately chased his birds out." He stopped then slowly and deliberately granda repeated the statement.

"I knew Roger would never have deliberately chased his birds out," and once again the room was silent.

"So," he said raising his voice.

"I thought something must have happened to him, perhaps he'd had a bad turn. We all know Roger has been unable to work for years. We all know he cannot help any of us on the gardens because of his illnesses."

I could hear smug laughter and sniggers.

"So," he said again and I could visualise him pulling himself up erect and staring at each of the club members individually.

"I went round to his loft to check that he was alright."

The burst of laughter from within the clubhouse was deafening and I had to see what was happening. Slowly I raised myself up and peeped through the window. Sure enough standing on the small stage with a table in front of him, erect and stern was granda. He was staring at the members a number of whom where rocking back and forward laughing. Alongside granda sat Pincher Martin and the Chairman of the club Dixie Dean. Dixie was a very quiet man and he got on with everyone, he never disagreed with granda and now he sat in silence staring at the gathered club members. Dixie was also chairman and in charge of the basketing committee.

"Now then, now then," granda said, "this is a serious matter."

He stopped talking until silence had returned to the room then he continued.

"I went into Roger's garden and was delighted when I saw him coming out of his loft safe and sound. But, he did seem unsteady on his feet."

"Drunk," someone shouted.

"Here now let's be fair," said granda chastising the culprit, as he spoke his face never changed no smile just complete sincerity.

"As Roger came out of his loft I climbed onto the gantry to help him, it was then that I saw the wasp on his shoulder."

The room was silent everyone was listening enthralled by the story.

"Biggest wasp I've ever seen, I thought it must have stung poor old Roger and instinctively I went to brush it off."

He stopped talking and glanced around the room, finally he concentrated his gaze on Rat Face.

"Unfortunately Roger you must have moved your head and I caught you on the side of the face."

Once again, the room erupted, only this time it was a mixture of laughter and ridicule.

"You lying old buggar, you punched him," someone shouted.

"Not bloody hard enough," someone else responded.

Men stood up, chairs fell over, and two clear groups of men quickly formed. Granda never moved from the stage he stood erect watching them then, abruptly, he brought his fist down onto the table in front of him.

"Sit down and shut up," his voice was booming.

I watched as his words sunk in and amazingly the groups broke up and everyone re-took their seats. I was so proud that he was my grandfather his presence completely dominated the meeting. Then with his voice still raised, he spoke again.

"Now, I've told you what happened. I am sorry that you Roger think that I deliberately punched you. I would only have done that if you'd deliberately chased your pigeons out in front of my blue hen and I'm sure you wouldn't have done that."

He stood staring directly at Rat Face challenging him to say something. Rat Face hesitated obviously thinking about what granda had said then he mumbled,

"accepted."

"Next item," announced granda.

"Propose that only two droppers, per loft, be allowed out on a race day," shouted Pincher Martin.

"Seconded," shouted my father.

"For," asked granda.

Hands shot up around the room.

"Against," asked granda.

Some of the club members, mainly Rat Face's friends, were clearly confused and hesitantly they glanced around the room. It was obvious to me that they weren't prepared for this proposal and a few hands were slowly raised.

"Hang on," someone shouted.

"Proposal passed, as from tomorrow only two droppers are allowed on the gantries during a race day. Anyone having more than two droppers or letting birds out will be stopped from racing for a year. Meeting closed," said granda and sat down.

I watched as the room erupted, granda, my father, Pincher Martin, Dixie Dean, Blanco and a number of other men stood up and walk towards the door. Suddenly I realised my own predicament and raced away from the clubhouse. I only made the corner of the fence when I heard the clubhouse door opening and with it came the sound of raised voices.

"Sammy this hasn't been discussed," someone shouted.

I heard my granda's voice clear and proud.

"It's just been discussed, it was listed as an item on the agenda, and you never said anything, you've had a vote, that's it."

I had run back to the loft and was standing on the gantry when they returned. Their return to the loft was neither triumphant nor downcast.

"Any trouble son?" my father asked.

I just shook my head.

Chapter Six

That meeting was never discussed in front of me but I soon realised that after the meeting the gardens had changed forever. Two groups had been formed; fortunately, the largest number of members seemed to support granda. The others whilst not openly hostile withdrew their friendship and their attitudes became unhelpful and surly. That night after the meeting granda had tried to return the club to normal. The job of basketing the pigeons for the next day's race was late and he'd pushed Dixie to get the job done as quickly as possible. The clock committee had accompanied him down to his house and, at nine o'clock they'd struck the clocks. My granny, desperately trying to find out what had been going on, pumped all of the committee members for information but none of them had taken the bait. I had waited with my father until all the jobs had been completed and the pigeons were on the transporter and were safely on their way to Doncaster. This was the second race point of the season a distance of about 110 miles from the Banwell club.

That 1956 old bird season was an average-racing year for the Baker loft. We won two inland races and much to our delight one channel race. Huwey, a two-year-old pigeon, was one of granda's favourite birds. He had won two previous inland races from Ashford and Redford. Both of these were long distance races but this year he excelled and won the race from Lillers a distance of about 440 miles. Granda was a good judge of all his pigeons flying capabilities and having seen Huwey on his return, from Lillers, had decided not to send him any further. However, that season other people did really excel Pincher Martin did well winning a channel race and four inland races. Blanco didn't race during the old bird season. He hadn't stop at the first round of young birds but had continued breeding taking a second round of youngsters. He was still settling his old birds and was relying on them to produce good young birds. He had started with four breeding pairs and by the end of May had a young bird loft containing sixteen young birds. Of course, his second round of youngsters were too young for the first young bird races so he concentrated on his first eight youngins. Granda warned him that he'd lose them. Eight birds was a very small kit of flyers and granda told him really he should think to the future and the next breeding year when he could use the youngins for breeding stock. However, Blanco had the bit between his teeth; he was stung by the racing bug and wanted the excitement of racing his own birds.

Training youngins for the racing season was always a worrying time. The same procedure as for the old birds was adopted but, when the birds returned, granda always tried to be at the loft. It was important that the youngins were taught to drop as soon as they arrived home. If no one was there, the birds would fly for hours. The youngins were also very nervous and any movement in the loft or on the gantry could scare them into the sky. If this happened quite often, they'd join other flocks of young birds and be dragged miles away from the gardens. Young pigeons were always getting lost and the notice board was full of notes.

Red hen No 7654 lost Saturday. Pincher Martin
Blue cock No 8176 missing. Topper Brown.
Chequered hen with white tail No 8285 lost Sunday. Donkey Smith

The list was endless.

A large number of these missing young birds did turn up. Quite often, they would be attracted down into other fancier's lofts by their pigeons. Any outsider pigeons or 'strangers' as granda called them landing in our loft were always treated kindly. He always caught and personally returned the birds. Other club members were not as helpful they just chased the birds back into the sky. Some were attracted to the church tower and frustrated fanciers would watch their pigeons, their pride and joys, flying around with the skemmies. Others were reported lost from all over the North East of England. Some big-hearted youngster would find an exhausted bird in a field or on a street. They'd keep it in a box then they'd give the ring number to the police or to a local pigeon club. In turn, they would ring The Union who had all the records of the birds. They would inform granda, and he would inform the owner. Many of the members didn't want the expense of having the pigeons returned. If the bird was found outside the Newcastle area, quite often it meant it had to be returned in a box, on the train, and being informed of a found bird could turn into an expensive exercise. In addition, the fact that the bird had been kept elsewhere than in their own loft might have jeopardised their homing instinct. Moreover, men were reluctant to pay out large amounts of money to have birds returned that could prove to be unreliable. Granda always helped by asking the lorry drivers from work to pick up birds when they were out making deliveries. This was usually the best way to collect strays and only cost owners the price of a packet of cigarettes.

The Scottish pigeon clubs, like the North East clubs, always raced from South to North. Very often on Saturday afternoons, as we stood gazing into the sky, we'd see large flocks of birds flying through on their way back to their Scottish homes. Occasionally, on very hot days, exhausted Scottish birds would be looking for water and would drop into anyone's loft. This happened occasionally on the gardens and the birds would stop to drink from the water troughs. I always felt privileged when this happened in our garden. It amazed me to think that this bird was flying to Scotland and during its journey was using us as a watering hole. Granda never encouraged these pigeons. Feeding and watering them encouraged them to hang around and sometimes Scotsmen would stop for a drink and then try to stay for good. If this occurred, he would catch them and hold their heads under the water in the trough. The poor bird would fight frantically for its life but granda wouldn't stop, only when the bird was about to drown would he lift it out and throw it into the air. Believe me, very quickly, those pigeons had their homing instincts restored and left the gardens. However, their belief in Geordie hospitality must have been completely destroyed.

Surprisingly Blanco never lost one young bird. Some of the members said he was lucky but that wasn't true. Blanco was dedicated; he treated his young birds like children. He took no chances, he took his time familiarising the birds with the loft, then the gardens, then the area, then and only then did he allow them to fly with the other pigeons. His birds always looked fit and well. For him that 1956 young bird season was a great success and much to everyone's surprise, he won two races. Granda couldn't believe it and shaking his head he would stand on the gantry and watch Blanco's youngins flying.

"We've dropped in here son," he'd say under his breath. "That blue hen there she's off that old cock. That bird never flew for me but that youngins flying well for Blanco."

However, that year I believe the highlight for granda was not our wins or Blanco's successes. During one of the channel races an incident occurred, which I believe gave him as much satisfaction as actually winning the race. The channel races were the real tests of the racing season and to win one was a real achievement. In these races pigeons were no longer just racing for places in their clubs, the real prizes were for placings in the Federation. Lofts from every club in the North of England entered birds and the competition was intense. We had Huwey and some other good channel birds but, apart from Huwey's win, for some reason, that year, they were performing very poorly. Granda and father had discussed it and decided not to send Huwey. This race was the longest channel race, Huey had won once and they felt that was sufficient for the year.

Rat Face did have a good channel bird, it was his pride and joy and he only raced it in the longest channel races. That year the big race was from Le Bourget and it was the last old bird race of the season. No one on the gardens knew where Le Bourget was, sufficient to know it was in

France. Le Bourget race was proving to be a real highlight. Throughout the Federation of the Northern Clubs, some 4600 birds, being carried in 260 race baskets, were entered. Because of the time involved in collecting the baskets from different clubs, then transporting them to the airport the basketing of the race pigeons took place on a Thursday night. The Federation had organised a transporter plane to fly the baskets to an airfield at the race point and they would be liberated on the Saturday morning. The race was about 550 miles from Le Bourget to Newcastle and depending on the weather should have been completed on the Saturday. That year Rat face turned up at the clubhouse carrying his bird, a nice looking red hen, he was confident and swaggered down the path.

"Not entering Huwey?" he said cockily to granda as he pushed past him to get into the clubhouse.

"Not this time Roger, just giving him a rest, plenty more races to be won," replied granda.

We had entered two birds but granda wasn't hopeful for their success. Inside the clubhouse, Rat Face handed in his single bird. He'd nominate it with a halfcrown, one shilling, sixpence and thrupence to win, which proved he was confident. The nominating system for the pigeons always confused me, but I knew that a pigeon fully nominated, like Rat Face's, if it did win, would win all the 'nom' money and the prize money.

As a smaller number of birds were sent from the club to the channel races, basketing at the club, for these races didn't take long and usually the members finished up in the local pub. Granda never went to the pub but occasionally my father would go then report back to granda giving him all the news. That Thursday night as he came into granny's living room he said,

"Bloody Rat Face is full of it; he's shouting the odds in the bar. Because we didn't send Huwey, he reckons we've chickened out. He reckons that bird of his will walk the race."

Granda just smiled.

Rat Face did have good reason for his confidence. His red hen was good; it had won one previous channel race and been second in another. It was rumoured that he'd turned down an offer of one hundred pounds for the bird from a man in Leicester who was starting up a pigeon stud.

"Well he does have good reason to be confident," granda eventually replied, "that bird's done well in the past. However, channel races are hard son, a lot of things can happen to a bird. They reckon them Frenchmen are shooting the pigeons and eating them."

The thought of rows of Frenchmen, wearing berets, lined up with guns and shooting at our pigeons as they left the baskets suddenly appalled me.

"And," granda continued, "the weather across the channel can be bad. Saturday's forecast isn't the best, best bet, wait and see," he said.

Channel races were long and drawn out events. The excitement of seeing lots of birds arriving, racing home, wasn't there. The birds were liberated very early in the morning and usually they weren't due home until late in the afternoon. If for some reason the liberation was delayed then the birds would turn up on the Sunday morning. If this was the case, men with birds in the race had to get up early, usually at sunrise, just to ensure that they didn't miss their bird's return. Nothing was more disappointing for a fancier than to arrive at the gardens to find a race bird sitting on the loft waiting for him.

I remember that channel race very well. The birds were delayed; the weather in France was poor. A hold over, especially in a channel race, was always bad news. The pigeons would have to wait, confined in the race baskets, for another day and the race would drag over into Sunday or even Monday. The conveyors who travelled with the birds were very aware of this and if a break in the weather did occur they would, if possible, liberate the pigeons. It was early afternoon when the conveyors took that chance. They said the clouds cleared and for a brief period, the sun had shone. They'd opened the baskets and liberated the birds. Unfortunately, the pigeons must have flown straight into the bad weather and no pigeons from any of the clubs in the Federation returned home that night. We waited in the garden until the sun had gone and it was dark.

The next morning my father and I were up early and I remember the gorgeous blue sky as we hurried along the West Road towards the gardens. It was six o'clock when we arrived, we could see the time on the church clock and granda was already there.

"Anything?" father asked.

"Nothing yet son," granda replied.

I climbed onto the fence and looked around the gardens. A number of the lofts were open with their owners sitting in the early morning sunshine. I glanced at Rat Face's loft and sure enough, he was there. Further along the row of lofts I could see Pincher on his gantry scanning the sky.

"Check the clocks son," granda said to my father and he went into the loft, lifted the clock and inspecting the dial.

"Aye it's fine dad," he said, "where's the spare?"

"In the shed son," granda replied.

For some reason granda always called my father, my brother and me, son, and occasionally it did cause confusion. I watched the clock checking ritual with interest. The spare clock was always placed in my shed and now my father went in and checked it.

"Blanco's here, he's just feeding his youngins," granda said.

That spoilt my morning; I knew that when any pigeons arrived home Blanco would be sharing my shed.

Patiently we waited, the hands on the church clock moved slowly. Our two droppers played around on the gantry then took a bath in the large pot hand basin sunk into the grass. This basin had served as a bath for the pigeons as long as I could remember. Sometimes granda added potassium crystals.

"Acts as a disinfectant," he told me. "Kills all the mites," he'd said.

I was none the wiser I just knew that the purple colour fascinated me.

Suddenly Pincher's voice rang out.

"Here's one, high, highest I've ever seen them," he shouted.

We all craned our necks and stared in the direction of the Tyne Valley. Usually birds returning from the channel races flew directly North then West along the Tyne Valley.

"Going straight through, probably a Scotsman," someone shouted.

"No way, it's for the gardens," responded Pincher. He sounded quite upset that someone was questioning his opinion.

Although the sky was still perfectly clear and blue we still couldn't see the bird. Suddenly Blanco came running into the garden.

"Shed," granda said and Blanco and I like well-trained dogs complied.

Standing alongside Blanco I scoured the sky and far away, high over the valley I could see a small black speck.

"There, there it is," I shouted excitedly, "it's coming this way."

"Aye it's for the gardens," Pincher, determined to prove himself right, shouted.

As it approached the gardens, the black speck grew larger. It was high and it was difficult to see its colouring. The bird suddenly pulled its wings tight behind it and started to drop from the sky. I have seen many majestic sights but that morning seeing that bird returning from France and dropping like a stone, from the clear blue sky, astounded me. I knew Blanco had the same feeling as he whistled through his teeth.

"Its mine, it's mine," Rat Face started to shout.

My heart dropped, I so wanted that magnificent bird to be one of ours.

"Aye looks like Roger's red hen," Pincher called out.

For us the scare was over and Blanco and I left the shed. We climbed onto the gantry alongside granda to watch the bird complete its flight from France. The disappointment could be felt on the gardens; everyone knew that once the bird was timed in, it would take all the winnings. I watched enviously as the bird, still dropping like a stone, never strayed from its course towards Rat Face's loft. It definitely was Rat Face's and it streaked along the front row of lofts then turned straight into his loft. Rat Face charged in after it and slammed the loft doors.

I was disappointed and I climbed down from the gantry it was all over. The gardens were strangely silent and time seemed to stand still. I gazed into the sky in the direction from which Rat Face's pigeon had come, hoping that one of our birds would appear, but there was nothing there. All of a sudden there was a commotion, a door was slamming and someone was shouting.

"Shite, shite, shite."

I knew the voice but couldn't understand why he was swearing; after all he'd just won the race.

"My clocks stopped, my shitting clocks stopped."

It was Rat Face.

Suddenly everyone realised that the race wasn't over and a new feeling of optimism swept across the gardens.

"Sammy, Sammy I need your spare clock," Rat face shouted.

Granda never moved from his place on the gantry. We couldn't see Rat Face but we knew he would be charging along the front of the gardens towards our loft. No one spoke and the four of us standing in the garden, staring at the gate, waited for the inevitable entry of Rat Face. During a race, to stop anyone entering and scaring the pigeons, granda always locked the garden gate. I realised this and intrigued I glanced at him but he never move to unlock the gate and neither did we. Rat Face oblivious to the locked gate charged straight into it. The railings and the gate rocked as he slammed into the wooden gate.

"Shite," he screamed, "Sammy I need your spare clock, open the bloody gate."

Granda still didn't move.

"Who is it?" he asked.

We all turned and, in amazement, looked at him; we all knew who it was.

"Sammy it's me Roger, open the bloody gate I need your spare clock."

Slowly granda climbed down from the gantry and made his way towards the gate; on his way, he stopped to kick some pigeon droppings off the path.

"Sammy, Sammy what are you doing? I need the clock," Rat Face was panicking and screaming.

"Hold on Roger," said granda slowly withdrawing the bolt from the gate.

Rat Face nearly knocked my grandfather to the ground as he pushed the gate open.

"Your spare clock Sammy, where is it?" he pleaded.

I was making my way back towards the shed, to get the spare clock, when I heard my granda's reply.

"Sorry, Roger it's stopped, it's not working."

The small amount of colour in Rat Face's face slowly drained away.

"You lying shite, it's not stopped," he said.

Granda now stood directly in front of him and was stopping him from moving up the garden.

"It's stopped Roger; I've just checked it and it's just stopped. The boy there must have moved it when he came out of the shed, the dial must be stuck."

"You lying old bastard," Rat Face responded.

The gardens were silent, I don't know if the other members could hear what was happening but suddenly Pincher's voice rang out.

"Another bird, just as high and definitely for the gardens."

The two men, granda and Rat Face, stood facing each other and suddenly the urgency of the situation dawned on Rat Face.

"Please let me use your clock Sammy," he pleaded.

Granda still looking him straight in the eyes said, "this bird could be mine Roger, and, until I see whether I need it or not, I cannot allow you to touch my clock. Let's see who the bird is for, then if it's not for me I'll time your bird in on my clock."

I didn't know which way to look. I had glanced at the sky and seen the pigeon approaching the gardens but I was also fascinated with the stand off between the two men.

"It's mine, it's mine, it's for me," Pincher was screaming excitedly.

"Clock me in Sammy, it's Pincher's bird, please Sammy, come on Sammy, the birds not for you, I can still win, please clock me in," pleaded Rat Face.

Granda climbed onto the gantry and watched the fast, approaching pigeon. There was no doubt that the bird was heading for Pincher's loft.

"Could be our red cock," granda said, "what do you think son?"

Slowly my father climbed onto the gantry and watched as the pigeon landed in Pincher's loft. Now a totally dejected Rat Face followed him to the edge of the gantry.

"No dad, it's too light, I think it is Pincher's, clock Roger's bird in," father said.

Slowly granda took Rat Face's thimble containing the rubber race ring, which the pigeon had carried on its leg all the way from France, and went into the loft. After a few seconds there was a dull thud as he struck the clock.

"It's timed in Roger, you can relax," said granda as he came out of the loft.

For what seemed an eternity dumbstruck and seething Rat Face stood in the garden. He was obviously furious and struggling for words and we all stood and stared at him. Eventually my father went into the shed and returned with the spare clock.

"See here Roger," he said holding the clock out, "the dials stuck, it happens sometimes when it's moved."

Slowly Rat Face started to shake his head.

"You lying old bastard," he said pointing at granda. "You've just cost me the race and a lot of money."

"Here now, no swearing, look at the clock it's stopped," said my father holding the clock out towards him.

Rat Face grabbed the clock and stared at the motionless dial.

"See it's stopped," repeated father.

Rat Face shook the clock and for a moment I thought he was going to throw it to the ground but then, gently, he placed it on the path, slowly turned and left the garden. We all stood in silence watching as the gate swung and closed.

"Bloody shame," said granda, "that's a lovely pigeon it deserves better. Roger should have checked his clock first thing this morning just to see that it was working. Oh and by the way," he continued, "we'll have to get that spare clock serviced. It seems to be sticking a lot, it just takes one big shake and it stops. Still, Pincher will be happy I know his red hen bird was fully nominated."

Pincher won the Federation and his bird was fully nominated. Later that Sunday night granda and Harry Walker, from Westerhope, the president of the Federation met. They used The Unions pre-set tables to calculate the over-fly and under-fly times for all the clubs and the lofts.

Then they calculated the velocities of each bird and decided which was the fastest bird back to its loft. Pincher beat Rat Face by 30 seconds.

The other memorable event that occurred, on the gardens, that year was Beryl Morris had a baby. This did not particularly interest me but after Sunday dinner at my granny's, the news caused great consternation. The dog along with my brother and I were ushered out of the living room and into the front room. Here, unusually, the gas fire had been lit and we were told to stay there. However, my brother didn't like being told what to do and along with the dog, we crept back to the living room door and listened. With our ears pressed against the door we heard granny say,
"old Jack hasn't got it in him."
My mother and my aunty both laughed.
"Well she's definitely had it in her, I only hope it is Jack's," replied my aunty.
My brother laughed but I didn't see the joke.

Chapter Seven

The racing season finished in September and the gardens went quiet. Every day granda still went to the loft to water, clean out and feed the birds. Cleaning out the loft wasn't just a question of cleanliness it was also the time when granda inspected all the droppings. This was one of his ways of checking the health of all the birds. Sometimes as he raked the floor, he'd mutter to himself, "something dropping slime here."

Then he would inspect nest boxes and perches to find the pigeon that was dropping loose green slime. Once he'd found the bird he'd isolate it and treat it. This wasn't his only way of assessing the health of the birds. Regularly he'd catch them and inspect their wings and their body feathers. He was an expert and could quickly identify any bird that wasn't too well. As the end of the year drew nearer granda no longer let the pigeons fly every day, instead he exercised them once or twice a week.

At the bottom of his garden Blanco had built himself a shed. It was a haphazard effort but he was proud of it and inside his two certificates were now stuck proudly to the wall. Pigeon men never drew attention to their certificates but they always placed them in positions where it was impossible not to see them. Granda had his installed inside the loft, in a small side section, which was closed off from the main loft by a lattice door. It contained bags of feed, a first aid kit for the pigeons, and his certificates. They filled each wall and from within the loft they were impossible to miss.

This side section was a fascinating annexe to the loft. It was always slightly dusty and smelt of corn, beans and maize. Stacked on the floor, along the walls, were brown paper bags filled with different types of feed. Just inside the door was an old bread bin, which we used to hold the mixed feed. When the birds were racing, we fed them a mixture of tic beans, maize, maple peas and white peas. The mix was predominantly made up of beans with small amounts of the other ingredients added. The young birds when they were weaned and feeding for themselves received a richer mix made up of different mixes of wheat, maple peas, white peas, red dari, blue peas, white dari, safflor seed, tares, maize and mung beans. The names fascinated me they all sounded so exotic. How much of each ingredient was mixed with the beans was granda's secret. Every week he carefully mixed a large batch measuring out the ingredients then filled the bread bin. The corn tin, an old tea caddie with the lid removed, was then used to measure out the feed. Through years of use the paint on the sides of the tin, where granda held it, and where it scraped through the corn when it was being filled, had worn off. The tin was used for measuring the feed, and for rattling to attract the birds' attention, it was an antique but an integral part of our loft.

Screwed to the wall of the annexe was a cupboard in which there were boxes and bottles containing all types of interesting mixtures. These were granda's secret recipes and healing potions and I wasn't allowed to touch any of them. One night he accidentally locked a pigeon in the annexe. That night for some reason the lid had been left off the bread bin and the pigeon got into the bin and started eating. It must have eaten all night because the next morning, when we found it, its crop was crammed with beans and maize the poor bird could hardly breathe or walk.

"Some times these birds can be so greedy and stupid," granda said as he retrieved the bird from the corn bin.

I stood and marvelled at the size of the bird's crop. It had packed so many beans in that it looked like a massive, inflated swelling on the front of the bird. Granda let me touch the crop and it was as hard as concrete.

Through the tight skin of the crop, I could actually feel the shapes of the beans and the maize packed into the bird.

"I'll have to operate to save its life," granda said dramatically, "it's eaten that much its system will never digest that amount of corn."

I watched fascinated as granda took out his first aid kit and removed a brand new Gillette razor blade. Then he unfolded the blue paper and exposed the new silver blade. The pigeon had eaten so much that it could not fly and it just stood on the top of the bread bin, head cocked to one side, suspiciously watching him. Even when he picked the bird up and plucked feathers off its crop, it didn't resist. He held the bird tightly in one hand and with the other hand he took the Gillette blade and expertly slit open the bird's crop. I expected blood to fly everywhere but nothing happened. The corn was so tightly packed that any blood flow must have been stopped and long before he had finished the cut, the bird's crop was forcing itself open. I was amazed, the corn was that tightly packed it was pushing its way out of the crop. The corn had not been digested in any way and it popped out of the now open cut. Granda used his finger to pull the remaining beans and maize out of the bird's crop. Then having removed the corn, he returned to his first aid kit and removed a needle and thread.

The bird, with the release of pressure from its crop, now seemed relieved and was beginning to struggle. I didn't blame it, I would have struggled seeing granda approach me with a needle and thread in his hand. Anyway, slowly and methodically he pushed the needle through both sides of the skin of the crop and pulled the cut together. Then using the needle he tied a knot and snapped the thread between his teeth. He repeated the procedure five times finishing up with five neatly tied knots, which now effectively closed up the cut. Unlike other birds, when pain is inflicted upon them, pigeons don't squawk or make a noise but they do struggle and try to flap their wings to escape. However, that day that pigeon did neither. Either it trusted my granda, or the relief of having the corn removed from its crop was such that it accepted what was happening. Two weeks later, again, we caught the bird and using small scissors cut the thread then pulled the stitches out. It was a perfect healing job, the feathers were growing back over the scar and the pigeon appeared perfectly happy. I noticed the smile on my granda's face and I knew he was pleased with his work.

At the end of the racing season, I always looked forward to Christmas. Christmas time on the gardens was always quiet. The birds didn't need much exercise and quite often it was too cold to let them out and our interest moved from the pigeons to the family. Christmas at my grandparent's house was always great. The fire in the hearth was always roaring and the smell of roasting turkey was always mouth watering. The sweets, nuts, fruit and presents were great and feelings of safety, security and happiness were always there. However, that Christmas nineteen fifty-six was the last time I would experience those feelings.

With the start of the New Year, everyone's thoughts turned to the breeding season. We usually paired up on February 14th 'Valentine's Day,' and during January my father and granda would discuss which birds should be paired together. January was also the time when my father started building up the birds. Feeding the birds was becoming expensive. However, granda insisted on only feeding them the best beans. We often visited the corn merchants and granda would inspect the beans. He would run his hands through them tut and shake his head. I loved to copy him, I would push my hands and arms deep into the bags of beans, then lift them out with my hands full of beans and let them run through my fingers back into the bag.
"Beans should be brown in colour," he would say, "never light brown or beige they still contain water. Old beans are brown they've dried out. Beans mustn't be wet or contain water, old beans about three years old are the best." Even now, years later, I can still hear his voice.
Apart from their regular feed, at this time of the year, we also increased their intake of vitamins. Once a week we caught every pigeon and pushed a cod liver oil capsule into its beak. Then we held their beaks shut until the bird swallowed.

This was also the time of the year when, much to my mother's disgust, my father also insisted on baking a cake for the birds. The cake was usually cooked in old biscuit tins and contained maple peas, millet, maize, tic beans, eggs, sherry, sugar, linseed and anything else he thought would do the pigeons some good. His one secret ingredient was a sprinkling of a concentrated Calcium powder, which he bought for eight shillings and sixpence but never ever told my mother. The smell of the cake, cooking in the oven, was dreadful and our flat smelt for days afterwards. This cake was precious and wasn't just fed willy-nilly to the birds. Over the months of January and February, it was rationed out to them so that when they were paired up, for mating, they would be in the best possible condition.

During the weekdays of the early months of the year, we didn't see many of the club members. Sunday was the one-day of the week when all of the members assembled on the gardens. They handed in their money for the numbers draw to granda or Pincher Martin. Then having checked the numbers on the notice board they'd congregated, around fires, on the hill of pigeon muck at the front of the gardens. Although pleasantries were exchanged between Rat Face and my granda, the rift between them was still there and the two camps of men still existed. The hill was the social centre of the gardens and men stood or sat on buckets, around a fire, cracking jokes or just talking about pigeons. However, an incident was about to occur that would widen the rift between Rat Face and my granda but it would also reduce Rat Face's credibility.

At this time of the year, the gardeners on the bottom allotment section of the site always manured their gardens. Fresh pigeon droppings contain too much lime to be used as manure. However, pigeon muck, which has been stacked up for a number of years, does lose its lime content and does make reasonably good manure. The sand mixed with the droppings from the pigeon lofts was also good for breaking down the soil and any clay that was there. However, probably the most attractive feature for the gardeners was the fact that the muck hill in the pigeon gardens provided free manure. My uncle was one of the gardeners. He wasn't interested in the pigeons but did like gardening. Every January the gardeners would arrive at the muck hill pushing their wheelbarrows and start digging out the pigeon droppings. It was usually a good time when both sets of men talked and cracked jokes. It also served a purpose insomuch as the huge pile of rotting pigeon droppings was reduced.

My uncle Peter was a quiet man and it took a lot for him to lose his temper. He was also a joiner like my father and grandfather. That year, 1957, one Sunday morning, he arrived at the muck hill on his own and started to dig out the old manure. Rat Face and some of his friends were sitting around a fire and watched him with interest.

"What dee yee think yee're deeing?" Rat Face had eventually asked him mockingly.

Uncle Peter was a nice man and always got on with everyone.

"It's that time of year again," he'd replied smiling at Rat Face, "the gardens need the manure."

Rat Face's friends all knew who he was and they had all smiled back. However, Rat Face had continued in his sarcastic tone of voice.

"That's wor pigeon muck and sand, yee shouldn't be taking it. We pay for the sand, and the corn to feed the pigeons then when it comes oot the other end, yee think yee can have it for nowt."

Uncle Peter had stopped digging and smiled at Rat Face. He told us later that he thought it was a joke.

"I'm not smiling," Rat Face had said, "what you're deeing is stealing, yee should pay for that."

Uncle Peter had stood for a while looking at the men then said.

"Seriously, are asking me to pay?"

"Yes we bloody are and all your bloody gardener friends too, corn costs us money and yee should pay for that manure," Rat Face had replied.

Uncle Peter told us that he'd stood for a while looking at the men then he'd shrugged his shoulders, picked up his shovel and wheelbarrow and left.

"Yee bloody Bakers, yee think yee own these bloody gardens," Rat Face had shouted after him.

Uncle Peter told us the story at Sunday dinner and granda just shook his head.

However, the story soon spread throughout the gardens and some of the pigeon men thought it was a good idea that the gardeners should pay for the manure. Others just shook their heads and walked away. The gardeners also heard the story and stayed away from the hill of pigeon muck. On the Thursday morning after the confrontation had taken place a council official arrived on the gardens. This was not unusual as occasionally the council did check the gardens. However, on this occasional the young man arrived with plans of the gardens and two joiners. A small number of pigeon men were sitting on the hill and watched with interest as the official walked the boundary fence checking the location on his plan. Eventually he arrived at the gate installed between the allotments and the pigeon gardens. He stood for a while consulting his plans then opened the gate and approached the pigeon men.

"How long has the gate been here?" he asked.

"Always been there," one of the pigeon men replied.

"Shouldn't be there," the council man replied, "this isn't a bridle path or a right of way. There should be no direct route through from Elwick Road to the West Road."

The pigeon men just smiled at him.

"What you going to do then, close it?" one of the pigeon men asked sarcastically.

"Afraid so," the council official replied.

The pigeon men just stared at the young man in disbelief.

Granda, had just returned from work for his lunch, and was at home when the two pigeon men arrived and knocked on his door.

"Sammy you got to come to the gardens. The councils closing off the gate between the allotments and the pigeon gardens, you know all the rules and regulations, come up and sort it out," they said.

Granda just looked at them, and then shrugging his shoulders replied, "not much I can do over thirty years ago I installed that gate and really it shouldn't be there."

When the two men returned to the gardens, the two council joiners were removing the lock and screwing the gate closed.

"We'll be back on Monday to replace the fencing," they told the pigeon men.

For the pigeon fanciers living off Elwick Road the news was stunning. The short cut through the allotments had been closed and for the men this now meant a half-mile walk around the streets to the West Road entrance. Many of these men were Rat Face's friends and eventually they asked him the questions. "Whose fault is this? and how has this happened?"

"Bloody gardeners have done this," Rat Face answered, "them Bakers is behind this."

When he made the comment Pincher Martin was there and straight away, he had pointed out the obvious.

"Sammy Baker lives off Elwick Road, now he's got to walk round to the West Road and remember it was Sammy that actually installed the gate. Do you really think he'd have anything to do with closing it off? besides," he'd continued, "Sammy and his family don't do selfish things like that. Any of the gardeners could have complained to the council. If you hadn't opened your big mouth and upset the gardeners we'd still have the gate."

Much to Rat Face's annoyance, everyone listening to Pincher had agreed with him.

On the Monday morning, true to their word, the council joiners returned and replaced the gate with a new section of fencing. Two days later, just to add insult to injury, a tractor pulling a trailer, piled high with cow manure, turned up at the allotments and, backing right up to the fence, tipped the full load of manure against the new fencing, this effectively sealed off the footpath. Now no one would now be able to climb over the fence without being covered in manure.

Pincher was right the closing of the gate was an inconvenience for granda, and for a week, whilst Uncle Peter was busy in his allotment, granda walked to the West Road entrance. Peter's allotment was at the very west end of the allotments and backed onto the fence dividing the allotments from the pigeon gardens. Between the first row of lofts, our row, and the dividing fence there was a space of about fifteen feet. At the west end of the row of lofts, virtually outside our garden, the bushes had been allowed to grow and they overhung Peter's allotment. Peter was a good joiner and he made an excellent job of cutting a small gate into the fence. The gate opened into the bushes and, anyone using it, was completely hidden from the muck hill and the other lofts. We all used the bushes as a toilet so the other pigeon men were used to seeing us going in and out of the bushes. This new gate became The Baker's private entrance to the pigeon gardens.

None of our family had complained to the council about the gate and no one else ever admitted complaining to the council. However, granda did visit the council to try and find out what had happened. An official in the council gardens department told him that the council was checking on all footpaths, which crossed their land. They were concerned that a footpath between Elwick Road and the West Road could be seen as a right of way and could jeopardise any future building on the site. They told him that really the path, between the allotments and the pigeon gardens, should have been closed off at least once a year to establish the council's control of the path. However, now that they had removed the gate if the pigeon men wished to challenge their decision, they would have to go to the courts. It appeared that the council man's visit might well have been just a coincidence. Granda passed this information on to Dixie Dean and Pincher Martin knowing that they would circulate it to the other pigeon men.

The closing of the gate changed the routine of many of the pigeon club members. With the gate closed off, they no longer used the muck hill as their meeting point. Now, the top gate onto the West Road, the only official gate off the pigeon gardens, became their meeting point. This benefited all the lofts on the front row, as groups of men waiting to go to the pub no longer overlooked them. The area was quieter and cleaner and with Uncle Peter's secret gate the situation suited us. However, the walk to the pub, for the other club members, was now half a mile longer and they complained bitterly to Rat Face about his big mouth.

Chapter Eight

The health of the pigeons and the control of pests were most important on the gardens. During the racing season pigeons from different lofts were placed in race baskets together and diseases, infections and pests were easily passed on. Before, during and just after the breeding season when the adult pigeons were feeding young birds, cleanliness and health were crucial. We regularly caught our birds and inspected their wings, eyes and beaks. Once a week the bath in front of the loft was filled and sprinkled with potassium crystals, then each bird was encouraged to take a bath. Often they didn't need much encouragement. They enjoyed the bath and splashed around spreading their wings and dropping their heads into the water. Any pigeons not bathing were caught and unceremoniously dumped in the bath. Occasionally we caught the birds and dusted their wings with a powder disinfectant. This we did by using a small blower. The disinfectant powder was placed in the blower then when the rubber ball was pressed; the powder was blown onto the birds wings. Ticks were dreaded and fortunately, I only saw two or three pigeons with them. These small black creatures burrowed into the quills of the pigeon's feathers and to remove them was a real problem. The infested pigeon was isolated and daily the powder blower was used on them. Once I even saw granda resorting to pricking through the quill of the bird's feather, with a needle, in and attempt to kill them.

Just before and during the breeding season my father's cake and the cod liver oil capsules were given regularly to the birds. The breeding pairs of birds were allocated nest boxes and then locked in. Most times the happy couples settled down but occasionally a couple would fight and we'd have to split them up. Blanco, who was just starting his breeding programme, watched all of these procedures. He never said much but it was obvious that all the time he was learning and a powder blower and bottles of different disinfectants soon appeared in his loft. Once the breeding season was underway Blanco threw himself into caring for his pigeons. The previous year, in his loft, Blanco had paired the same coloured birds together. Now all the pigeons in his loft were mostly blues and we noticed that, once again, he adopted the same policy.

"That pairing doesn't necessarily guarantee the same coloured birds, or the best," said granda, "but I suppose with a loft full of blues it makes them easy to spot."

Following the introduction of the new rule about droppers, Blanco's two white fantails became his permanent droppers. During his first season, when he'd been racing his young birds, they had served him well, now they were very much part of his loft and the gardens. He didn't allow these pigeons to breed but kept them purely as droppers. I liked the birds, and they had become personalities on the gardens. Their inability to fly with the rest of the pigeons always made them stand out, and I felt sorry for them. They flopped around on the front of Blanco's loft and if I went into his garden, they were very friendly. I disgusted my father and granda by asking if we could have some fantails.

"Bloody fantails, nothing but pets, it costs enough for corn to feed the racing pigeons without keeping pets," my granda said and that was the end of my suggestion.

The breeding season was a busy time but a good time and all of the birds were in good condition. The cock birds, nodding their heads back and forward, strutted around the loft. To impress the hens they confidently blew out their crops and chased them. The hen birds in true feminine style, just keeping out of reach, led them on. The cocks would drive the hens around the garden and eventually the hen birds would succumb to the cocks displaying and would drop down allowing the cocks to mount them. Granda watched these performances with interest. He knew exactly which cock was paired with which hen, and with his shoe, would quickly discourage any cock bird that was getting amorous with a different hen.

Thankfully, during February and March Rat Face stayed away from our garden. Blanco regularly called in asking for advice from granda and I only went to the garden at weekends. The atmosphere on the gardens was good, the weather was warm, the breeding season was in full swing, and the racing season was just about to start. It was a good time for me but, unbeknown to me, my world was about to crumble. Until that Wednesday night, when I returned home early from school, I can never remember hearing my mother and father quarrelling. The teacher had allowed our class to leave school early she told us that she had a meeting to attend. Obviously, the class was delighted and, along with some of my friends, I decided to go to the swimming baths so I raced home to get my bathers. As I ran along the back yard towards the kitchen, I was surprised to hear my father's voice. Then as I entered the back door into the kitchen I could clearly hear my father's raised voice in the living room.

"Of course it's not mine," he shouted.

"But Mary, from across the road, heard Roger Black's wife telling the woman on the bread counter at the Co-op that it is yours," my mother replied.

I opened the door and the discussion stopped. I was shocked, my mother was sitting in front of the fire crying and my father was standing beside her. When I entered they both turned away, my mother hiding her tears and my father just shaking his head.

"What's wrong?" I asked.

"Nothing son, just adult stuff, what do you want?" my father replied.

I went to my mother; she'd stopped crying and was wiping her face. I didn't know what to do; I was confused, this was the first time I had been in this situation.

"Are you alright?" I asked her, by now I was nearly in tears.

She as always re-assured me, found my bathers and pushed me out of the back door. As I passed my father he pushed sixpence into my hand.

"Enjoy the baths," he said.

I didn't enjoy the baths. I knew something terrible had happened I had heard my mother use Rat Face's proper name in our house.

During the following week, there was a lot of whispering between my mother and father. There was also tension and, when my brother or I entered the room conversations between them regularly stopped. At the end of the week, my mother called us both into the living room and sat us on the settee.

"Your dad's going to stay with granda and granny Baker," she said.

"Why? Can we go?" my brother asked.

My mother couldn't answer, her eyes filled with tears and she started to cry.

I missed my dad but at the pigeon garden I did see him. However, the atmosphere in the garden had also changed; granda was abrupt with father and occasionally he even ignored him. Occasionally Beryl Morris called at the garden to see father, she always brought her baby and my granda ignored her. I knew the trouble that was now burdening my whole family had somehow started with Beryl and I hated her. Rat Face and his friends, once again started to meet on the muck hill and took great delight in making comments to my father and granda. One Saturday as I walked down the path leading into the gardens Rat Face and some of his friends passed me, as they passed Rat Face asked how my brother was.

"He's fine he's playing for the Newcastle under fourteens," I replied proudly.

Rat Face burst out laughing.

"By God he's a quick developer," he said.

His friends also burst out laughing and I ran off. I didn't understand what was happening but ideas were forming in my head. I didn't really know where babies came from or how they were created. I had watched the cock birds treading on the hen birds backs, mating with them, and I knew that eggs and young pigeons eventually materialised but I couldn't relate this to mothers and fathers.

My brother was growing up much faster than me. Having failed to pass his eleven plus examination, he had moved on from the primary school to the secondary school. His interest and knowledge of girls was also increasing. In addition, as he had been selected to play for the Newcastle under fourteen's football team, the girls seemed to be more interested in him. Father moving out of the flat hadn't bothered him as much as it had me. He of course was always at football training or chasing girls. The pigeon garden held no interest for him. At night, in our bedroom, we seldom talked. I think, because I was younger, he looked down on me and treated me as a kid. One Sunday night, as we lay in bed listening to the top twenty on radio Luxembourg on his portable wireless, I asked him what had happened to our parents. The Luxembourg programme as usual faded away then crackling came back.

"Mam thinks Beryl Morris's baby is dads," he replied.

"How can that be?" I replied, "Beryl Morris and dad aren't married?"

"You don't have to be married to have babies," my brother replied smugly, "you've seen the pigeons shagging, well people do the same."

I was horrified. The thought of my father chasing Beryl around the garden then her squatting down and him climbing onto her back shocked me. I couldn't reply I was stunned. I knew deep down there was more to it than that, but my brother was sniggering and I didn't want to hear any more of his tales. That night I lay for a long time trying to work out just what had happened.

For the next few weeks, whenever I was at the garden, I watched closely when Beryl came to see my father. I never saw her parading around in front of him or him blowing his chest out, Infact they were always subdued and talked in whispers. Father still came to our flat to see my mother; I think to give her money. We never went short, every Friday night pocket money was still presented to us and apart from losing father from the house we continued, very much, as we had always done. However, Sunday lunches at my granny's had stopped. My mother had not visited my granny or granda since father had left home.

Chapter Nine

Blanco didn't pay any attention to my family's predicament. He continued raising his young birds and when the racing season started his old birds, last years youngins, were entered for every race. We never questioned Blanco about his family or his background. He never spoke about family and we obeyed the unwritten rule of the gardens and didn't enquire. However, Blanco did have an irritating habit, he collected everything; nothing was left to go to waste. At the clubhouse, he would pick up old, unused seals from the baskets and any old rubber race rings left lying around disappeared into his pocket.

"It's his background," granda explained, "he's had nothing and can't see anything go to waste. He told me he collects the seals and when he has enough he melts them down and makes fishing line weights then he sells them at work. The rubber race rings he puts on the ends of pencils and uses them to rub out mistakes just like proper rubbers."

Granda seemed quite impressed; I could understand this but felt sorry for Blanco. However, his kleptomania did have good points; it meant that the clubhouse floor was kept clean.

That year the first old bird race was, once again, from Selby. This time granda's blue hen, unimpeded, won the race and we were delighted.

Blanco's pigeons did well and he finished in fifth place, a very respectable start to his old bird career. After the race, Blanco came to our garden and it was obvious that he was upset.

"What's wrong?" granda asked him.

"The window has a fallen and hit my a mother on the head," Blanco replied.

I was amazed; this was probably the most I had ever heard Blanco say.

"The sash cord will have snapped," granda replied.

"But who will a mend it?" Blanco asked.

"See the landlord," my father interjected.

"He says a no, he say we a break, we a fix, I a not know how," Blanco said miserably.

I noticed an exchange of glances between granda and my father then father sighed.

"I'll fix it, Blanco where do you live?" he said.

The next day was Sunday and once again I was roped into being labourer. I met my father at the pigeon garden and, with father carrying his joiner's bag we set of for Blanco's house. My father's big, brown joiner's holdall always fascinated me it contained everything, tools, screws, nails, fittings and window sash cord. The cord was used everywhere in our flat and in granda's house. It was used as washing line in the back yard and lane and everywhere in granda's garden and shed. At work father was always fitting and adjusting windows and he had collected a few spare rolls. The small shed built in our back yard was where he stored it and there were numerous rolls stacked under the bench.

Blanco lived off Scotswood Road in an old-fashioned house that had been converted into flats. The main door into the building was wide open and we climbed the stairs to the top floor and knocked on his door. Blanco, dressed in his raincoat, opened the door and silently beckoned us inside. The flat seemed empty, there were no carpets or lino on the floors and the floorboards creaked as we walked along the passage towards the living room at the front of the house. Blanco opened the living room door and an old woman dressed nearly identically to Blanco greeted us. Her raincoat, the same colour as Blanco's, went all the way to the floor and completely covered her feet. I wondered if she had feet and if she did, did she wear white sandshoes. However, the most noticeable thing about her was the bandage, which was wrapped around her head. Obviously, the window, when it had fallen, had cut her head. Frighteningly, between the collar of her raincoat and the bandage an old, unsmiling, crinkled face looked out.

The living room contained two armchairs, a table, a piano and a stool. In the hearth, a fire was burning and immediately I could feel the heat from it. However, the fire wasn't the conventional coal type fire. The ends of two long floorboards had been pushed into the hearth and set on fire and, it was obvious that, as the floorboards burned away, they were pushed further in. My father just seemed to accept all this, ignored it, and went straight to the window. As I went to pass the old lady, she placed her hand on my shoulder, stopped me and silently guided me towards the piano. In front of the piano, very slowly, she lowered herself onto the small stool and spread her hands out on the piano keys. I just stared amazed at how smooth and white her hands were. My family wasn't particularly musical; we listened to the wireless and occasionally when my father got drunk he sang, but music had never really figured in our lives. As I watched the old lady's hands moved across the keys and the piano came to life. Her fingers caressed the keys and moved quickly and confidently from key to key. The music she created was deep and mournful. Her left hand slowly striking the keys created a rhythm, and her right hand flashing from key to key drove forward some classical musical piece. My father had already opened the window and started dismantling the boxing containing the sash cord. Now He stopped working, turned and watched. I stood transfixed, never before had I listened to such a wonderful sound. At school, I had listened to the teacher playing the morning hymns and occasionally she would play music for us to dance to but never before had I stood alongside a piano and heard and seen music being created so passionately. All four of us delighted in the music. Then as abruptly as she had started, she stopped, got up from the stool and shuffled her way to the door.

"Hold this window son," my father said as I stared after her.

Re-sashing the window was easy for father. He knew exactly how to break open the boxing, take out the lead weight then secure a new sash cord to the window. Re-securing the weight and greasing the boxing with candle wax took some more time. Blanco, as I had watched his mother playing the piano, watched in wonderment as my father worked. The job took about an hour and when he had finished no one would have known that he'd worked on the window. Like a child with a new toy, Blanco slid the window up and down and my father and I stood and smiled.

"A how a much is a that?" eventually he asked.

My father was taken aback.

"No charge Blanco," he replied.

"Oh a yes, a you must a charge me," replied Blanco, "you a cannot work for nothing."

I had had visions of receiving at least a halfcrown for my mornings work but sadly, I now realised it wasn't to be.

"No charge Blanco," my father repeated.

"Oh a yes, I a must a pay you," replied Blanco.

Father having put all his tools back into his holdall was moving towards the door and I followed.

"My mother she a give a your boy a piano lessons for a four weeks, a free of charge, that's a fair," said Blanco.

"Okay that's a deal," replied father.

I was shocked, he'd never consulted me and I really didn't want to learn to play the piano. However, it looked as if I had been volunteered. Walking back to the garden I told my father I wasn't interested in learning to play the piano and asked about payment for my work.

"One day son," he replied, "you'll thank me; you never know when a musical talent will help you. Believe me those lessons are worth more than a halfcrown."

That was the end of the conversation and for the next four weeks, on Thursday nights, I was committed to piano lessons.

The second old bird race of the season was from Doncaster a distance of about 110 miles and much to everyone's amazement Blanco won it. His bird was fully nominated and none of the other fanciers on the gardens could believe it. To win the second old bird race of the season in your first year of racing was unheard of. Not only did his bird win the race it romped home a good fifteen minutes ahead of the other pigeons. Granda and my father had stood, shocked and amazed when the bird arrived. I had mixed feelings; I wished it had been one of our pigeons but I was pleased it was Blanco's and not Rat Face's.

The next Thursday night I had my first piano lesson from Blanco's mother and I wasn't impressed. She spent the whole hour making me practice scales and five-finger exercises. She beat out the time with a wooden ruler and after half an hour, if I made a mistake, she wrapped my fingers with the ruler. It certainly was not my idea of fun and I certainly wasn't looking forward to the second lesson. My mother was also worried about me. The area Blanco lived in was not the best in the city and I had to agree that I would go to Blanco's straight after school and then return straight home.

The following Saturday the pigeon race was from Grantham, about 160 miles from Newcastle, and Pincher Martin's pigeon was first, Rat Face was second and we were third. Blanco's pigeons were well behind and everyone on the gardens sighed with relief.

"Last week Blanco probably just got lucky," Pincher, said when he visited our garden.

"Wait and see," granda replied.

On the Thursday morning of the next week it was raining, that night I was due my second piano lesson and much to my disgust, mother made me wear my new Burberry raincoat. I hated it; it was a kid's coat, the blue material was heavy and the belt with the big buckle stuck in my stomach. Anyway, after school the rain had stopped and I made my way to Blanco's carrying my Burberry. When I entered the house, at the head of the staircase, the old lady was waiting for me. She never said a word just beckoned me inside the flat then pointed to one of the chairs and I threw my Burberry over it.

"E-every, G-good, B-boy, D-deserves, F-fruit;" she said pointing at the keys on the piano.

I think it was the first time I had heard her speak and her voice was thin and croaky. She said the words quickly as she pointed towards the keys and I realised, very quickly, that this lesson wasn't going to be any better than the first. Once again, she set of with the ruler and the scales and, as she regularly wrapped my knuckles, I plodded on getting more and more distressed. However, after an hour I was quite good at the scales. I had even started moving my fingers up and down the keyboard doing three and four finger exercises.

"Enough," Blanco's mother suddenly announced.

She was right, it was enough for me, and I was off. I shot off the piano stool and dashed down the stairs and out of the house. I only looked back once and saw the old lady at the window watching me as I ran up the street.

The next morning once again it was raining.

"Put your Burberry on," my mother said.

That was when I realised I had left the Burberry in Blanco's flat. Mother was not impressed, the Burberry mackintosh had cost a lot of money, she was quite proud of her son decked out in his fashionable rainwear, and now she was annoyed.

"After school you get yourself down there and get that mack," she said and reluctantly I agreed.

My brother, who had been listening, quickly offered to share his Burberry with me. His secondary school was just further down the road from my primary school and his Burberry was also a great embarrassment to him. So it was a relief for both of us when we set off for school both sheltering under his Burberry. He was pleased because he also hated his raincoat and wearing it over our heads was a lot less formal. At my school I nipped out from under the coat and he continued down the road with the treasured Burberry blowing in the wind behind him. After school, I returned to Blanco's but the front door was closed and locked and despite knocking and knocking, I couldn't get an answer.

"Blanco will definitely bring it to the gardens tomorrow," I reassured my mother when I returned home.

That Saturday the race was from Peterborough about 200 miles from Newcastle and I went to the gardens early. I was praying that Blanco would bring my Burberry with him. However, when eventually I saw him walking along in front of the lofts he wasn't carrying anything. The pigeons were not due for another hour and I explained to granda about the Burberry. He laughed and told me to get off and get the mack before the pigeons arrived so, reluctantly, I set off for Blanco's flat.

Blanco's mother really frightened me and as I made my way to the old house, I was nervous. As I approached the house I could see the window, which my father had fixed was now wide open. I kept looking up admiring his work when suddenly Blanco's mother appeared holding a pigeon. I stepped into the front doorway, out of view of the window, and was just able to watch as she threw the pigeon into the air. It was a blue hen bird; I could tell that much and I watched it circle the old house then head off in the direction of the gardens. Slowly I climbed the stairs and knocked on the door of the flat. Blanco's mother answered my knock and seemed surprised to see me.

"I left my Burberry mack," I said.

She just stared at me; she seemed shocked to see me.

"My mack, my mam says I've got to get it," I said.

The old lady stepped aside and I dashed down the passage into the living room. The mack was still lying on the chair where I had thrown it. I grabbed it and dashed back along the passage and past the old lady.

"Thanks," I said as I jumped down the stairs.

I ran all the way back to the gardens and knocked quietly on granda's garden gate.

"It's unlocked," he shouted.

I was surprised; he always locked the gate during a race.

"Come in son, the winners already in," he continued.

I opened the gate and went into the garden, my father and granda sat on the bench alongside the loft.

"Blanco's got the first bird home and it's fully nominated," my father said, "once again he's left us all standing and he only sent two pigeons to the race."

"One more, over the church," Pincher Martin shouted, "red cock could be Sammy's," he continued.

The urgency was over but I still went into the shed and watched as the red cock dived into our loft. Granda followed it in and the familiar clunk of the clock told me it was safely timed in and it was safe for me to come out of the shed.

"Fully nominated and it's knackered" granda said as he came out of the loft, "bloody Blanco, God knows what he's feeding those birds on. That blue hen of his didn't even look tired when it came home."

I listened to his comments then suddenly I remembered Blanco's mother throwing the pigeon into the air.

"I saw Blanco's mother throwing a blue hen out of her flat window," I said.

They both looked at me.

"Aye that'll be right," granda replied, "Blanco said he'd taken a Scotsman home; it dropped in last week lost and absolutely flown down. He's been nursing it at home, said his mother would throw it up during today's race and hopefully it would team up with some Scotsmen and find its way home."

I stayed in the garden and watched as the other pigeons returned from the race. From the state of the birds, it was obvious that it had been a hard race and that they had encountered bad weather, all of them looked tired and wet. Granda was happy with his second place but the memory of Blanco's mother throwing the pigeon out of the window still haunted me. Eventually I asked my father if it was possible for someone to liberate a pigeon without it actually going to the race point. He wasn't in a good mood; Beryl had just left the garden crying. They had been in the shed arguing for some time and I had heard her mention my name and saw her pointing at me through the window. The week before I had seen her outside the clubhouse, and despite her calling my name, I had ignored her and now I thought I might be in trouble.

"Not now son," he said abruptly, "I've got to see your mother."

Chapter Ten

The situation between my mother and father was starting to have an effect upon my brother and me. My mother was always breaking down in tears and kept asking my brother to go and find father. My brother was also becoming rebellious, he stayed out late and I knew he was smoking cigarettes. I also had suspicions that he was drinking beer. I tried to stay loyal to both my parents and tried not to take sides but it was becoming increasingly difficult. I respected my father but looking back, I now realise that he was a very passive person and he relied upon granda. I suppose both of granda's sons respected him and relied upon him perhaps too much for men of their age. He had found them their jobs, they worked alongside him at the same building company, and whenever they had a problem and needed a decision, they always turned to him.

During my visits to the pigeon garden, I tried not to listen to the conversations between granda and my father but sometimes curiosity did get the better of me. My brother's comments about Beryl's baby still nagged at me and occasionally I would sneak around the garden and listen when the two men were talking. It was on one of these occasions that I heard my granda laying the law down to father.

"Son you've got to sort it out," I heard him say; "you know that bairn's not yours. Just look at its hair and its face, surely it remind you of someone? That bloody Beryl has seen more cock-ends than weekends. She's just taking you for a ride; you're paying her money when you've no need. Old Jack Morris threw her out he knows what she is; Jack even says the bairn's the spit of Rat Face."

I was shocked; I knew that whenever Rat Face's name was mentioned in connection with our family there was always trouble.

The next day I had been to the water tap getting water for the pigeons. I was carrying two full watering cans back to the garden when I saw Beryl. She was pushing the baby in a pram and I asked her if I could look at him. She was delighted to show him off to me, even took him out of the pram and gave him to me. I looked at his face from both sides, and then I held him at arms length and looked at him from a distance. Finally, I got up real close and looked into his face.

"You'll recognise him next time you see him," Beryl said.

"Looks like Rat Face," I said innocently.

"Buggar off," replied Beryl.

This encounter had been the reason why I had ignored her outside the clubhouse.

That Saturday after the race my father left me in the garden with granda, he insisted that I stayed and accompanied granda to my granny's. It was obvious to me that something was going on.

"You stay with me, we'll go down and see your granny and Tiny, might even take him for a walk eh?" granda said.

This was the first time granda had ever invited me to take the dog out for a walk with him. I was surprised but agreed. When we did go to the house, to collect the dog, there was a lot of whispering and nodding between granda and granny. I wasn't supposed to see it but it was pretty obvious. We took the dog for a walk but granda said little and the dog didn't really want to be out, so we returned early.

That night when I returned home, my father, mother and brother were sitting around the table, obviously waiting for me, and there was an empty chair at one side of the table.

"Come in son," father said, "sit down, Mam and I want to talk to you and your brother."

I felt quite important but when I glanced at my brother, he pulled a face and lifted his eyes towards the ceiling. I moved round the table and sat on the empty chair and father started.

"Mam and I have been talking and I'm moving back in, we think it'll be best for all of us."

I looked at my brother who, once again, raised his eyes and looked at the ceiling. I ignored him, after all, they had waited for me and were involving me in the discussion and I felt quite important. I felt that I was being treated like an adult and that I should contribute something to the conversation.

"That's good Dad," I said, "I've missed you."

Both my parents looked at me and smiled and I felt very proud. I glanced at my brother; he stuck out his tongue as if being sick. I knew what he thought of me, just a kid. Well, I thought, I'll show you how grown up I am and what I know.

"That's really good dad," I continued, "because that Beryl Morris has seen more cock-ends than weekends."

The smiles disappeared from my parents' faces and my brother screamed with laughter.

With father being back at home it was easier for me to talk to him. The memory of Blanco's mother throwing the pigeon out of the window was still troubling me and later in the week, once again, I asked him about the possibility of someone liberating a pigeon, without it actually going to the race point.

"Be difficult," he said, "all the birds are counted into the race baskets and they're all race rung. I really don't know how anyone could do it."

I accepted his explanation and tried to put Blanco's mother out of my mind.

The piano lessons continued and I still had two free lessons to endure. At the very start of the lessons, I'd had visions of being able to play like Winifred Atwell or Russ Conway but, monotonously, the scales continued and the ruler still whacked down on my fingers. During my visits to the flat, I never saw Blanco, he must have been working and his mother said very little. She was always dressed the same with her overcoat fastened to her neck but now the bandage on her head had disappeared and had been replaced by a woollen hat. The hat, I am sure, was really a tea cosy as there were two holes in it. She never smiled or talked, just pointed to the piano seat and then to individual keys to give me directions. I was pleased when the four free lessons were finally over. However, as I left the flat after the fourth lesson she stopped me and said.

"Your Pa Pa can arrange more a lessons for a halfcrown with my son if he wishes."

I was dumbfounded; this was only the second time I had ever heard her speak. I never told my father about her offer, I had already decided that piano playing wasn't for me and that was the end of my musical career.

The old bird races continued, but our placings and also Blanco's, deteriorated. Rat Face won the next race from Hitchin about 250 miles and then Mattie Walker won the Hatfield race, which was from a distance of about 260 miles. Pincher Martin was still flying well, he was always in the top five and obviously, he was delighted. By now, I detested Rat Face. Whenever he won, he bragged about it and the rift between him, his friends and our family was growing. I had noticed that Beryl was now a regular visitor to his garden and this cheered me slightly. The next race was from Redford and this was always a good race point. Redford was a good distance from Newcastle, about 320 miles, and the birds usually took about seven hours to fly home. Blanco was complaining that his birds weren't fit and he'd decided to send only two birds.

For every race, club members needed to know at what time the birds were liberated from the race points. This enabled them to work out roughly what time the birds would return. Informing them of the liberation time had become my granny's job. The club paid granda's telephone bill and part of the agreement granda had with the club, was that he would organise for the liberation times to be available to all the members. When the conveyors, who travelled with the pigeons, liberated the birds at the race points, they would ring granda and tell him the time of release. He would then ring the weather bureau in Newcastle and find out the direction of the prevailing wind. Then he would work out a rough velocity, which he thought the birds would fly at, and when the members telephoned, along with an estimation of the pigeons return time, he would give them this information. Every Saturday morning, during the racing season, he made the call and worked out the times. He would write the times down and then when he left the house my granny would be left in charge of the telephone.

Occasionally if I was at my granny's she would let me answer the telephone and usually a voice would say,
"What time they up?"
I would read off the piece of paper.
"Liberated at six o'clock, strong North-West wind probably home about two o'clock."
The pigeon men loved to argue about their pigeons flying capabilities and they all thought they were the experts. Of course, different weather conditions, the wind and the condition of the bird all contributed to the bird's capability. Sometimes the members would disagree about the time for the return of the birds.
"From Redford with a strong North-West, nee way will they take eight hours."
If this happened, I'd panic, I'd beckon to my granny and she'd grab the telephone.
"Who is this?" she would shout down the telephone, they all knew better than to argue with granny and the line would go dead.

On the day of that old bird Redford race, at two o'clock, we were all patiently waiting in the garden. The wind was blowing strong and it was a dull, cold day.
"They'll not do eight hours," granda grumbled. "That wind's on their noses and it's bloody cold, could be ten hours, they're really ganna struggle."
Even Pincher keeping his look out was beginning to doubt the eight-hour flight time.
"Sammy your time's way out today," he shouted.
Granda pretended to ignore the comment but after a while he whispered to father, "bloody clown," and I smiled.

"One out of the valley," as usual Pincher was off with his commentary.

Everyone turned and looked down into the valley and corn tins all over the gardens started to rattle.

"Coming this way, it's for the gardens," Pincher's commentary continued, "blue cock, could be Blanco's, Blanco looks like it's yours, looks in good nick mind."

I had retired to the shed and watched as the pigeon circled the gardens. I was amazed, the bird definitely did not want to drop and it looked as if it really was enjoying itself.

"Christ that birds fit," granda said, "you'd think it had never been away."

Blanco continued calling the bird and the two fantails fluttered around the front of his loft but the bird still would not drop.

Pincher, now all excited, was continuing with his vigil.

"Two more same direction," he suddenly called out.

All eyes returned to the valley and once again the corn tins started rattling.

"They're bloody skemmies Pincher, they're heading for the church, they're the vicars," someone shouted and laughter rippled around the gardens.

Pincher, insulted and deflated, didn't answer and sure enough the two birds dropped onto the church roof. Blanco's pigeon was still enjoying itself. It circled the gardens and, as if to humiliate everyone, cruised along in front of the lofts. Everyone, wishing it were their bird, watched it, then suddenly it dropped into Blanco's loft and he followed it inside.

"That bird's never flown from Redford," my father said.

Filled with anticipation all of the club members waited for Blanco to emerge from his loft. The gardens were silent and not saying a word, everyone continued to wait. Granda and all of us waited, I had left the shed and now stood beside him just waiting. The hands on the church clock moved slowly and club members started to shout comments over to Blanco.

"Is it from the race Blanco?" someone shouted.

"What states the bird in Blanco?" someone else shouted. "Has it been through rain? Is it flown down? Is it knackered?" other club members joined in.

Eventually Blanco came out of his loft and replied.

"Yes it's a from the race and it's a bery, bery tired," he shouted.

"It's bery bery jammy," someone shouted back.

One hour after Blanco's pigeon arrived, Pincher now wanting to redeem himself, started again.

"Two birds over the clock."

"Sure they're not for the vicar," someone shouted and the gardens echoed with laughter.

"Mattie's chequered cock, and could be Sammy's red cock," called out Pincher.

I ran back into the shed and watched as the birds approached, both of them were flown down and struggled towards the gardens.

"They're knacked," someone shouted.

He was right the two birds didn't circle the gardens. They flew low and straight towards the gardens then turned right and flew straight into their lofts. Granda was waiting and clocked the bird in and, as he held it in his hands, I ran out of the shed and looked at the bird. Its feathers were soaked and its head was down. It was obvious that the bird had flown through a storm and was exhausted.

"Blanco's bird must have just beaten the storm," granda said.

On that Saturday, that Redford race, once again placed the doubt back in my mind. It also created doubts in other people's minds and whispers went around the gardens. No one could believe that Blanco's bird could have out flown a storm and returned so fit. Some of the members even asked granda about the race ring. After the race, in the clubhouse when he checked the clocks and calculated the placings, he had removed the ring from Blanco's clock.

"Of course it's genuine," he replied, "what are you trying to say? How could Blanco have fixed the bloody race? You saw the bird come home, you saw the bird basketed, how could anyone fix a race?" He was obviously annoyed at the suggestion that Blanco had cheated.

Nevertheless, later sitting in granda's living room, I listened as he and my father discussed the race.

"Son, for having flown that distance that bird was in remarkably good condition," he said.

"I know that dad," my father replied, "but how could anyone fix a race. The bird must just have got lucky and beat the storm. You could check with the conveyors and see if any of the pigeons got out of the baskets early. Otherwise, I can't see how it was fixed and besides Blanco wouldn't do anything dishonest."

On Sunday morning when the conveyors returned the race baskets to the clubhouse granda was waiting for them.

"No way does any bird ever get out of the baskets early Sammy," one of the conveyors said, "you know us Sammy we've done this job long enough and if it did happen we'd tell you. All the baskets are on the lorry and before the seals are broken rods are pushed through the loops on the front doors of the baskets. Then when we're going to liberate, we cut the seals and at the right time pull a lever, this forces the rods down and all the basket fronts open together. The birds, usually in a bunch, circle once or twice then break for home. We have never had a bird get away early. If we had Sammy, I'd tell you. Honestly, it was a good liberation the basket fronts all dropped together, there were no problems."

Chapter Eleven

Times and attitudes were changing on the gardens. Originally the pigeon club had been established, by the working men of the area, purely for recreation. For the local pitmen, factory workers, shipyard workers, labourers and the unemployed, the gardens provided a place of safety and escape. The fresh air cleaned the industrial dust from their lungs and the friendship on the gardens provided an escape from their wives and families. They didn't have much money. The nomination system meant that their knowledge of their birds dictated, that the small amount they did have, was only used on their best birds.

The original pigeon races had been purely for sport and friendly competition. Now, as the prize money was growing the attitude of the members was changing and a different type of member was being attracted to the club. Previously, the question of cheating had never been an issue and as far as we were aware, no one had ever cheated. The gardens had always been a friendly place. Occasionally certain members had fallen out but usually, very quickly, they would shake hands and the friendship would return. This had not happened with granda and Rat Face and the rift between their groups of supporters had grown even wider. On top of this, the allotment holders no longer spoke to the pigeon fanciers.

Before Rat Face's interference, both groups of men had been friends and talked. The pigeon fanciers often scrounged vegetables and flowers from the gardeners and in return, the gardeners collected the muck from the muck hill, this had all stopped. A new culture based purely on winning money was creeping in. Accompanying this new culture was suspicion, and envy and the general feeling on the gardens reflected these qualities. Perhaps it was just that times were changing, I don't know, but there wasn't much we could do to change the situation.

All of the club members knew that the membership of the club was going to increase. The council had consulted the club and they had agreed that a further row of lofts could be built at the back of the gardens. Now, to everyone's interest, the construction of three new lofts was already underway. These lofts were not the traditional, single skinned timber constructions, identical to all the other lofts on the gardens. The new members had rented two plots each, so the new lofts were twice the size of the existing lofts. They were being built on concrete rafts. The walls were double skinned with insulation in-between. The windows where now fitted with metal bars with shutters installed, and the roofs were insulated and double felted. The men building the lofts were not the owners. The builders were being paid and would not discuss who the owners were.

Granda knew who the owners were, they had already applied for membership of the club and he had read their application forms.
"There's money coming onto the gardens son," he said one day as we were cleaning out the loft.
My father nodded and replied.
"You can see that from the lofts being built at the back. Pincher Martin was telling me that they're putting loft managers in charge of the new lofts."
"Wouldn't surprise me, one scrap man and two road haulage men have applied to join the club," granda said, "and they're spending a lot of money on those lofts, all insulated and with shutters. Even heard a rumour that they're talking about some form of heating. The birds will have better living conditions than half the population of Newcastle."
I listened fascinated.

"Why would you heat a pigeon loft?" I asked.

"To bring forward the breeding season," granda replied, "two or three weeks make a lot difference in the size and strength of the young birds. If you heat the loft, the pigeons will pair up earlier and produce youngins earlier. And, before they start racing, the old birds will have had longer to recuperate after bringing up the youngins."

"I heard they've been down to Leicester to look at that stud loft trying to buy birds," father said.

"Wouldn't be surprised," granda replied.

Later that day, when our loft was clean and the birds had been fed and watered, we walked round to where the lofts were being built. The area in front of the three lofts had become a regular meeting place for club members and a number of members were leaning on the fencing admiring the building work.

"Some size eh Sammy?" one of the men said, "are they allowed two garden spaces?" he continued as he looked at granda.

We just looked at the lofts in amazement; each loft took up two regular garden spaces. The front gantries seemed massive they stretched out and across in front of the lofts. Each loft was sectioned off, into compartments, for cocks, hens and old and young birds. Two smaller compartments had been installed and we guessed they were for food storage and what looked like a small office.

"I suppose there's nothing stopping anyone renting two garden spaces," granda eventually replied, "we've just never thought of it before. Mind you I've seen worse built bungalows," granda said shaking his head.

We admired the lofts for a further ten minutes then walked down to granda's house.

"Times are changing son," granda said and my father and I both nodded our heads.

We knew that the new lofts would not be ready for that seasons racing. However, they were creating a lot of curiosity amongst the members and they were taking the interest away from Blanco and his winning blue cock.

Times were also changing for me. Recently at school, I had sat the eleven plus examination. It had been no big deal; I was quite good at English and arithmetic. The pigeons and gardens had helped me. Regularly I had helped granda count the birds. I had read his notices, weighed out corn, and helped him with his records. The actual eleven plus test had not seemed difficult and I don't even think my parents knew I had taken it. One morning the teacher had arrived in the classroom and given out the papers, and we had completed the sums and the English. My education on the gardens obviously hadn't benefited me as I had failed and was allocated a place at the same school as my brother.

That years racing season continued. Blanco had no more winners and for some reason his birds appeared to slow down and he wasn't placed in any of the races. We had a couple of seconds then much to our delight we actually won one of the channel races. 'Huwey' was now three years old and granda's favourite pigeon. The race was, once again, from Lillers in France. The liberation was delayed and it turned into a two-day event. For some reason Rat Face hadn't entered his channel pigeon for the race and there was much discussion on the gardens as to whether he'd lost it. However, that was nothing to do with us and having waited all day on the Saturday race day, once again on the Sunday morning, we were at the garden at six o'clock. Much to our delight Huwey arrived at seven. Just to see him dropping out of the clear blue sky made the early start worthwhile. Of course, we were all delighted and, for a further half hour, he was the only bird on the gardens. My only regret was that Rat Face's loft stayed shut and he wasn't there to see our triumph.

"Might win the Fed Sammy?" someone shouted over.

We did not want to build up our hopes but we did fancy our chances.

"We'll see," replied granda modestly.

The new dropper rules stated that three hours after the first pigeon from the race arrived on the gardens, the other club members could let their pigeons out to exercise. Having won the race we cleaned the loft and when the other lofts opened up and released their pigeons, we proudly walked round to have another look at the new lofts. One of the lofts was completed and actually had pigeons inside. The new owner, and now club member, was standing on the gantry with an older man alongside him. When he saw granda, he called over.

"Hey Sammy, good win today, come inside and have a look around."

This was unique and unusual and we jumped at the opportunity. As we entered the loft we gasped, it was breathtakingly large, spacious and immaculately clean. One of the compartments was fitted with nesting boxes with removable fronts. The fittings and workmanship were very professional and had obviously been completed by qualified tradesmen. I gazed through the lattice interior doors and did a quick count of the pigeons inside. I calculated that in two compartments there were about sixty pigeons with plenty of room for more.

Granda talking to the new member was referring to him as Mr Clarke. This confused me slightly as it was the first time I had ever heard him refer to a member as mister. Usually, very quickly, new members received a nickname or everyone used their first names. As we toured the loft it became obvious to father and me that Mister Clarke wanted to speak to granda alone, and he guided him away from us towards the other end of the loft. It didn't matter as it gave us time to nose through the different compartments. Father knew the older man, he called him Tommy and he followed us and pointed out certain birds.

"Yorkshire bird, won Midlands Fed last year from Lillers," he said proudly as he pointed at a chequered hen, "she'll not fly a race again. Next year we'll put her straight down on eggs; she's been bought for breeding. She'll stay in the loft, a prisoner for a year. We'll take two sets of youngins from her, sell some of her eggs, and then she'll be loft trained."

Father asked if he could handle her, the old man looked at him shocked.

"Nee way, nee one touches them birds, Mister Clarke and me's the only one's handling them."

We were just leaving that section of the loft when father leaned over and looked into a nest box.

"By god that looks like Roger Black's channel bird the red hen," he said.

"That's right," replied Tommy, "George bought him a week ago. Roger's a greedy buggar asked two hundred and fifty pounds for her but George got her for two hundred."

Father stepped back.

"Seriously Tommy, Rat Face sold his channel bird to you?" he said.

"Aye that's it there, mind he wants two eggs when it's paired up that was part of the deal. I'm surprised you never realised that Rat Face had money, haven't you seen that Beryl dame walking around in her new outfit, pushing her new pram," replied Tommy smiling.

The mention of Beryl's name seemed to shock father and he shook his head and went quiet.

Eventually granda returned to us and we set off making our way back to our garden.

"Bloody impressive set up," my father said, "the old loft manager is Tommy Wright he use to fly pigeons at Westerhope. I've met him before at a prize giving; he knows what he's doing. And" he said sighing, "they've also got Rat Face's red hen, Clarke bought her a week ago for two hundred pounds. Bloody greedy buggar that Rat Face he'd sell his mother for a price."

"Clarke offered me two hundred pounds for Huwey," granda said.

We all stopped dead in our tracks.

"He did what?" father said.

"He offered me two hundred pounds for Huwey," granda repeated, "I knocked him back."

I had already noticed that granda had dropped the mister and was now referring to George Clarke with some distain.

"It's a bad time for the gardens when men can spend that amount of money on pigeons," he continued, "he's buying up every decent bird on the gardens, and did you see how many birds he had in that loft. What really worries me is he's only the first. There are another two new members going to do the same thing and certainly, with those numbers of pigeons, it'll be mob flying on these gardens next year."

Later back at the loft, I was allowed to handle Huwey. The bird was thin and it was clear that he'd had a long hard flight. Nevertheless, I was allowed to hold him and I handled him gently and with great respect. We had never had a pigeon worth two hundred pounds before.

We never won the Federation; two pigeons had arrived at lofts in Walker before Huwey. It meant that our prize money was smaller than we had hoped for but we still had the pleasure of being first on the gardens. That night as we walked home I asked my father what granda had meant by mob flying.

"Well son," he replied, "the more pigeons you put into a race the better chance you have of winning. Of course that is assuming that the pigeons are reasonably good birds. If you have money, you can buy good birds, enter them for the races, and nominate a large number of them. That will greatly increase your chances of winning more prize money. At the moment most of the lofts have one or two good pigeons but if the new men buy them pigeons they'll probably win everything."

"Can't you stop them?" I asked.

"Difficult son," father replied, "at this point in time there are no restrictions on the number of birds you can enter for a race and we can't stop anyone from buying pigeons."

Chapter Twelve

The year was passing and my time at the primary school was fast ending. In the last week of the school term, I was invited to a party. One of the girls had decided to have a party at her house for all of the class. Her father was a manager at one of the big stores in Newcastle and compared to us they had money. Anyway, on the Saturday night, of the final week of school, the whole class was invited to her house. She told us there would be music, food and a magician and we were all excited and looking forward it.

That Saturday I went to the garden watched the pigeons return home, and then ran home myself. At five o'clock, dressed in a clean shirt and shorts, I walked with a few of my friends to the girl's house. This particular girl lived in the west of Newcastle in a large semi detached house. It was bigger than our flat and even bigger than granda's house. There was a dining room, a living room, and a kitchen. Girls always seemed to get excited about parties. I wasn't too keen on parties. I had been to a few and in my limited experience, they always seemed to finish up with the girls wanting to play catchy kissy or postman's knock. However, the food was good and her father had some large black records, which he played on his new gramophone in the dining room. The party had been going for about an hour when her father made an announcement.

"The magician will be appearing in the living room in two minutes."

Thirty kids rushed to cram into the living room. Some of the furniture had been removed and a number of the kids sat crossed legged on the floor. I was one of the last in and stood at the back. The magician had placed a small table, at the front of the living room, directly in front of the window with a top hat placed on it. With great expectation, we all stared at the table and the hat. Suddenly the door opened and a big man dressed in a clown's outfit pushed his way into the room. It was not what we had expected; somehow, we had thought the magician would appear from the top hat. The size and presence of the man dressed in the clown's outfit quite scared me. A number of the kids sitting at the front obviously felt the same and moved back. The clown never spoke just made his way to the table, then magically, from somewhere, flowers appeared, and everyone was surprised and gasped.

I looked hard at the clown; there was something vaguely familiar about him. However, his face was completely painted with a traditional sad face, which masked his identity. He performed a few tricks, pulling cards from behind kid's ears, dropping pennies out of their noses and I have to admit that he was clever. The flowers he had originally produced he had placed on the table, now he picked them up, and they disappeared. Then magically they re-appeared out of a pocket of one of the kids in the front row and I was impressed. The clown costume he was wearing was a traditionally, oversized, all in one costume with wide sleeves. However, as I watched him perform his tricks there was something naggingly familiar about him.

I watched closely and suddenly he pulled a white pigeon from out of the hat. The sudden introduction of pigeons really caught my attention and I watched how he handled the bird. It was a white fantail cock bird and it lay perfectly still in his hands then suddenly it disappeared. How he did it I don't know, one minute it was there and then it was gone. All the kids gasped and I leaned forward to try and spot where the bird was hidden. The clown's face changed from the sad, crying face to a happy smiling face and it was obvious that he was pleased with himself. He looked around the room and I watched intrigued by his white face and the big red lips painted on it. Then I looked at his eyes and saw the pot eye, I gasped, it was Blanco.

Still smiling confidently the clown continued looking around the room. If he saw me, he didn't seem to recognise me and I thought I must be wrong. Then from out of the top hat he produced a second bird a white fantail hen pigeon. I knew then that it was Blanco; the two pigeons were his droppers, but I still had a slight doubt and I had to be sure. I stood on my toes and looked down at the clown's feet and yes, he was wearing sandshoes. I wasn't sure what to do. I felt quite proud that I knew the magician but also, for some reason, I thought that Blanco wouldn't be too pleased to see me.

The show continued and both pigeons disappeared then re-appeared out of the top hat. Kids gasped in amazement and I have to admit that I was very impressed. I couldn't see how he did it; the birds were there one minute and the next they had gone. The kids all started clapping, the clown acknowledged the applause, and once again his eyes travelled around the room. This time, just for a second his good eye halted on me and I felt his stare. That was it, no recognition, no nods of friendship, and no familiarity whatsoever, just a stare and at that moment, I knew he did not want me to recognise him. I knew he definitely did not want me to talk to him and, trying to move out of his stare, I stood back and moved behind another kid. Despite this disturbing moment, I have to admit that the show was good and I enjoyed it. No one in the room knew where the pigeons, the flowers, the strings of flags, the cards or the pennies came from or went to. He held everyone's attention and the room was quiet, which really was a first for my classmates. At the end of the show, everyone was sad to see the clown leave the room and as he pushed his way back through the kids, I noticed he glanced in my direction but I looked away.

Some of the children followed the clown out of the room but I waited. I knew he would have to come back to collect his table and the rest of his props and I did not want to see him and, somehow, I knew he did not want to see me. After a few minutes, I made my way back into the dining room where the girls were organising a game of postman's knock. That was my signal to leave and unnoticed I made my way to the front door and let myself out. I had enjoyed the party, the food and the clown had been good but as I walked home, I knew that my presence and my recognition of Blanco had not been welcome.

That night sitting watching the black and white television I told father what I had seen.
"Are you sure it was Blanco," he asked.
"He had a pot eye," I replied.
"Lots of people have pot eyes son," he said, "anyway if it was Blanco it's not a problem, good luck to him. He's only trying to raise some money, if you enjoyed the show that's all that's important."
It wasn't all that was important and I knew it, my father seemed to be missing the point. If Blanco could make pigeons disappear then re-appear he could also stop then from going to the race points, and he could possibly make them re-appear on the gardens. However, when I pointed this out to father he thought about it then dismissed it saying,
"The system works son, the birds are put into the race baskets and counted and no pigeons can be taken out. What's more no one should be race basketing their own birds."
I still had doubts and whilst he wouldn't admit it, I think my father also shared those doubts.

Chapter Thirteen

I moved to the senior school and life continued. On my first day at the senior school, a number of the teachers approached me and asked if I was related to the Baker boy in the class three years above. I was quite pleased at being recognised and proudly told them that I was. However, they all said the same thing, 'just remember we'll be keeping an eye on you.'

I didn't know whether this was a good thing or a bad thing.

The 1957 pigeon-racing season finished. The three new lofts were completed and all three now contained pigeons and had loft managers. Blanco didn't win any more races that season and my doubts about him started to diminish.

Christmas day arrived, only this year it was different, we didn't go to granda's for dinner. Since my father had returned home, my mother had not been to my grandparent's home. My brother and I hadn't noticed this and it was only at Christmas we realised that there was still something wrong. For a short time the security that I had previously felt in my family home had returned but now, at Christmas, this security seemed to be threatened. Christmas had always been a time for all of the family to be together and I missed the familiar smells, the laughter, granda, granny, and even the dog. We spent Christmas day in our own house and my parents worked hard trying to ensure that we had a good time but something was missing.

    Mother told us that for the first time the Queen was making a Christmas speech on the television and she was very keen for the whole family to watch it. Father seemed interested but my brother and I weren't looking forward to it. For Christmas dinner we had a small turkey and all the trimmings. We all enjoyed it. Then mother announced that she hadn't made a Christmas pudding, instead she'd made a jelly trifle. This pleased me because I didn't like raisins and father didn't eat Christmas pudding anyway. We all sat around the table and mother proudly placed her trifle, in the centre of the table. It was nicely turned out on a plate and covered in cream it looked really good. Mother had tried to finish the dinner before the Queen began her speech. Unfortunately, we were late and the Queen was due to make her speech. Nevertheless, we were all feeling happy. Father sat back and said that after lunch he thought he would go down to the garden and check the pigeons. I thought this was a good idea and asked if I could go with him. Obviously, my mother didn't share my sentiments and suddenly she erupted.

"Garden, bloody garden, bloody pigeons, I'm sick of it, it's Christmas day, surely you can stay in with your family, I'm fed up with it."

She stopped shouting just long enough to wipe her eyes then she continued screaming the words at father.

"You prefer the pigeons to us, for all I know you could be going to see your hussy. You probably are going to see her. I feel like going to that damned loft and letting all the birds out."

I interrupted her.

"Mam it's Huwey that won the Lillers race not Hussy and it's a cock bird. And, if you let the birds out they'd just come back, they're homing pigeons," I said.

My mother stared at me in disbelief.

"God" she screamed, "you've brainwashed and transformed your son into a miniature Sammy Baker and you've ruined our marriage. Look at him he talks like your father, he walks like your father and he idolises your father."

I just sat still; I was amazed at my mother's outburst. I looked at my brother. I didn't, for a minute, think he looked like granda but obviously mother did. My brother just sniffed and I continued to stare at him. Unbelievably my brother was watching the Queen on the television she was just about to start her speech.

I had never seen my father lose his temper before but suddenly he reacted.
"Enough," he shouted and jumped out of his chair.
We all jumped in our chairs.
"Enough, I've had enough," he said pointing at mother. "You give me nothing, I made a mistake, I've apologised but you'll never forgive me. Every night we sleep in the same bed and every night you turn your back on me. This isn't a marriage it's a bloody constant battle, well I'm sick of it."
With that he slammed his hand down onto the trifle. Cream, jelly, tinned fruit and custard splattered all over the room and us.
"You swine," my mother shouted, "you bloody swine."
Father never replied. Covered in trifle, he turned and, slamming the door behind him, he left the room. I listened to his footsteps in the passage then after a few minutes I heard the front door slam. I sat, my bottom lip quivering, staring at my mother. The Queen, now blurred through my tears and a piece of trifle stuck to the television screen, was speaking. She was telling us that twenty-five years ago the first Royal Christmas message had been broadcast to the nation on the wireless. She said she was happy with the commonwealth, and her family and her were enjoying Christmas. How I wished I was. My brother, unperturbed and still watching the Queen, was using his spoon to eat the trifle off his new Christmas jumper. My mother, head down on the table, was sobbing and I, completely confused, sat frozen in my chair. Then unable to control myself I broke into tears. Christmas was dead, the whole thing was destroyed and I dashed into the bedroom, collapsed on my bed, and cried. I expected my mother to come in and console me but she never did and eventually I must have fallen asleep.

When I awoke it was dark and I was tucked up in bed and wearing my pyjamas. Mother must have come through, undressed me, and put me into bed. But there was something else, something disturbing; the bed was wet as were my pyjama bottoms. I knew what it was, it had been years since I had wet the bed but the old memories came flooding back. Trying desperately not to wake my brother, I slipped off my pyjama bottoms and kicked them to the bottom of the bed, then I pulled the top sheet down and lay on top of it. The blanket was rough on my skin but it was drier. I lay in the darkness feeling thoroughly ashamed of myself and wondering what to do. Slowly the dampness seeped through the bottom sheet and once again I could feel the cold creeping into my body. I knew it was early in the morning and I could not lie there all night. Quietly, I climbed out of bed and crept to my mother's room. Slowly, I opened the bedroom door and entered. I was surprised at what I found. A fire was burning in the fire grate in the room. This fire was usually only lit when someone was ill. However, the warmth from the fire was welcoming and I crept to the side of mother's bed. Father and mother lay in the bed covered by the covers but I could see that they were wrapped in each other's arms.

The movement in the room must have woken my mother as she turned and whispered.
"What's wrong son?"
"I've wet the bed," I whispered.
She sighed and pulled the covers up on her side of the bed. I climbed over her and pushed my way in between her and my father. He never said a word just turned his back to me and started snoring. The warmth from their bodies and the fire soon warmed me and I fell asleep.

"Baby, piss bed," someone was whispering in my ear.
I turned my head to find my brother leaning over me. He punched me, climbed over me, and snuggled into the warm bed alongside me. Mother and Father had gone and through the curtains, I could see that it was getting light.
"Mam's stripping your bed baby," my brother said, and kicked out at me.
I didn't care, we now had the big bed for just the two of us and it was warm and comfortable. The next thing I remember was the smell, bacon and eggs. I had fallen back to sleep, as had my brother, but the

smell had woken me. I climbed out of the bed and made my way through into our bedroom. My mattress had been turned over and clean sheets, along with clean pyjamas lay folded at the bottom of the bed. I grabbed the clean pyjama bottoms, pulled them on and went through into the living room.

"Good morning son," my father said, "mam's cooking bacon and eggs with dripping fried bread."

He never mentioned the wet bed, the row or the trifle, neither did mother and as we ate breakfast she was smiling. The trifle had been wiped off the walls and the TV and it wasn't discussed; it was just as if nothing had happened.

"After breakfast we'll get dressed and go to the garden, then we'll meet your mam at granda's for dinner," father said.

I was confused this was a very different story from yesterday and I had no idea what had brought on this transformation.

My brother had decided he would accompany us to the garden and in the privacy of our bedroom, as we got ready, I asked him what was going on and what had happened when I'd gone to bed.

His reply was cocky, "I just watched the telly, mam cleaned the living room then she went and lit the fire in her bedroom. Later dad came back and I was ordered to bed. I listened hard at the wall but couldn't hear what they were saying but when they went to bed their bed was creaking and banging. I reckon they were having a right old shag."

Once again his crudeness shocked me but not wanting to appear ignorant I asked no more questions. My brother was now fourteen and was big for his age. He was playing centre half for Newcastle boys and this had developed him. However, he was crude but he did seem to know a lot about life.

Usually we spent Boxing Day at our house and it was usually a boring day. The presents were always played out and during the day there was nothing on the telly. However, this year it was different, just walking to the gardens was a pleasure. At the gardens, there were a few pigeon lofts open and only a few pigeons were flying.

"Too cold to let the birds out," father said, as he started to clean the loft. He looked in the small corn area and picked some things off the window ledge.

"Here get rid of these," he said.

He handed me a handful of old rubber race rings and my brother eight pigeon eggs. The race rings and the eggs were from last year. The rings granda had been taken off the birds' legs when they had returned from the races. The eggs, as soon as they had been laid, had been taken away from the birds. They had been lying in a small tin box for the past six months. My brother gave me four of the eggs and he kept four. I pushed the race rings into my trouser pocket and then we walked along the gantry to the end of the loft. Standing there because he was taller than I was, he could peer over the fence.

"Be quiet and stand back," he said, pushing me backwards out of the way.

He took one of his eggs and threw it high in the air along the fronts of the other lofts.

"What you doing?" I asked.

"Shut up," he replied.

The second egg he threw was lower, but in the same direction, then he stepped back and he threw his last two eggs roughly in the same direction.

"Bastards," someone shouted, "who's throwing eggs about?" The voice was familiar and I knew it was Rat Face.

"Quick come here," my brother said, dragging me off the gantry and down towards the garden gate. He opened the gate. "Get rid of your eggs," he said and I threw the eggs outside.

"I see you, you little bastards," shouted Rat Face.

I peeked around the gatepost and saw Rat Face; he was running towards our garden and looked very annoyed.

"You've hit me with them stinking eggs," he shouted as he waved his fists in the air.

My brother looked back towards our loft. The gantry was deserted and it was obvious that father hadn't heard the commotion. He grabbed me and pushed me out of the garden and he followed, Rat Face was still running towards us. My brother, holding my arm, strode boldly towards him.

"We're sorry Roger, we didn't realise you were outside your loft," he said as Rat Face stopped in front of us. "We'll clean any mess up."

Rat Face was furious; there was slime in his hair and it was obvious that one of the eggs had hit him on the head. Suddenly his hand shot out and he tried to grab me. I, terrified, jumped back out of his reach.

"Lay off him Roger," my brother said.

"You what? You little twatt," Roger stuttered.

"There are two of us Rat Face and we'll do you," my brother continued.

I glanced around to see who had joined us and who the other person was, then, shocked, I realised he was talking about me.

My brother's words not only shocked me they also shocked Rat Face. He stepped back and eyed the two of us up and down. My brother was slightly taller than Rat Face; he had broad shoulders and, from all the football, was fit. I, still terrified, stepped alongside my brother and the two of us stared at Rat Face.

"What's going on?"

It was my father.

"Your boys have been throwing eggs around and one of them hit me," Rat Face said.

"I'll deal with it Roger," father replied.

Rat Face stared at us, we had just faced him down and he seemed unsure what to do.

"Make sure you do then, them boys is getting out of control," Rat Face spat the words out at father. Then, slowly, he eyed us both up and down. "Next time you'll not be so lucky," he snarled pointing at me, then he turned and walked away.

I couldn't believe it; my admiration for my brother had just risen by one hundred per cent.

"Stupid beggars," father said as he clipped us round the ears, "you're acting like little kids, help me finish up in the loft then we'll get down to granda's."

I couldn't believe father was letting us off so lightly, and as we followed him back to the loft I thought I could see his shoulders rocking as if he was laughing.

We fed the birds then went down to granda's. Tiny, the little dog went wild; it always did when all the family were together. Once again, my brother and I were pushed into the front room, the fire was on and granny's and Uncle Peter's Christmas presents were still there unopened. The four adults went through into the living, room; it was obvious they wished to talk. This time we didn't go to the door and listen. I was content to read my new Broon's Annual and my brother had a football book to read.

That Boxing Day was one of the best ever. I was pleased that the argument between my parents appeared to be over and my mother was once again talking to my grandparents. I was delighted with my Christmas presents but most of all I had seen Rat Face forced to back down by my brother. However, that night, as I lay in bed, between clean sheets, I realised that my brother wouldn't always be with me at the gardens. My fear of Rat Face returned and I hoped I wouldn't meet him. I also hoped and prayed that I wouldn't wet the bed again.

Chapter Fourteen

The New Year arrived and once again our thoughts turned to pairing the birds up. However, something else seemed to be bothering granda and I overheard a conversation between him and my father.

"Well we could discuss it at the AGM," granda said.

"There's nothing to discuss dad," father replied, "you know there's never been any restriction on how many birds one member can enter for a race."

"That's right son," said granda, "but do you think the others realise what's going to happen. The new lofts will be sending ten times as many birds as any of the old lofts and the old member's chances of winning will be greatly reduced. The new men will be dominating the gardens."

"Well then put it on the agenda just to be discussed," replied father, "I know Pincher Martin is keen to discuss it, he was talking to me the other day about it and, if you want, he'll submit it as an agenda item. I'll ask him."

I knew they were talking about mob flying. Secretly I was quite looking forward to the racing season and seeing the three new lofts in action. They had already started settling their birds and the number of pigeons circling the gardens on a Saturday afternoon had greatly increased.

The AGM of the club always took place in early February in the clubhouse and was usually a quiet affair. Granda, Pincher Martin and Dixie Dean were always nominated as the three officials and no one ever opposed them. I attended the AGMs purely as a spectator and father always told me to keep my mouth shut. Just after Christmas, the agenda was always pinned on the club notice board and everyone was aware of the date, time and the items to be discussed.

That year, as I had done in the past, I accompanied my father to the meeting. The meetings always took place on a Sunday morning and usually lasted for half an hour then most of the men disappeared to the local pub. This year as we entered the clubhouse there was a different atmosphere. The three new members sat confidently and prominently at the very back of the room. They were noticeable by their dress; they were wearing expensive suits and sat smoking cigars. A few of the members, including Rat Face and his friends, were sat alongside them and seemed keen to talk to them. I had not read the agenda and expected the usual no trouble meeting.

The chairman, Dixie Dean, opened the meeting. He thanked members for their support over the past year and made comments about last year's races. He welcomed the new members to the club and all three nodded in acknowledgement then he handed over to granda.
"Minutes of last AGM, you've all had copies can I have a proposal to say they're a true record," granda said. "I've not had a fuckin copy," said Billy Spratt.
The other members had nicknamed Billy, 'Billy Bucket Head' but no one ever called him that to his face. Billy was just a little slow, at least that's what granda said, but I really think it was an attempt by granda to justify Billy's swearing. Most of the men used 'bloody' as their chosen swear word. Fuck was seldom used and was shocking, not only because it was swearing but, because of its sexual implication. Why Billy chose it, I don't know perhaps it just chose him. Apart from his swearing, Billy was a real nice man and I liked him.
This claim by Billy was not unusual Billy made the same comment every year.

"Billy, mind your language," replied granda, "and you did get a copy. I stood at the gate and handed them out and members signed to say they had received their copy. I remember you rolled yours up into a telescope and watched the pigeons through it."

"Fuck me, sorry Sammy you're fuckin right," said Billy triumphantly. "Now I fuckin remember, fuck it, I'll propose they're a true record."

Billy's use of the fuck word was quite funny, it was the only swear word he ever used and occasionally he even split words up to introduce it. The one big word that Billy used a lot was incidentally and in Billy's vocabulary, it became inci-fuckin-dentally.

No one disagreed that the minutes weren't a true record and someone shouted, "Seconded." The rest of the members grunted, which meant get on with the business.

"Matters arising from those minutes?" asked Dixie Dean.

No one spoke.

"No matters arising, next item, treasurer's report," said Dixie.

Pincher Martin had produced his usual financial report and copies had been circulated. Pincher was a very thorough person, his report was very accurate, and usually very little discussion took place on it.

"You've all had copies of the report," said Pincher, "if there are any questions I'll be pleased to answer them."

The room was silent and everyone stared at their sheets of paper. It was doubtful if half the men in the room understood Pincher's report.

"Mister Treasurer, under miscellaneous expenditure there is no explanation as to what this money has been spent on," said a voice from the back.

Pincher looked stunned, someone was actually questioning the detail of his report and immediately everyone, looking for miscellaneous expenditure, shuffled their papers.

"Of course it doesn't," replied Pincher, "the total is only three pounds and it's been spent on things like string, cardboard tags for the baskets, pencils and other small miscellaneous items. If I detailed them all there would be a long list."

"I would have expected all items that have member's funds spent on them to be accounted for," said the voice from the back and everyone turned to see who was making the comments.

George Clarke was standing, with the treasurer's report in his hand, staring at Pincher. Pincher just glared back at the new member.

"He's right you know," interrupted Rat Face, "it's wor money and you should be telling us what you've been doing with it."

"Every year for the past thirty years I've put in miscellaneous expenditure and no one has ever questioned it before. If you think I am detailing every pencil, ball of string, tin of paint or bottle of ink you are wrong. However, if you want to see the receipts I will provide them for you. The only receipt I don't have is one from you for that replacement glass for the notice board," replied Pincher glaring at Rat Face.

Everyone in the room knew that Rat Face's brother worked in a glazier's shop and he got pieces of glass for nothing. Dixie Dean, sensing the tension that was building in the room, interrupted.

"I think Pincher's report, as usual, contains enough information and I have no reason to question it. Pincher has said that he has all of the receipts and if anyone wants to see them he'll provide them, and that should be more than enough for any member. As for you Roger, you'll have to provide a receipt for that glass. If there are no more questions we'll move onto the next item on the agenda."

There was an embarrassed silence in the room and members rustled their papers. George Clarke smiled and nodded at Dixie then sat down.

"Next item, nomination of officials," announced Dixie.

"Nominate Mister Clarke as chairman," shouted Rat Face.

The room now went deathly quiet. Dixie stared at the room full of men and they all stared back, it was obvious to me that Dixie wasn't expecting this.

"You'll need a seconder for that nomination," said Dixie in a quiet voice.

"Seconded," came a voice from the back of the room. I glanced over and just saw Jimmy the labourer, sitting alongside Rat Face, sheepishly lowering his hand.

"Any other nominations?" asked Dixie.

"Nominate Dixie Dean," shouted Mattie Walker.

"Seconded," came a voice from the front of the room.
"Well that means we'll have to vote on it," said Dixie.

It was obvious to me, and probably to the majority of the members, that none of the three officials had expected any voting to take place. The usual "vote to elect all three officials back into office," had not come. Now granda stood up and Dixie sat down.

"There are two nominations for the position of chairman, any more?" asked granda.

The room was silent. However, men sitting at the front of the room started turning round to get a look at Mr Clarke then they started muttering. Rat Face and his friends sat at the back of the room smiling triumphantly. Mr Clarke and the two other new members just stared straight ahead.

"Anyone want to speak for or against any of the nominations," granda asked.

Rat Face jumped up.

"Yes I'd just like to say Nobby is new to the club, but."

He was stopped mid sentence by Mr Clarke's voice.

"You can cut that crap out, my name's George or Mr Clarke, definitely not Nobby."

Rat Face was stunned.

"I was just saying that George is new to the club but is used to running a business, and I think we need new management at the top of the club," he stuttered then abruptly he sat down.

Blanco sitting at the front of the room raised his hand and granda nodded at him. Slowly Blanco stood up and turned to face the members. I suppose, standing at the front of the room, he was an imposing figure but his raincoat lost him some credibility. However, as he stood alone in front of all those men I had to admire his courage.

"I am a young in this a pigeon club, I a listen and am a ashamed. Mister Dixie Dean is a fine man; he is a friend and a gentleman. Mr Clarke is a new and has a never flown a pigeon in the club. He a may be a fine man but I a no likee," with that Blanco sat down.

The other members exchanged glances and it was obvious that no one else wished to speak. The vote did not take long and Dixie was voted back in. However, a number of the members, mainly Rat Face's friends, voted for Mr Clarke. Granda and Pincher Martin were re-elected as secretary and treasurer but, the writing was on the wall and everyone knew that next year there would be more nominations.

The meeting continued and a number of items, race points and over-fly times were discussed. Then the final item 'Restricting numbers of birds per member, per race' was introduced. Granda explained how the club had never restricted members entering any number of pigeons for any race. But now, he explained, with the new lofts and their capability to contain and fly very large numbers of birds, the members might feel that certain lofts will have an advantage. Everyone turned and glanced back at the three new members. They sat undisturbed and at ease smoking their cigars.

"Really it's an item just for discussion," said granda, "but we would like your opinion on it."

"Mister Secretary," a voice boomed from the back and everyone jumped.

George Clarke was once again standing and he was an impressive figure.

"Mister Secretary," he repeated, "I have a simple question for you. Last year, how many birds did you send to the Peterborough race when Blanco won?"

"Ten," replied granda.

"And how many birds did Blanco send?" continued George Clarke?"

"Two," replied granda.

"Well then, tell me what is the difference between me sending fifty birds, you ten and Blanco two? You sent five times as many birds as Blanco so what's wrong with me sending five times as many birds as you?"

"Bloody frightened they'll lose control of the gardens," shouted Rat Face.

George Clarke looked at him and Rat Face shrunk into his seat.

"And remember mister secretary," George Clarke continued, "the more pigeons I put in, and nominate, the more prize money there is."

Talk of increased prize money stirred everyone.

"I think he's fuckin right Sammy," interrupted Billy Bucket Head.

"Mind I won't be sending fifty birds per race," said George Clarke staring at granda, "so really I won't have the same advantage as you had over Blanco," with that he sat down.

It seemed to have become a personal thing between granda and George Clarke and both men stared at each other.

"We're wasting good drinking time," someone shouted from the back.

"Anyone else want to speak on the matter?" asked granda.

Once again, the room was silent and men shook their heads.

Dixie glanced around the room then stood up and declared the meeting closed.

When all the members had gone, father, the three officials and I were the only people left in the clubhouse. Usually at this point, in previous meetings, there had been a good feeling and we would all be looking forward to a new season.

"I smell trouble," said Pincher.

"I think your right," replied granda, "but we've tried to be fair, we've tried to discuss the matter but time moves on and we, as officials of the club, must move with it."

Dixie never said anything; it was obvious to all of us that the votes against him had hurt him.

"Don't take it to heart Dixie," said Pincher, "it was only Rat Face trying to cause trouble; you saw how he was with me. The members voted you in, they know you're the best man for the job."

Dixie just smiled and left the clubhouse. When we left all three of the new members were standing outside talking. George Clarke was in the road haulage business as was one of the other new members Tommy Tippins. The third new member was a younger scrap merchant called Malcolm Ash. I didn't like him he was a wide lad, always had an answer a bit like my brother.

"No hard feelings Sammy," George said.

"None taken George," said granda.

Back at the loft, granda and father discussed which birds they would be pairing together.

"The three new lofts are already paired up," said granda.

"How do you know?" asked father.

"For the last week all the shutters have been closed and during the week, when it was frosty, there was no frost on top of those three lofts. They've installed some form of paraffin heating system," replied granda.

"Can't be paraffin dad, you wouldn't put paraffin heaters in the loft. The fumes would affect the birds breathing and besides its bloody dangerous leaving lit paraffin heaters in the loft."

"They're not inside the lofts son; they're in small corrugated iron sheds alongside the lofts. They're heating some water pipes that they've installed underneath the lofts with header tanks inside the corrugated sheds," replied granda.

I could see the look of amazement on my father's face.

"They'll be two weeks ahead of all the gardens with their breeding programme then," said father.

"That's right son, they'll be flying big youngins and their oldins will be well through the feeding period by the time of the first race," said granda.

Whilst the whole family had gone to granny's at Christmas, my mother had still not agreed to return to the old days and go every Sunday for dinner. That Sunday when we left granda at the garden instead of going straight home, out of curiosity, we went round to the new lofts. Mattie Walker and Billy Spratt were standing staring at the lofts and as we approached them, they smiled at us.

Mattie Walker nodded at father and said, "funny meeting this morning, felt a bit sorry for Dixie, not the usual friendly atmosphere."

Then he nodded towards the new lofts.

"Sammy doesn't want to buy eggs does he?" he asked.

"What?" replied father.

"Eggs, the new lads are taking orders for eggs. Fifty quid gets you two eggs from that Yorkshire, Lillers winner. Five quid gets you an egg from Blanco's Peterborough bird."

Once again I saw a look of amazement on father's face.

"Blanco's not selling eggs?" he said.

"Not Blanco," replied Mattie laughing, "George Clarke, he bought Blanco's blue hen. The lads reckon Blanco got fifty quid for it. That's what surprised us when he spoke against George this morning."

It was obvious to Mattie that all of this was news to us and he seemed pleased to be passing it on.

"Seen the heating system?" he continued and pointed towards George Clarke's loft. "See the pipes underneath the loft; they're carrying hot water from that corrugated iron shed at the side of the loft. Paraffin heaters are heating the boiler in the shed and hot water is circulating through the pipes."

"Fuckin Clever eh?" interrupted Billy, "I'm going to do my fuckin loft"

"Billy you'll burn your loft down, don't go messing with paraffin heaters," said father.

Having spent some time with Mattie and Billy, discussing the benefits of heating the lofts, we eventually made our way home. Walking down the West Road father shook his head and said.

"I cannot believe Blanco sold that blue hen, he was going to keep it and breed from her, I'm shocked."

Blanco appeared to be unpredictable and once again the doubts about him came into my head and I decided to watch him closely during the coming racing season.

The shock of realising that the new lofts had already paired up their birds spread like wildfire throughout the gardens. Men started to board up their loft windows and mysterious paraffin heater devices appeared in greenhouses and tin shacks hurriedly built alongside the lofts.

"We'll pair up on the fourteenth of February as usual," said granda.

We had come to the garden that Monday night because father was keen to tell granda about Blanco selling his blue hen. We stood on the gantry looking down the Tyne Valley admiring the streetlights.

"I'll not be rushed into changing my ways," granda said glancing at my father, "and yes, I did know that Blanco had sold his blue hen. He came to tell me that George Clarke had offered him fifty pounds for the bird. His mother's not well and he needed to buy her some warm clothing and extra food. I told him to take the money and get his priorities right."

My father just shook his head and said, "George Clarke is buying every bird that's won a race on these gardens. Once he's bred off them and starts racing them he'll win everything."

"Nothing we can do to stop him buying pigeons," replied granda, "and besides he hasn't bought every pigeon that's won a race. He didn't get Huwey and Pincher Martin's knocked him back, he wouldn't sell George any of his birds. There are a few men who will still be racing quality birds. I suppose George will argue that, by breeding from proven, quality birds, he is improving the bloodstock on the gardens. He is selling eggs and men are buying them, so it seems it is what the members want. Although I cannot see how you can prove which egg came from which bird."

I just listened to the conversation with interest.

Chapter Fifteen

Because the three new lofts had paired up early, they were the first lofts that granda visited to record the ring numbers of the young birds. One week after we had paired up and settled our birds in their nesting boxes he called at the three new lofts. He said he was doing them a favour, but really, I think he was bursting with curiosity to see how their young birds had turned out. We waited at our loft for him to return and were surprised when, after a very short period, looking shocked, he came back through the garden gate clutching three pieces of paper.

"Just gave me a list of ring numbers, never seen the birds or the youngins," he said disappointedly.

"Can they do that?" asked father.

"No reason why not, there's nothing written down by The Union saying I have to see the birds," replied granda.

However, the incident did not go unnoticed and weeks later, when granda visited the remainder of the club member's lofts he was not made welcome. At some, he just received lists of numbers; this of course was mostly from Rat Face and his friends.

The rift between granda and Rat Face, my doubts about Blanco, the introduction of the new members, the voting at the AGM and the change in attitude towards our family were all having an effect upon me. My previous feelings of security and safety whilst at the gardens were slowly being eroded. The gardens no longer felt welcoming and I was beginning to feel threatened. Granda never mentioned the changes but I knew he was worried. One afternoon when we were sitting watching the pigeons as they played around the bath he said,

"Do you know why I started breeding and racing pigeons?"

I just looked at him; it was unusual for him to talk about himself or his past.

"No," I answered, "I've never really thought about it."

It was true, granda and pigeons were synonymous and I had never thought to question how or why.

"During the war, in the trenches, the signallers used cables and Morse code to pass messages, it worked but frequently the cables got snapped or blown up."

Now he really had my attention. Granda had never talked to me about the war and although I had tried to question him, he would never be drawn.

"Sometimes instead of running cables through the trenches they'd use pigeons. The officers had set up lofts behind the trenches and the birds would home to these lofts."

I was enthralled, pigeons at war; it was fascinating.

"Well, they'd bring small pannier baskets of pigeons into the trenches and we'd have to spot for the German big guns being fired. Then, on a slip of paper, our officer would make a note of the location of the guns and attach it to the bird's leg. We would sit in the trench and watch as the officer threw the bird up. In that completely dead landscape, a bird that was free to fly where it wanted was the most wonderful thing to watch. The pigeons would circle then head off back behind our lines to the loft. Unfortunately, the Germans were always watching and their snipers would start shooting at the birds. They shot quite a few but some did get away. Then a few hours later our artillery would open up and shells would whistle over our heads into the German positions."

He stopped talking and stared at the pigeons then very quietly, he started again.

"I remember one particular day when the trench floor was just a mess of thick, clinging mud but we'd laid our trench capes on top of the mud and along with the rest of our kit, we were lying in the sun. It was the first day in a week when it hadn't rained and it was an opportunity for all of us to try to dry everything. The sky, a clear cloudless blue, was magnificent and the silence was intense. Suddenly three pigeons, liberated by one of our officers, flew along the trench. Desperately the birds flapped their wings and tried to gain height. Enviously all of us in the trenches watched those pigeons. Unlike us, they were free. As they gained height and climbed into the sky, to all the troops, they were symbols of freedom and hope. Two of the birds, still trying to gain height, veered to the left and circled. The third bird veered right and sped off behind our lines. All of us, including the Germans, cheered. We all knew that fastened to the birds' legs was a message giving the co-ordinates of the German big guns. It didn't matter to any of us, the front line troops on both sides didn't care; we were so well dug in that even the big guns couldn't get at us.

The German snipers were slow. Like us, they must have been enjoying the sunshine but then shots rang out. The two pigeons still circling turned into balls of feathers and fell back to earth behind the enemy lines. The third bird, now just a dot in the sky, flew on and we all cheered. How we wished that, like that bird, we could fly back to our homes and our waiting families. That one bird had what you must look for in a good racing pigeon. It was capable of thinking for itself, it didn't follow the others, and it knew where it was going and went for it."

Granda hesitated and I waited, I had hung on his every word, then suddenly he laughed and continued.

"I remember once in the winter when we were freezing and starving the signallers arrived with a basket of six pigeons and some corn. As soon as they left, we stole the lot, basket, pigeons and corn. Ten of us ate them pigeons and the corn; for us it was like a Christmas dinner, only better. To fool the officers we put the heads, wings and feathers back into the basket and blew it up. I have always regretted eating those wonderful birds. I don't know if the officers knew what we'd done but there was no trouble over it. Since those days son I've always respected and admired the birds."

I was stunned this was the first occasion when I'd heard granda talk about the war, but I knew he wasn't talking to me he was thinking out loud. His eyes were glazed and he was back in the trenches. He must have realised what he had been saying and suddenly he appeared embarrassed.

"Take no notice of me son, just a sentimental, old man reminiscing," he said, "but," he continued, "always, remember this, three things change everything, money, power and time."

I was taken by surprise and confused so I asked him what he meant.

"Nothing son," he said, "just thinking out loud again."

Slowly he got up from the seat and I watched him as he chased the birds back into the loft. His movement was less sprightly than usual, his shoulders seemed stooped and there was an air of disappointment and frustration about him. I knew he didn't want to talk anymore so I helped him lock the loft then made my way home.

Before the racing season started the council wrote to granda asking if he would attend a meeting at the Town Hall. He went to the meeting and when he returned to the gardens everyone was keen to know what was going on.

"Nothing to worry about," he said, "the council is releasing more land at the back of the gardens. There will be sufficient land for another ten lofts. The plots are going to be bigger and if any of the existing members want to change plots, the council will give them priority. A number of the existing members, mainly the younger men, were keen to take up the offer.

"What do you think dad?" my father asked, "we could move, build a bigger and better loft, put in heating and even build the loft using bricks or concrete. We could really build a loft to be proud of."

I could see the disappointment in granda's eyes.

"Are you not proud of this loft son?" he asked.

Father must have realised what he had said.

"I never meant it that way dad," he replied.

However, the damage had been done. Granda left the garden and I watched him from the gantry as he slowly walked round to the back of the gardens to look at the land that would be released.

We did not move the loft; we stayed on our old site. Two other members did opt to move to the new garden sites at the back of the gardens. I think my father realised how thoughtless his comments had been and how much he'd hurt granda and it was only then that I understood how vulnerable the old man was. I say old man because it was only now that I was beginning to realise that granda was getting older and time was taking its toll on him.

There was no doubt that times were changing. That year, 1958, the first race from Selby attracted 550 birds from the club. Usually because this was the first race of the season it was popular and about 400 birds were entered. The majority of the extra birds all came from the three new lofts.

"They're mental," Pincher Martin said when he and granda were discussing the race, "those birds have never raced to the lofts. They were only home trained last year. Granted they have had youngins, which should be an incentive, but probably half of them will return to their old lofts. They're just throwing pigeons away."

"Don't be so sure," replied granda, "those three loft managers are experienced race men; they should know what they're doing."

That Selby race was a new experience for everyone. The birds were liberated on time and it was a clear sunny day. Pincher, as usual, standing in his look out position, was staring out over the Tyne Valley.

"Here they come," he shouted, "bloody cavalry charge, about thirty birds and they're all for the gardens."

His inability to positively identify any of the birds must have annoyed him, because suddenly he started again and I felt he was trying to regain some of his credibility.

"Sammy's red cock is there and there's one for me," he shouted excitedly.

We watched as the flock of birds, at first just black dots, flew along the valley then turned to approach the gardens.

"One more on its own over the church," Pincher called out and everyone glanced towards the church, "Blanco's blue cock, gannin like a train," he shouted breathlessly.

The gardens erupted, corn tins rattled; men shouted and kicked out at their droppers. Blanco's white fantails fluttered up then dropped back onto his gantry. The atmosphere was electric and the noise deafening, men called out, "how way, how way, come on."

Pincher was right it was like a cavalry charge but Blanco's pigeon was going to win. The bird was a good twenty seconds in front of the flock but they were catching it. I had to admit it was exciting and the introduction of more pigeons had certainly made the race thrilling. Every club member must have believed they had a pigeon in that flock as they were all shouting and the noise was deafening.

Blanco's pigeon, well in the lead, approached his loft, clapped its wings together and turned right to sweep back along the fronts of the other lofts.

"God that bird's fit, it still wants to fly," gasped granda.

However, his attention quickly returned to the rapidly approaching flock. Birds spun out of the formation, some circled and others, like stones, dropped straight into their lofts. To actually see who had won was impossible and without Pincher's commentary, no one knew who had pigeons home. The 'clunk' of clocks being struck, as fanciers timed in their birds, could be heard all over the gardens. Granda was definitely amongst the winners; his red cock bird had left the flock and dived straight into the loft. I had watched amazed as the pigeons arrived and I knew that some of the birds had flown straight to the new lofts at the rear of the gardens.

"Did you see the winner?" granda asked.

"Couldn't tell," I replied, "there were so many birds and they were diving all over the place but we'll not be far away."

Granda was standing on the gantry and gazing around the gardens trying hard to see who was celebrating but everyone seemed stunned. Birds had been clocked in all over the gardens and to say who had the first pigeon was impossible. However, one pigeon was still flying. Blanco's blue cock was soaring high in the sky then swooping down to skim along the front of the lofts; obviously, it was still enjoying itself.

"You'll never drop that bird Blanco unless you shoot it," someone shouted and laughter rippled from some of the lofts.

"That bird has never raced from Selby," said granda, "the bloody thing's just starting to enjoy itself."

I watched the bird as it flew higher and higher into the sky, it certainly appeared to be enjoying itself.

Later when everyone gathered in the clubhouse, the atmosphere was electric. Men were queuing with their clocks and talking excitedly. The clock committee was taking its time opening the clocks and thoroughly examining every circular dial of timing paper. Everyone realised how close the race had been and father and I stood quietly near the back of the room. We knew that the times would be close and seconds would count.

"Bloody great race Sammy," someone said.

We turned to see George Clarke standing behind us.

"So much for your theory that more birds will spoil the racing. Everyone here says it's the best race they've ever seen."

Granda smiled.

"It was a good race," he replied.

The clock committee eventually finished examining the dials and compiled the result list.

"First Pincher Martin, second, one second after Pincher, Sammy Baker, third George Clarke."

Everyone agreed that it had been a great race and we were pleased to have taken second place. George Clarke was disappointed with his third place; I really think he expected to win that first race. However, I knew that, for weeks to come, everybody would be talking about the excitement of the finish. Amidst all this excitement it seemed to me that everyone had forgotten about one thing. During the clock opening Blanco had stood alongside us, his pigeon had eventually dropped but far too late to be clocked in and he had come to the clubhouse purely out of curiosity. A couple of the men had joked with him about the pigeon.

"You're over-feeding them, that bird wasn't hungry, it was full of corn, the bird was enjoying itself," they said. No one seemed to question the credibility of Blanco's bird or have any doubts about it, but I did.

Back in the security of our garden, once again, I raised the question of Blanco's birds with granda and my father.

"I know it is queer how his pigeons are always so fit," said granda, "sometimes I think they haven't been to the race points but I can't think of a way that he could fiddle the system. The birds are all taken to the clubhouse in baskets and owners aren't allowed to race basket they're own birds. All the owner's baskets are placed on the floor then the basketing committee takes over. Each bird is removed and the rubber race ring goes onto its leg. The race rings all come in one box and the ring itself is on a piece of cardboard with the ring's number on it. The rubber ring goes onto the bird's leg and the cardboard with the number on goes back into the box. The committee keep a record of the numbers against the owner's names. The birds are then placed in the race baskets; cocks and hens are separated. The baskets are sealed and the seals are checked before the race baskets go onto the conveyors lorries."

"I've thought about it," interrupted father, "the pigeon would have to be removed from the basket before the conveyors collected the baskets and I don't know how that's possible."

"Tell you what young man," said granda ruffling my hair, "next few races you and I will watch the basketing committee at work. If anything is going on we'll spot it."

Chapter Sixteen

The second race of the season was once again from Doncaster. Blanco had won this race last year with his blue hen. These early races were always short and were a good start to the season. It re-introduced the birds to the race baskets and the liberation procedure and a short race also created greater interest for the club members. Following the first Selby cavalry charge, everyone was fired up for the second Doncaster race. That Friday night as the basketing took place everyone was excited.

Club members were not allowed into the clubhouse when the pigeons were being ringed and transferred into the race baskets. The members brought their baskets with their nametags on and left them in the clubhouse then the basketing committee took over. Granda explained to me that once members had paid their nomination money to Dixie Dean, they had to leave the clubhouse. No members were allowed to stay in the clubhouse when the birds were being race basketed. At one time, they had been allowed to stay but they had made too much noise and had been a distraction for the basketing committee. However, as granda was secretary of the club he was allowed to watch. To check the procedures, officials of the club, could stand at the back and watch and none of the basketing committee seemed surprised to see us. They never questioned our presence and set to work recording race ring numbers and placing the pigeons in the race baskets. I watched fascinated.

Because of the excitement and success of the first race it seemed that every member had entered more pigeons for this race and baskets of birds covered the clubhouse floor. The rumour, that because many birds would be entered the prize money would be high, had obviously spread throughout the gardens. We, as normal, would enter ten birds. We basketed our birds in the loft then went to Blanco's loft and he put his three birds into the second compartment of granda's small basket. Even though we had doubts about Blanco, granda insisted that we continued as normal. He would not prejudge Blanco and I think he still valued his friendship.

"It's about time you were buying your own basket Blanco," granda said.

We had lent Blanco one big old basket for his training flights but it was too big just to carry birds to the clubhouse. Since he had arrived on the gardens, for race basketing, we had always allowed him to put his birds into the second compartment of our sectioned off small basket. Granda liked this small divided basket. When he was training the birds it allowed him to keep the cock and hen birds apart.

"I a know Sammy," Blanco replied. "But I'm a still a trying to get a mee mama better. She's a still wheezing and needs medicine and warm clothing, this season if I a win I'm a gona buy a basket."

Granda had just shrugged and watched as Blanco placed his three birds into the basket.

In the clubhouse, I stood quietly at the back, fascinated by the race ringing procedure. Dixie Dean sat at a table with a huge ledger in front of him. Billy Bucket Head had the job of removing the pigeons from each member's baskets. He would take a bird out of a basket, then holding the bird still he would offer its left legs forward to Mattie Walker. Mattie was operating the ringing machine. This ringing machine was a stainless steel device, which screwed onto the top of a table and, fitted at the back was a handle, which when turned opened a set of pointed jaws. As Billy lifted the birds out of the baskets he read the number from the metal ring on the bird's leg. Then, amazingly without swearing, he called out the number that was on the metal ring and Dixie made a note of it in the ledger. From a box on the table, Dixie removed a slip of cardboard with a race ring on it. He removed the rubber race ring and handed it to Mattie, Mattie then stretched it over the pointed jaws of the ringing machine. As Mattie turned the handle at the back of the machine the jaws opened stretching the rubber race ring wide open. Billy placed the bird's leg between the jaws and Mattie slowly turned the handle closing the jaws. The machine's jaws were silver and slippery and as the jaws closed the rubber ring slid off onto the bird's leg. The jaws never fully closed and the ring always slid off long before the bird's leg could be trapped. The bird was never harmed and Mattie would shout out the number on the rubber race ring. Dixie in his slow methodical way recorded the race ring number against the metal ring number and the name of the member whose pigeon it was.

The pigeon was then passed to Blanco who stood, imposingly in his overcoat alongside the race baskets, obviously pleased with his position of authority. He accepted the pigeon from Billy in his right hand, opened the small trap door on the top of the race basket with his left hand, and placed the pigeon inside. There were always two baskets alongside Blanco, one for cock birds and one for hen birds. Each basket took twenty-five pigeons and Blanco counted them as he placed them in the baskets. When a basket was full Jack Morris stepped forward threaded a wire through the front basket door and using a device not unlike a pair of pliers crushed a lead seal onto the wire, this effectively sealed the basket. He then placed an empty basket alongside Blanco, took the full basket and placed it alongside the clubhouse door. Here the baskets stayed awaiting the arrival of the transporter. The procedure worked liked clockwork.

The committee involved in the ringing worked quickly and efficiently. Whether this was because we were watching or not I don't know. However, I do know that I was impressed. Billy for all of his shortcomings could handle pigeons very well. The birds struggled as he caught them but calmed as he held them and read off the ring numbers. What was noticeable was the difference in handling between Billy and Blanco.

When Billy passed the birds to Blanco any fighting or resistance they had offered disappeared. In his usual confidant way Blanco held out his huge right hand and accepted the birds from Billy. Then he stroked them, only once with his left hand and the birds stopped struggling and lay calm in his hand. Quickly his left hand opened the small trap door on top of the basket and his right hand disappeared into the race basket then it reappeared empty. Even when he'd placed the pigeons in the race baskets, for a few minutes, they appeared calm and docile. Blanco's movements reminded me of the party and his magician's act and I looked twice at his face to see if he was wearing his clown's makeup.

"What do you think?" granda asked.

I just smiled; the whole procedure looked foolproof and impressive.

The success of last week's race was obvious. Once again, there were five hundred and fifty birds to be recorded and basketed. The workers that made up the basketing committee plodded on and slowly the pile of member's baskets grew smaller. I watched as our basket was opened and Billy started removing birds.

"Red Cock 6952 Sammy Baker," he shouted and held the bird out to have its race ring fitted.

Blanco held out his right hand and accepted the red cock bird from Billy; he smiled at granda and placed the bird into the race basket.

"Let's hope that's the winner," granda said winking at me.

Our birds were basketed and Billy opened the second compartment of the basket and removed Blanco's pigeons. I watched as, one by one, the three blue pigeons were taken out, their numbers recorded and race rings placed on their legs. Blanco's routine never changed his right hand accepted the bird, he opened the small trap door on the basket with his left hand, place the bird in the basket and removed his right hand. I watched until he accepted the last bird then something changed. It did, I was sure of it I definitely saw it. For some reason Blanco accepted the last blue pigeon with his left hand but he still opened the small basket trap door with his left hand and placed a bird into the race basket with his right hand. I nearly didn't see it. No one else noticed anything and I, very confused, stared at Blanco. Why had he changed his rhythm? Why had he changed hands? The questions raced through my head.

Granda was watching Billy and I tugged at his coat sleeve.

"Did you see it?" I whispered.

"See what?" he answered.

Not wanting anyone to hear I whispered,

"Blanco changed hands."

"He did what?" granda asked.

"He changed hands," I replied.

Granda stared at me.

"Sorry son you've lost me, what did he do?" he said.

I glanced across towards Blanco; he was still doing his job accepting the pigeons from Billy. Only now, he was smiling and staring at me and suddenly I was afraid. Blanco's smile wasn't friendly it was intense and intimidating and I felt the hairs on the back of my neck rising. Granda was also staring at me waiting for an answer to his question.

I felt like crying, I felt so helpless. I knew something had happened but what had I seen? I really didn't know the answer. I knew that Blanco had done something, his stare told me so but his stare was also threatening 'You saw nothing,' it said.

"What's up?" granda said interrupting my thoughts.

"Nothing," I whispered, "can we go outside?"

We left the clubhouse and made our way back to our loft.

"Whatever's wrong boy?" granda asked as we entered the garden, "you've gone as white as a sheet."

I tried to explain to granda what I had seen.

"Blanco took all of the other pigeons in his right hand. Then when it came to his last bird, the blue cock, the one that came for him last week, he took it in his left hand but, he put it into the basket with his right hand."

I could see the puzzled look on granda's face and I knew he didn't share my doubts.

"But you saw the bird go into the basket?" he asked.

I nodded.

"And it was a blue cock bird."

I nodded.

"Well I think so," I said quickly, "it was definitely a blue pigeon."

"Well what's the problem?"

I was nearly in tears, I was so frustrated, I knew there was a problem; I knew that Blanco had done something. His defiant look had told me so his arrogance, his threatening smile, everything had been so bold. He was treating me like a child, he thought I couldn't harm him and I was hurt.

"Tell you what, we'll go and count the birds in the race baskets see if any are missing," granda said.

I wasn't sure; the last thing I wanted was to draw attention to myself and hesitantly, probably cowardly, I replied.

"I'll wait here."

Granda left the garden and I feeling miserable, sat on the bench outside the loft watching the pigeons picking at bits of sand and corn. I didn't know what to think, it was obvious that granda had doubts about my story. The fact that Blanco had changed hands didn't seem to bother him. I waited hoping that a problem would be found and my credibility in granda's eyes would be restored. Eventually, the garden gate swung open and I, expecting granda to be there, jumped from the bench. It wasn't him, Blanco stood in the doorway smiling at me.

"Is a Sammy here?" he asked.

Open mouthed I just stared at him.

"No, eh no, he's gone to the clubhouse," I stuttered.

"Oh that's a shame, but you a must a feel a very grown up boy looking after the loft," Blanco said.

I nodded.

"Did you enjoy a watching the basketing?" he asked.

The smile on his face told me it wasn't just a question, he was gloating.

"It's good," I replied.

"Tomorrow I a think I a will win. My a blue cock will a drop when he comes a home you a just a watch and see."

With that Blanco turned and left the garden and once again, alone and nearly in tears, I stood shaking just staring at the gate.

Ten minutes later, I was still looking at the gate when it swung open and I jumped back.

"Checked all the race baskets, they all have twenty five birds in, they're all sealed and now loaded onto the transporter, can't see anything wrong."

It was granda and he pushed past me and chased the pigeons back into the loft.

"Come on we'll go home and set the clocks," he said.

For him that seemed to be the end of the matter but for me, it wasn't. My hatred of Blanco was now complete. I knew he had done something dishonest and not only was he fixing the races, he was also threatening me and treating me like a child and that was too much.

Chapter Seventeen

Saturday morning dawned clear and bright. Unlike my brother, I hadn't gained a place on the school football team so I had all morning to think over my situation. I was frightened to go to the gardens but I knew I had to. I knew Blanco would win, he had told me so last night. I knew last night, when he stood in the garden, he was bragging. He had beaten me, he'd fooled all the basketing committee and granda and he'd come to the garden to gloat. He must have seen granda leave and he knew I would be on my own.

Reluctantly I made my way to the gardens. As I walked down the path from the West Road to our garden I could feel the tension in the air. All the lofts were open and there was a buzz of conversation between different lofts.

"Today's my day," someone shouted.

"Nee chance," a voice replied.

Nervously, as I walked, I looked around but thankfully, I was on my own. My father always worked Saturday mornings and made his way straight to the garden from work. As I approached Blanco's loft I could see that the loft was open and the two fantails were playing around on the gantry, but luckily, there was no sign of Blanco. With my head down I hurried past Blanco's loft and dashed into the safety of our garden.

"Someone chasing you?" granda said.

I smiled then noticed Blanco standing behind him.

"Eee's a fine a boy your grandson Sammy. Never play the a piano but one a day he be a famous pigeon man," Blanco said.

Granda look at him and grunted. It was unusual for Blanco to make such a long statement.

"I a go," Blanco said and walked towards the gate. As he passed me he ruffled my hair and I stepped back shocked by his confidence.

"Thinks he's going to win today," granda said, "seems bloody confident that he's going to win. Worst thing we ever did giving him that old blue hen, she must be producing good youngins now."

I said nothing.

The birds were on time and as usual, Pincher announced their arrival.

"One bird over the church looks like Blanco's blue cock." The disappointment could be heard in his voice and the gardens fell silent. It was Blanco's blue cock and it flew straight along the front of the gardens and dropped straight into his loft. Everyone watched in silence as the pigeon dropped and the thump of Blanco's clock, being struck, was heard.

"That bird wasn't going to mess about," granda said, "the bloody thing looked tired and half starved."

"Out of the valley," it was Pincher again, "whole flock of them, like a swarm of bees."

The excitement had returned to his voice but the impact had gone. Everyone knew Blanco's blue cock was fully nominated and all the big money had gone.

"Sammy's red cocks amongst them, so'ssss mine," chanted Pincher comically.

Then, as the pigeons arrived, all hell broke loose. To get to their lofts birds darted across one another and men cursed and swore as their pigeons refused to drop. However, once again, the Baker family's red cock dropped like a stone straight through the doors into the back of the loft and granda clocked him in.

The clubhouse was full when we arrived with our clock and everyone was talking. Blanco was at the front handing in his clock.

"By god that pigeon didn't mess around this week," someone said to him.

"No he's a good a bird just a needs a training to drop," replied Blanco.

"Best fuckin way to train him to drop is put a small piece of fuckin lead in the left side of his fuckin head," the voice replied.

"Eh a how can I a do that," asked Blanco.

"With a fucking shotgun," the voice replied.

Everyone knew who the comedian was and burst out laughing.

"Bird looked knackered," said granda as Blanco passed us on his way out of the clubhouse.

"Yes he's a had a hard flight," Replied Blanco.

"My red cock birds in good condition but your bird looked flown out, I didn't think it had been a hard race," said granda.

"Different birds, a different a condition," replied Blanco as he hurried past us.

Father and I waited outside the clubhouse with the rest of the members until Dixie Dean came out with granda and stuck the results on the notice board. Blanco was first Pincher was second again, and George Clark was third, we were fourth.

"Tell you one thing," granda said as we walked back to the loft, "the man with the best pigeons on these gardens is Pincher Martin. He's always in the first three and has birds for every distance."

I was frustrated because no one had mentioned Blanco and eventually when we were standing in the garden, I couldn't contain myself.

"Granda, Blanco's bird was knackered, yet ours and Pincher's were in good condition, how can that be?"

He knew what I was suggesting.

"I'm tired of this argument about Blanco," he said, "I know how suspicious you are but I cannot prove anything. Moreover, I can't think of any way that Blanco could be fiddling the system. The best we can do is keep watching him and the basketing committee."

We watched the basketing of the pigeons for the next three races and nothing seemed untoward. However, Blanco stopped winning and much to everyone's delight his birds weren't in the first ten places. Infact he sent no pigeons to one of the races.

"Ah Sammy my birds are a tired I a no likee," he said as he discussed his birds with granda, "I a give them a week off, next week they's at Hatfield and I a think I's a got a chance."

Whilst Blanco went backwards in the winnings stakes, George Clarke moved forward. He won the third race of the season from Grantham, 160 miles, just beating Pincher. Then in the fourth race from Peterborough, 200 miles, he was second to Topper Brown. We were third and granda was pleased. The other two new lofts were also starting to make an impact Tommy Tippins had two bird in the first ten from both race points and Malcolm Ash took first and fourth places from Hitchin, 250 miles, the fifth race point. Both of them seemed happy with the way things were going.

The council released the extra garden sites at the back of the gardens and the lofts were to be built, as a final row of ten, which when completed would fill the pigeon club site. A number of men had been making enquiries with granda about the sites and he was of the opinion that the gardens would be filled quickly.

"Be bloody good prize money when all the gardens are filled," George Clarke said as we went into the clubhouse.

He met us as we were going to watch the basketing for the sixth race of the season from Hatfield, 260 miles.

"Will be," said granda dismissively.

"Be nearly fifty members Sammy, the club's becoming big business," continued George cockily, "think we should have a meeting with the council; see if they won't turn some of the allotments into pigeon gardens."

Granda stopped in his tracks. George Clarke knew that the other members, gathered at the door, had heard what he had said and now they were all listening.

"No point in being small minded Sammy," George continued, "the allotments are doing nothing and our club's taking off. Do you want me to set up a meeting? I know a lot of the councillors."

Granda never turned to face George Clarke and I knew he was furious but he controlled himself.

"George you're not an official of the club. Any arrangements for meetings will be done properly and after all the members have been consulted. If you want to make a suggestion put it in writing and the committee will discuss it," granda replied.

With that granda pushed through the door into the clubhouse dragging me behind him.

As we took up our positions at the back of the clubhouse, he whispered to me.

"This is the last time we'll watch this procedure. I've got enough problems with men like George Clarke trying to take over the club without you trying to discredit Blanco."

His words hurt me but it was obvious that he was annoyed, his hands were shaking and he was breathing heavily. I was hurt but could understand his sentiment. George Clarke could not have picked a more public place to try to embarrass granda. Everyone had heard George and there was no doubt that the idea of throwing the allotment men off the site and expanding the pigeon club would now be discussed all over the gardens.

Following the euphoria of the first two races, the impact of bigger prize money was starting to wear off. Over the following three weeks, men had lost pigeons and everyone was re-assessing their situations. This meant that the numbers of birds entered for the Hatfield race was smaller. Nevertheless, still more than before the three new lofts had started racing.

Once again, standing at the back and leaning against the clubhouse wall we watched the basketing committee in action.

"Back again Sammy?" asked Dixie Dean.

"Aye just like to watch you lads in action," replied granda.

Dixie smiled and opened his race ledger.

"Okay let's start," he said.

Once again Billy removed the pigeons from the baskets. Mattie placed the race rings on their legs and Blanco put them into the race baskets. Dixie in his methodical way sat at the desk and recorded all the numbers and Jack Morris moved the baskets. I could tell that granda's mind wasn't on watching the procedure. George Clarke had upset him and he leant against the wall just staring at the men. I guessed he was thinking about what George had said.

I was still impressed with the smooth way that the committee worked. As they drew near to our basket, which also contained Blanco's three birds, my interest grew.

"Ours next," I said to granda.

"Aye alright," he replied.

Billy removed our birds one at a time. They were race rung and then passed to Blanco. He as usual received them with his right hand, opened the small top trap door of the race basket with his left hand, and placed the bird inside the basket. No problem I thought. Billy opened the second compartment of our small basket and, one at a time, took out Blanco's birds. As usual, Blanco continued receiving the first two birds in his right hand, but when he received the third bird, he changed and took it with his left hand. To me the change in his procedure stuck out a mile.

"Did you see what he did?" I whispered to granda.

Annoyed he replied, "what?"

"Blanco changed hands."

"Never seen it," granda said, "but so what? He gets tired and changes hands, the birds are still rung and in the baskets." I could hear the annoyance in his voice.

No one was taking any notice of our whispered conversation and Jack Morris had moved the race basket containing Blanco's birds and placed it with the others alongside the door. Granda took my arm and moved me towards the door.

"I think we've seen enough," he said.

I could tell by his voice that he was annoyed and I allowed him to guide me to the door.

"What's George Clarke shouting about Sammy?" asked Dixie.

We stopped in front of the door, just alongside the race baskets, and granda turned to answer the question.

"Oh some idea he's got about taking over the allotments. Thinks we should be expanding the club. I've told him to put it in writing to the committee. It'll upset the allotment lads and we don't want any more friction on the gardens."

As granda had turned away from me, I knelt down beside the race basket containing Blanco's pigeons. I peered in and scanned each bird trying to find his.

I knew I didn't have much time. The more granda discussed George Clarke's proposal the more annoyed he became. The pigeons in the race basket seemed to know what was happening, they had found spaces and squatted down. Only occasionally, a bird would move and upset a neighbouring bird and they would flap their wings. I spotted Blanco's birds they weren't together but I was able to count them. They were all there, three blue pigeons looking in good health.

"Come on," granda interrupted me.

Then, just as he was pushing me away from the basket, I saw it. One of the birds wasn't race rung. The rubber ring, which should have been on its left leg, wasn't there.

"Granda," I said.

But granda was in no mood for messing about.

"Come on," he demanded as he pushed me through the door.

Outside Rat Face, George Clarke and their cronies were gathered.

"Going down the pub Sammy fancy a pint?" Rat Face said unpleasantly.

He knew fine well that on a Friday, before a race, granda never drank and as yet, he still had to set the clocks.

"Not tonight," said granda as he dragged me down the path and along to our loft.

Back in the garden, I could see that granda was in a foul mood. I tried to talk to him but he ignored me. However, when he did finally speak to me he was apologetic.

"Sorry son just give me a few minutes," was all he said.

I did, I knew talking to him then would only upset him more and I waited until he'd locked the birds in the loft and picked up his clock.

"Best get down to granny's and set the clocks," he said.

From the tone of his voice, I knew he had calmed down and I breathed a sigh of relief and spoke up.

"I know what Blanco's doing," I said.

Granda looked at me, his look said, 'not again,' but I knew what I had seen and so I continued.

"One of Blanco's birds in the race basket wasn't race rung," I said.

Granda's eyes shot open.

"What? can't be, I saw them all rung and put in the baskets," he said.

"I know but Blanco's switching birds," I said.

I was pleading with him to understand.

"The pigeon that Billy passed to Blanco isn't the same bird that is in the basket. He's a magician, the bird Billy gave him went up his left sleeve and a bird from his right sleeve went into the basket."

Granda just stood looking at me in amazement.

"Why?" he asked.

"Because then on the race day his mother lets the pigeon go from their flat on Scotswood Road and it flies back here."

It was all so simple, I could see it clearly now and he had done it so easily. Granda stood staring at me.

"Are you sure there was a bird in the race basket without a race ring?" he asked.

"I'm positive," I replied.

Even then he never moved.

We stood facing each other saying nothing. Granda was obviously trying to decide what to do; father entered the garden and broke the silence.

"What's the matter?" he asked.

"Tell your father what you've just told me," said granda.

I repeated my story and my father listened intently.

"Are you sure?" he asked.

I, now nearly in tears, nodded.

"What you going to do?" father asked looking at granda.

"I suppose I'll go and check the race baskets, see if the boys right. That's about all I can do. I'll say one of my birds was ill and I need to take it out, makes me look like a fool though."

"Transporters gone," replied father, "it was just pulling away from the top gate when I came in. There's no one at the clubhouse. The clock committee's probably waiting at your house now."

I saw granda's face drop.

"Right come with me," he said.

The three of us set off for granda's house. He was deep in thought, I was smiling excited at being involved in something so grown up and dishonest and father just followed us. As we passed Blanco's loft he was locking up.

"Good a night a Sammy, I'll a pick up those magazines tomorrow. I'll a be here about a one o'clock," he shouted.

Granda just muttered something and walked on; I turned and smiled at Blanco.

My father and I waited in the front room whilst granda and the clock committee set the clocks. Granny as usual had been pumping them for information and when we entered, she started on granda.

"The men have been waiting, where have you been?"

Granda ignored her and went straight into the living room. My father and I sat in the front room and he lit the small gas fire.

"Are you really sure about the race ring?" he asked.

"Dad, I saw it, one of Blanco's blue birds didn't have a race ring on its leg."

Once again, because I was so frustrated, I was nearly in tears.

After ten minutes, carrying the clocks with them, the clock committee left the house and granda came into the front room.

"Well at least they're all happy," he said, "but we have a problem. The conveyors will not contact me until tomorrow morning when they liberate the birds. They only contact me if there is a problem and there'll be no problems tonight."

"Then you contact the conveyors, tell them to open the baskets and check the birds," said father.

"Son do you have any idea what would happen if I tried to do that. First, how the hell am I going to contact the conveyors? Call the police and tell them to stop the lorry on the road? I really don't think so. I'd have to explain all of this to the police and they'd probably just laugh at me. Then, even if they did stop the transporter, which basket is the bird in? They'd have to open a few until they find the bird. In addition, any open unsealed baskets would disqualify all the birds in those baskets from the race. On the gardens, there would be bloody hell on and what if we are wrong? How are we going to explain all of that to the committee and the club? What about all the nom money riding on those birds? Finally what do you think Rat Face, George Clarke and his friends would make of all this. If Blanco is fiddling and we prove it, they'll have a field day. And if he's not fiddling and we stop the lorry and open baskets they'll still have a field day. We're damned if we do and we're damned if we don't. No son, contacting the conveyors is not an option."

The three of us sat staring into the gas fire. Granda eventually broke the silence.
"Whatever we do we must do it quietly and it must be our secret. If certain other members get to know that Blanco has been fiddling the races they'll lynch him. Also, my credibility as his friend and secretary of the club will be destroyed. I'd have to resign and if I go, believe me, Dixie and Pincher will go and then the new men will take over."
My father nodded agreeing with him, I disappointed, just stared into the fire.
"Okay," said granda, "now I'll tell you what we are going to do."
The tone of his voice had changed it was positive and confident. I was pleased and listened to him in awe.
"This will involve all of us, so tomorrow son you'll have to miss work and you young man better be right and be prepared to play your part."

Chapter Eighteen

That night I couldn't sleep. In the front room in front of the gas fire granda had laid out his plan and I had a key part to play. As he'd detailed his plan, I had seen the worry on his face and slowly doubts had crept into my mind. Had I really seen a bird without a race ring? God, they had asked me that question repeatedly. I had been sure, but lying in bed that night I began to doubt myself. Then I thought of Blanco and of the Friday night when he'd come to our garden and confronted me. He had known I was on my own and he was threatening me. The memory of his cockiness and confidence once again annoyed me. He had known then that I had seen what he did and he had been warning me. I decided then that I was right and I would go through with granda's plan.

I was up early and fully dressed when mother and father came into the living room.

"Are you not well son?" mother asked, "it's unusual for you to be up so early."

When we finished breakfast, father and I left for granda's house. Only when we were outside and walking along the West Road did father speak to me.

"Are you alright son?"

I nodded.

When the two of us arrived at the house and knocked on the door granny opened it and was taken aback.

"By God, the two of you are up before your clothes are on," she said.

"Come in," granda shouted, "stop blathering woman and let the lads in."

It was only eight o'clock and granda had heard nothing from the conveyors.

"They should have liberated the birds by now," he said.

The telephone rang, granda smiled and as he picked up the receiver, he winked at us.

"Five o'clock that's fine. No problems? No, well thanks. Are you coming straight back? Okay, see you tomorrow morning," with that he put down the receiver.

He looked at the list of telephone numbers lying alongside the telephone then he picked up the receiver and dialled.

"Aye Sammy Baker here Banwell Pigeon Club can you give me a forecast for today. Aye strong North-East wind, dry, good, thanks, bye."

He scribbled the information onto a sheet of paper and laid it alongside the telephone.

My granny had been watching us.

"What's going on?" she asked, "you're like a bunch of conspirators."

"I'm going to answer the telephone today," I chirped up.

She just looked at me mystified.

"Why? What's wrong with me? Don't you think your old granny can handle it?" she said.

"The boy needs more confidence, he's not speaking up for himself, he needs to communicate with adults more," said granda.

"Rubbish," replied granny, "he's full of confidence leave the lad alone. Don't listen son, I'll answer the phone you take the dog out."

"Woman, will you just leave things alone," interrupted granda.

I could see a big argument starting and spoke up.

"I want to do it, I asked to do it," I said.

She looked at me quizzically then shuffled out of the room.

Granda stationed me, sitting alongside the telephone, in front of the back living room window and I sat looking out into the back garden. I watched granny as she hung out her washing. She kept looking over her shoulder and staring at me suspiciously through the window. I glanced down at the piece of paper alongside the telephone and started rehearsing what to say when the telephone rang.

"The birds are up at five o'clock, strong North-East wind should be back about two o'clock." I repeated the sentence in my head.

Suddenly the telephone rang and I jumped.

"Bakers," I said confidently.

"What time's the birds up," a voice said.

"Birds are up at five o'clock, strong North-East wind probably about two o'clock when they get back."

"Never, bloody Hatfield in nine hours with a North-East wind right on their noses nee way. Those birds should have been liberated earlier."

I was stuck.

"Thank you for calling," I said and put the receiver down.

Granda and father smiled.

"That's the way son, now you know what to do. As soon as he's called come up to the garden," said father, "let's just hope he does call."

"Oh he'll call, he always does," replied granda.

When they had left for the garden my granny's maternal instincts took over. She brought me a cup of tea and a Kit Kat then fussed around.

"You don't have to answer the phone son, go on out, I'll do it," she said.

"No granny," I insisted, "I've said I'll do it and I will," I replied.

However, every time the telephone rang she rushed to my side her hand reaching out to take the receiver from me. I think she felt rejected, after all this was her regular Saturday job, and she had done it for years. The majority of the members ringing in were friendly and some even asked if it was me on the telephone. I was beginning to feel quite confident when Rat Face telephoned.

"Time the birds up," he demanded.

I passed the message.

"Who's this he asked.

I told him.

"How do yee know how long the birds will take," he asked.

"Sammy has left the message written down," I replied.

I realised that that was the first time I had used my granda's Christian name and suddenly I felt grown up.

"Well as usual he's bloody wrong," said Rat Face and slammed the phone down.

It was eleven o'clock when Blanco rang. Unfortunately, granny was now polishing the windows and was listening to everything I was saying.

"Mrs a Baker," Blanco said, "at a what a time is a the birds liberated."

"The birds were liberated at six o'clock, strong North-East wind, probably be about three o'clock before they get home," I said confidently.

"They're a late," Blanco replied.

My granny stopped polishing the windows and tried to grab the receiver from me.

"You've made a mistake," she hissed in my ear.

The dog, seeing granny trying to pull the receiver from my hand, started barking and pulling at my shorts. I had one hand clamped over the mouthpiece and one hand holding the receiver, Blanco was still talking in one ear, and my granny was whispering in the other.

"Are you a sure about the time," he asked.

"Definitely, conveyors had problems at the liberation point, sudden showers they had to hold the birds back, bye must go," with that I slammed the receiver back onto its cradle.

Granny and the dog stopped wrestling with me and stood staring at me.

"In over thirty years of answering the telephone," she said, "I've never made a mistake. You've just given someone the wrong time and the poor man could miss his birds."

The look on her face told me she was horrified.

"Don't worry granny it was a joke," I lied, "it was Blanco, I know he's going to the garden early, he's arranged to meet granda at one o'clock so he'll have plenty of time, it's only a joke."

The look of despair on her face deepened and I knew she did not appreciate the joke.

"I only hope your granda doesn't find out what you've done," she said.

I didn't like to tell her it was his idea.

After Blanco's call, I waited in the house and didn't go straight to the garden. After an hour nearly all of the club members had rung but just in case Blanco rang back I waited by the telephone. He didn't call back and after the hour I left and made my way up to the gardens. I think granny was glad to see me go. Before I left she sat down beside the telephone and placed her hand on the receiver. I realised then that it made her feel important, she was part of something; she was sharing a hobby with granda and had an important job to do. I suspected she had also missed trying to get gossip out of the callers.

At the garden granda was waiting for me.

"Well?" he said.

"He called; I told him the birds were up at six o'clock. He should be about an hour behind us."

Granda nodded.

"Your father's away down to Blanco's flat. He left about an hour ago but he'll have a long wait. Now when Blanco arrives on the gardens we have to catch him and stop him talking to any other club members."

We waited and watched for Blanco. It was a bit like waiting for the pigeons to return home. Then at one o'clock granda, who was standing on the gantry, announced.

"He's here."

I dashed into the shed and granda went to the garden gate.

"Hey Blanco," I heard him shout, "I've got them old pigeon racing gazettes if you want them."

Blanco took anything for nothing and I knew he would come straight to our loft.

Sitting inside the shed I could hear the two of them talking. Quite why I had opted to hide I don't know but having made the decision I couldn't just suddenly pop out, so I remained silent and listened.

"Birds is a late Sammy," Blanco said as he sat on the bench seat alongside the shed.

"Not too late Blanco," granda replied.

Then I heard them turning the pages of the magazines and granda occasionally making some comment about an article.

"It's a your grandson answering the phone today," Blanco said.

"Yes, missus isn't too well and he said he'd help out," replied granda.

I was impressed with his ability to lie and to sound so natural. Suddenly, Billy Bucket Head pushed his head around the garden gate and interrupted their discussion.

"Hey Sammy, that's fuckin never a North-Easterly wind, it's fuckin swung right round, I'll bet the fuckin birds are back by half past fuckin one."

I couldn't see Blanco but I could hear the distress in his voice.

"A half past a one, you're a boy said on the a telephone a three o'clock, how's he so wrong?"

"Hey Blanco that's the way it goes, the wind changes, the sun shines, the birds fly faster, really you should go and open up your loft," replied granda.

It was unusual for Billy to be right but this time he was and at half past one the gardens came to life. Blanco had left our garden and had opened his loft.

"Seemed terribly disappointed when he left," said granda as I emerged from the shed.

Now as Pincher started his commentary I darted back into the shed.

"Chequer hen and blue hen both for the gardens," announced Pincher.

"Chequer hen could be Billy's, blue hen could be minnnnne," Pincher dragged out the word mine.

"Cocky bastard," someone from the back lofts shouted.

As the two birds approached, the gardens fell silent; only two voices could be heard Pincher's and Billy's. It was unusual for Billy to be in the first three and the excitement was obviously getting to him. From the gantry outside our loft, we could just see into Billy's garden. I had left the shed and joined granda on the gantry. We watched as Billy, all excited, tried to jump onto his gantry, stubbed his toe and fell. His two droppers took off in fright and Billy's corn tin spilt all over the gantry.

"Are you alright," granda shouted.

"Fuckin fine Sammy lad, fuckin fine," replied Billy he was that excited I don't think he even knew he'd tripped.

Pincher won, Billy was second then a flock of about ten birds arrived and everyone was clocking in. One of our birds was in the flock and whilst we wouldn't be in the first five, it was nice to have a bird keeping up with the winners.

"How you doing Blanco," granda shouted when he came out of the loft having timed our bird in.

"Eh a nothing a yet Sammy," replied Blanco.

We both smiled.

"I wonder why," said granda.

By two o'clock, it was all over and a steady stream of birds was arriving home. Blanco came round to our garden, this time I didn't hide.

"No good Blanco?" granda asked.

"No good Sammy," replied Blanco, "but I a not understand, your boy here he gives me a the wrong times. I speak with Billy and he a say birds is up at a five o'clock so why a your boy tell me a six?"

"Ah Blanco he's only learning, he's bound to make mistakes. But, nothing lost you were here on time, you would have clocked your birds in if they'd returned," replied granda.

"I a know but a Sammy it's a not a right."

I interrupted him.

"Blanco I'm really sorry I got confused. People were ringing up and arguing with me about how long the birds would take and I just gave you the wrong time, I'm really sorry," I said.

I was quite impressed and realised I must have inherited my grandfather's ability to lie.

Blanco hung around our loft watching granda clean out, then he accompanied us to the clubhouse to put our clock in. Occasionally he glanced in my direction and I felt most uncomfortable. It was ten to three and we were walking back past his loft when a lone blue pigeon appeared from behind the church clock tower. Pincher must have been watching as he called out.

"Blanco here's your blue cock, he looks knackered."

Blanco shrugged and went into his garden, we continued towards our loft.

"Didn't seem surprised," said granda.

Half an hour later father arrived.

"Well?" asked granda.

We were both dying to hear what he had to say.

"You'll not believe this," said father as he sat down on the bench. "I waited outside Blanco's flat till half past two. Then out comes his mother with a shopping bag. Well, for a minute I was convinced we were wrong, she's going shopping I thought, and I nearly came back to the garden. However, I had been there for a couple of hours so I decided to follow her and see where she went. Well she's a nimble old buggar, there's nothing wrong with her, she shot off heading for the West Road and it took me all my time to follow her without her seeing me."

"And," interrupted granda impatiently.

"And," said father, "she stopped on the waste ground behind the church, opened her shopping bag and threw out a blue cock bird. I was stunned, I was still a good distance from her but the bird circled over me and I'm nearly sure it was race rung."

There was silence; I felt as if a great weight had been lifted from my shoulders, I had been right and I felt vindicated. All through the day, in the back of my mind, I'd had a nagging doubt that I may have been wrong.

"So what do we do?" I asked.

"We do nothing," replied granda, "you two forget about this, I'll deal with it."

I was disappointed. I had seen this type of thing on 'Dixon of Dock Green,' on the telly, and I wanted to march round to Blanco's loft and confront him with the evidence.

"You cannot let it go dad," said father.

"Do you really think I would?" replied granda "this isn't a game. Do you know what certain members of this club would do if they knew what Blanco has been up to? There are men on these gardens who beat their wives up for buying new shoes for the kids. What do you think they'll do to Blanco?"

Once again there was silence, then father who was obviously upset started again.

"He can't race again or be on the basketing committee, and how many times has he done this? He should pay back all his winnings, really dad you should call in the police," he said.

"Son I know all of that," granda replied, "but there's more involved here than just Blanco. The clubs under pressure, there are people who want to change it and they will cause trouble. All they need is an excuse to get rid of me. Remember I've always stood by Blanco he was my friend. I've told you, leave it with me, I'll deal with it."

This time when granda spoke, we knew it was the end of the discussion. His voice told us he was furious and our questioning wasn't helping. Without mentioning Blanco or the race we stayed at the loft for a further half hour. Then father and I left and when we passed Blanco's loft I noticed that it was locked and Blanco had gone.

The next day, being Sunday, as usual we went to the gardens I could hardly wait. I was expecting a big confrontation but it never happened. Blanco was nowhere to be seen and much to my disappointment, his loft and garden remained locked.

Chapter Nineteen

When you are young justice, guilt and retribution are all straightforward. I do something wrong, I am caught I am punished. It all seemed so simple to me. After all, every Saturday night, I watched it happening on Dixon of Dock Green. The Blanco situation, to me, was that simple and I longed to find out what had happened to him. The next race was the first of the channel races, the basketing was taking place on the Thursday night and after school, I went straight to the gardens. The race was from Lillers, France, about 440 miles across the channel and we were entering Huwey, which was another reason for my excitement. I hadn't seen or talked to granda since Sunday and when I entered the gardens, I was looking forward to seeing him. Confidently I strode down the path passed the clubhouse where a few of the members were standing. Rat Face was amongst them and I tried to ignore them. However, as I passed them I noticed that David was also with them.

David was a boy about my age and granda said he was a Mongol. I didn't know what that meant but appreciated that David was different. I had never really spoken to David he lived on the West Road and often visited the gardens. He usually stayed at the top of the gardens and seldom wandered down to the front row where our loft was. I think he was frightened of granda. Rat Face and his friends often talked to him and teased him. They had taught him to swear and introduced him to smoking and he stood outside the clubhouse with a cigarette in his hand. As I passed the group, I heard Rat Face say.

"Go on David give him a punch."

I knew he meant me and I quickened my pace.

"See David," I heard Rat Face say, "he's like all the Bakers, runs away."

The comment alarmed me but what shocked me even more was as I passed the clubhouse I saw one of the members coming out and I briefly glimpsed inside. To my horror, I saw Blanco basketing the pigeons.

I hurried to our garden and found granda, carrying his small basket, just about to leave.

"Just sending the two," he said.

"Can we watch the basketing," I asked.

Granda looked at me.

"Blanco's still basketing," he said, "but he can't basket his own birds. I've had a word with Dixie and told him that the rules prohibit any member from race basketing their own birds."

I was stunned; at the very least, I had expected Blanco to be marched off the gardens never to return. Granda must have seen the disappointment on my face.

"I'll tell you what's happened when your father gets here," he said.

We walked round to the clubhouse and I was relieved to see that Rat Face and his friends had gone. However, David was still there. He seemed pleased to see us, and his plump face creased into a big smile as we approached him.

"Channel race," he said to granda.

Granda nodded, "aye it's a big race David," he said.

"Cigarette," he said to me offering me a packet of five Woodbines.

"No I don't smoke," I replied.

He didn't listen but pushed the packet into my pocket and walked off.

"Suppose he's not a bad lad," said granda, "Rat Face and his friends are teaching him bad habits. Really his parents should stop him coming here."

I watched David walk away and felt sorry for him.

In the clubhouse, Blanco never looked at us, but I watched him and I could feel the tension between him and granda.

"Be a good race Sammy," said Dixie, "the three new lofts have entered ten birds each, it's more than I send to Selby. Blanco's bottled it though, haven't you Blanco?" he smiled as he said it I think he was trying to make a joke. "He says his birds are tired out."

Granda just nodded.

"My monies on Huwey or Pincher's hen," continued Dixie. "Huwey'll take some beating, am I right Sammy?"

Once again, granda nodded.

"Please yourself," said Dixie.

We waited until all the birds were in the race baskets and the transporter arrived to collect them. Blanco never acknowledged us and made his way back to his garden without speaking to us.

Just as we were finishing scraping out the loft father arrived. I could hardly wait to hear what granda had to say about Blanco.

"Well what's happened have you told him?" he said nodding towards me.

"No," replied granda, "I was waiting until you arrived."

Granda sat on the gantry and father and I sat on the bench.

"Well I don't know what you expected but the whole situation is complicated," said granda. "I caught Blanco on Monday night and told him what we'd seen and our suspicions. I told him that I didn't want to go to the police but I might have to, it depended on what the committee decided when I told them. I told him that a good alternative would be for him to leave the club."

I shuffled on the bench; the mention of police really got my interest and now I had visions of Blanco locked up in Durham Jail.

"He denied everything," granda continued, "I really have underestimated him. He said the bird his mother was releasing was another Scottish bird. Said he has had it for a week, took it off Dixie when it dropped into his place. I spoke to Dixie later and he confirms he gave Blanco a Scotsman, a blue cock bird." Granda shook his head. "Blanco was really upset that we didn't trust him, and even started crying. Then he accused me of plotting against him, giving him the wrong time of liberation. He accused me of trying to mislead him so that he would be late to clock in his bird. Said there was no problem with the basketing and all his birds were in the basket. And you know what, when you think about it he's right." Granda sighed and, as if to check that Blanco wasn't coming through it, he looked at the garden gate. Then he looked back at us and continued his tale.

"I know now that once we knew that an unrung bird was in the race basket we should have acted immediately. It's just a pity that the transporter had left before you told us about the bird."

I was stunned, God knows I had tried to tell him but he'd put me off, now he seemed to be shifting the blame towards me.

"I've thought about nothing else all week," he continued. "I cannot take my suspicions to the club committee, I have no proof. Blanco's story holds up. Dixie gave him a Scottish bird, which he says his mother liberated and on the race day, he finished no-where. If I tell them we deliberately gave him the wrong time it's me that'll be for the high jump."

Father and I looked at him.

"So what do we do?" I asked.

"Nothing," replied granda, "all we can do is watch him and hope that our intervention has stopped him cheating."

This was not what I had wanted to hear. Nothing had changed and Blanco was getting off the hook, I felt like crying.

Sitting in the garden we talked over the situation again and again. The more granda said the more we had to agree with him and eventually, although disheartened, we came to the same conclusion. However, the Blanco episode did have one good outcome, he stopped coming to our garden. He transferred his friendship to Billy, who seemed very pleased to have a new best friend.

That Saturday Huwey did it again and it was one of our greatest race days. The race took about nine and a half hours. The weather was good and there was a tail wind. It was the type of day Huwey loved. At half past three Pincher's commentary started.

"Bird in the valley, very high but coming this way."

We all stared down the Tyne Valley. The river was like a silver stream stretching away from us and we could see the rows of terraced house climbing up its banks. Obviously, the pigeons used these landmarks as part of their compass system to find their way home. This was Huwey's usual approach route to the gardens and we had seen it before but the sight still thrilled me. High, very high above the river was a black dot.

"That bloody Pincher has great eyesight," granda said and we had to agree.

"There he is," shouted father pointing at the small black dot.

"Could be Sammy's Huwey," shouted Pincher.

"No could be about it," whispered granda, "that's Huwey."

My chest swelled with pride. The black dot, still flying very high, was approaching the gardens and granda was on the gantry.

"How way son, how way," he called as he rattled the corn tin.

I believe the bird must have heard him, because it folded its wings behind it and started to drop. It was magnificent; the angle of its wings allowed it to drop like a stone but at the same time carried it forward like a bullet.

"That's my boy," shouted granda, "just look at him go."

We did and so did all the other pigeon club members. Because of the silence, they obviously knew it was our bird and they must have been impressed. No one else called for the bird, the gardens where silent, it was as if they were paying homage to a returning hero. Only granda's voice could be heard.

"Come on son," he said soothingly and Huwey did just that. About two hundred yards from the loft, he dropped out of the sky, straight towards us and unswerving, like a bullet fired from a gun, he shot through the doors and into the loft. It was a textbook return and granda, with great respect, followed him into the loft. Seconds later the clunk of the timing handle on the clock told us everything was in order.

I believe the gardens were stunned. No one shouted or asked if Huwey was fully nominated, they all knew he was. Moreover, his return home had been such a quality performance there was really nothing else to say. We were still drooling over Huwey's performance when Pincher's bird arrived. We heard him shouting but didn't watch. Nothing could surpass Huwey's magnificent arrival. The third, fourth and fifth places all went to birds from the three new lofts.

"Watch out next year," said father, "the new lofts will be there. They're flying bloody good birds and it'll not be long before they're winning every race."

I didn't care we had our hero, Huwey. He was fast becoming a legend on the gardens and I knew everyone of the members envied us.

It was unusual for Pincher to come to our garden but that Saturday afternoon he arrived out of breath.

"Magnificent Sammy," he said as he held out his hand to granda, "Huwey's worth a fortune, after a race like that everyone will want him or youngins off him."

I think all three of us, standing in the garden, were taken by surprise. We didn't fly for money, although the winnings did help with the corn bills.

"I'd never sell him," said granda.

"I know that," replied Pincher, "that Tommy Tippins has already been around to see if I'd sell him my hen. I'd only just timed her in and there he was, offered me three hundred pound for her."

We all looked at him.

"I'm like you Sammy I'd never sell her, but I have been thinking. George Clarke, Tommy and Malcolm Ash they are buying every good bird on these gardens. Soon it will only be you and I that are flying quality birds against them. Why don't we get together?"

Pincher was excited, his face was red and his hands were shaking. I knew very little about Pincher, overall he was a quiet man and he tended to keep himself to himself. I did know that his birds were his life. I had heard granda say that he was a postman, wasn't married and lived with his mother, but apart from that, I'd had little contact with him. Occasionally, with granda, I had visited his loft but he'd spoken very little to me.

"Not join together Sammy, just breed a few youngins from our birds. Imagine Huwey paired up with my hen. We'd take one round of youngins each and if you wanted we could sell eggs, we'd make a fortune."

It was obvious that the idea had never crossed granda's mind but I was impressed.

"I'll not rule it out," replied granda, "but I don't know about selling eggs. I don't want my bloodstock scattered all over the gardens."

That was enough for Pincher.

"That's all I wanted to hear Sammy," he said, "you'll give it some thought."

Tommy Tippins arrived very shortly after Pincher had left.

"Great bird Sammy," he said as he pushed his way into the garden.

His eyes were everywhere and he made his way straight towards the loft, he ignored my father and me. Granda stepped in front of him.

"Where are you going?" he asked.

"Just wanting to see the bird," Tommy replied.

"Not here Tommy, no one walks into my loft and if you want to see Huwey you ask me," he said.

As he spoke, he stood directly in front of Tommy blocking his view of the loft.

"No offence Sammy just thought we might talk a little business. That bird's a one off, you'll not be racing him again, two channel wins and a return like that, you can't afford to lose him."

"That's my decision," said granda.

"I'll buy him off you," said Tommy smugly, "I'll make you an offer you can't refuse. Three hundred pounds and next year when I've paired him up you get the first round of youngins."

"Not for sale," replied granda pushing Tommy towards the gate.

"Think about it Sammy, my offer will stand and I'll beat any other offers you get," called out Tommy as he opened the gate and left.

"Not for sale," granda shouted after him.

Chapter Twenty

We returned home triumphant. However, the Blanco situation had to remain a secret, we had agreed not to tell anyone including mother. She often met wives of the pigeon men in the local shops and if she knew, she might, by accident, talk about it. At least that's what father said. However, our feelings of euphoria were short lived. As we entered the living room is was apparent that all was not well. My brother sat in the armchair silently watching the television, and mother sat at the table with a crumpled packet of Woodbine cigarettes in front of her. I recognised the packet immediately, it was the one David had pushed into my pocket and I had left it in a draw in the bedroom.

"We won, Huwey won and Tommy Tippins offered granda three hundred pounds for him."

I couldn't contain myself but as I said it I saw the distress on father's face.

My mother was a good woman but, like all the wives of the nineteen fifties working men, her life was monotonous. She washed, cooked, baked, made the beds, shopped and stuck to her routine just to make a happy home.

"Three hundred pounds?" she said, "that's marvellous, we'll be able to have a holiday and maybe buy a new carpet."

My brother had lost interest in the television and was also taking an interest.

"You could buy a car dad and I need new football boots and a track suit," he piped up.

"Hold on," father replied, "Huwey will never be sold. Dad would never part with him; he's the best pigeon we've ever bred."

"It's not just his decision," mother said, "the loft is registered under Baker and son. You're always saying you're the son part of it and you're entitled to half the money."

Father looked at her and shook his head the silence, which followed, was frightening. No one spoke we all just glanced at each other, finally mother broke the silence.

"I found these in your son's pocket; you'd better sort it out because I'm just fed up with the lot of you."

She threw the packet of cigarettes at father and ran from the room. The triumph of the day was destroyed and I realised that I had opened an old wound and the old friction between my parents would return. My brother wasn't too concerned, he stood up to leave the room and I saw him slip the packet of Woodbines into his pocket.

Huwey did win the Fed but our win was marred by the death of Jack Morris. The Saturday night of our win Billy found Jack lying in his garden. Billy had been one of the last men on the gardens and had noticed Jack's birds still sitting around the loft. He had gone to investigate and found Jack on the grass in front of the loft. It appeared that he'd had a heart attack and had fallen off his loft gantry. I, of course knew none of this until the Tuesday night when granda called to see father at our house. My granda and granny very seldom visited our house and we were all surprised when mother opened the door and invited him in. My brother was out he had found a youth club, which held a dance on a Tuesday night, and he'd become a member. It didn't seem to bother him that it was a catholic club and only Catholics could join.

I sat and listened as granda told mother and father about Jack Morris's death. Jack had always been alright with me. After he'd thrown Beryl out he'd become more involved with the pigeons and I'd seen him a few times puffing and blowing carrying baskets of pigeons.

"What about his business?" mother asked.

"Word is Beryl gets the lot, business, house, pigeons everything. He never made a will and he'd never divorced her, so I suppose legally she's entitled," replied granda.

"There's no bloody justice in this world," said mother indignantly.

Granda, not used to hearing women swear, and with a look of surprise on his face, sat back in his chair.

"Bloody Beryl," continued mother, "never done a days work in her life. Some of us never bloody stop and apart from pigeons what do we get, bloody nothing. We couldn't get married between April and September because the two of you wouldn't come to the church when the birds were racing. We've never had a holiday, we just manage to get by on his wages and you'll not even sell a bloody pigeon to help us out."

The surprised look on granda's face turned to shock and his shoulders hunch slightly. I realised then that mother wasn't like granny Baker. She wasn't involved in father's hobby. She didn't meet people through his hobby, she didn't know the club members and she had no interest in his hobby. Granny Baker because she was married to Sammy Baker had status and respect and mother had none of this.

It was obvious that mother's outburst had taken granda by surprise.

"I'm sorry pet," he said, "I never thought to consider you when I refused Tommy's offer. All my life I've bred them pigeons, I produced the blood strain that created Huwey. It's been my life's work and I can't just sell him."

Once again I noticed how old and tired granda was looking.

"At the end of this year I'll retire," he continued, "I should get something from the firm for my retirement; they usually have a whip round. If you can wait until then I'm sure I can find something to give you."

If he was trying to make my mother feel guilty he was certainly succeeding, but somehow I didn't think he was.

"Enough," interrupted father, "I'll have no more of this talk. Huwey will not be sold and you'll give us nothing. This is my family and I'll provide for them."

It was the first time I had ever heard father raise his voice to granda. It was nice to have granda in the house but Jack's death and mother's outburst had destroyed the mood. He stayed for some supper but the atmosphere was strained and he left shortly afterwards.

Granda and father went to Jack's funeral. They said that Beryl was there all dressed in black and crying. The funeral was on the following Thursday and on Friday night granda told us that Rat Face and Beryl had been to the council to rent two of the new gardens. Beryl and Rat Face were living in a flat off the West Road. I knew that because I'd seen the two of them leaving the flat. They hadn't seen me and now, as much as possible, I made a point of avoiding the flat.

"They've even told the council they're giving up Rat Face's garden and Jacks garden and are going to build a brand new big loft on the new sites," said granda.

"Jack must have left a bob or two," replied father.

"Seems that way," replied granda.

I was quite pleased that Rat Face was moving from our front row of lofts. I hated passing his garden, Beryl had become a frequent visitor and I hated seeing her.

That Saturday the race was from Redford, about 320 miles, and we were entering ten birds. When we took the birds to the clubhouse for basketing there was a crowd of members outside the door. They were all talking excitedly. We pushed our way through them and went into the clubhouse. Dixie was just setting up the table and opening the race ledger.

"You'll have heard all the rumours Sammy," he said.

Granda smiled at him.

"You know me Dixie always last to know," he said.

Dixie smiled.

"You and me both Sammy, appears Rat Face and Beryl are going in for this new loft in a big way. They're stripping down both of their old lofts and joining them together on their new site. They going to insulate it and put an interior skin of eight by four sheets of timber on the inside."

Granda looked amazed.

"Rat Face is going to do all that?" he asked.

"No Sammy, come on Rat Face cannot tie his own shoe laces, he's hired a building company to do it."

"He's what?" replied granda shocked, "that'll cost a fair amount."

"Doesn't seem to bother him, all the lads say he was in the pub last night, dressed in a new suit, buying them drinks and telling them he was taking over Jack's furniture shop. Bloody Jack's just gone up the crematorium chimney and they're spending his money."

Dixie was keen to tell granda all the news and they discussed Rat Face and Beryl for a while. I looked around the clubhouse and noticed Blanco standing beside the race baskets. He glared at me but I ignored him. The small club, which I had known and loved was changing, the new members never acknowledged me, the friendships, which I had so treasured, had gone and I no longer felt safe and secure.

"What?"

I heard granda exclaim, "twenty pounds an egg I've never agreed to that."

"Aye, that's what Pincher said, twenty pounds an egg and no guarantees."

Dixie had finished setting out his table and was still talking to granda.

"I thought it was a bit steep Sammy but I've known you and Pincher a long time and I thought you wouldn't charge me full price."

I couldn't see granda's face but I knew he fuming.

"Leave them birds and come with me," he said grabbing me by the collar.

We both dashed from the clubhouse, granda striding out and me hurrying along behind him. It was evident that Pincher had decided to progress his idea about pairing up the two channel birds. Granda hadn't said no to the idea but he also hadn't said yes. However, Pincher obviously fired up by the idea, and unbeknown to granda, had been talking to certain club members offering to sell them eggs and youngins. The gardens were buzzing with rumours and it appeared that we were to be the last to hear them.

Pincher's loft and garden were always clean and tidy. The grass in front of his gantry was weed free and manicured. His small vegetable patch was filled with rows of leeks and cabbages and because of this tidiness; I always liked to visit him. As we approached the loft, I noticed that he had shaped the fencing around his loft into points to stop the birds landing on it. The points were all equally placed, spaced, and looked rather regimental. We didn't knock on the gate, granda just stormed through it. Pincher was sitting on the gantry watching his birds.

"Hello Sammy you're in hurry," he said.

"It's not me that's in a hurry," replied granda, "you've been talking about selling eggs and youngins and I've never agreed to your idea."

"Hold on," Pincher interrupted him, "I've been trying to find out if there's a market and believe me Sammy we can make a killing."

Pincher was bursting to tell us of his success. Unfortunately, granda didn't want to hear. He was annoyed that Pincher hadn't told him what he was going to do.

"Calm down Sammy," Pincher said, "I've done nothing wrong you didn't disagree with the idea and I was only trying to help. Believe me Sammy we are doing nothing wrong. George Clarke, Tippins and Ash are all doing the same thing; they're selling eggs and youngins. We can do better than they can. Our two birds are proven channel birds. They haven't just won one race they've been regular winners, everyone knows it and we're trusted and respected. We have been in the sport a long time and people value our judgement. Listen Sammy we don't even have to sell eggs from the birds, we've got similar coloured birds we could pair them up and sell their eggs, no one will know."

My grandfather's face turned red and I thought he was going to hit Pincher.

"Pincher what are you talking about? I've known you for thirty years and not once have I heard you utter a dishonest word. Now you're talking about deceiving other pigeon men just for money."

Granda's comments obviously hit home and Pincher's face dropped.

"Sammy what do you think Clarke and his friends are doing. How can anyone prove which pigeon produced which egg. Sammy I'm not too bothered we can do it honestly but it is a great way to make some money."

Granda listened.

"What about the bloodstock? We'll finish up racing against our own blood; surely you don't want to see that."

Pincher shook his head.

"Come on Sammy this isn't nineteen twenty, everyone has access to different bloodstocks. Throughout the country there are better pigeons than our two birds just breeding for egg sales, our bloodstock's good but it'll be beaten."

There was silence and granda was calming down. Perhaps he was also remembering my mother's comments from Tuesday night, I don't know but suddenly he seemed more interested.

"How many orders can you get?" he asked.

A huge grin appeared on Pincher's face and he smiled at me.

Chapter Twenty-One

Rat Face and Beryl entered no birds for that Redford race and on the Saturday morning of the race, the reason for their absence became clear. It was unusual for Rat Face to be on the gardens early and when I arrived, I was surprised to find four large baskets, full of his pigeons, placed outside his garden. Inside the garden four men were dismantling his loft and Rat Face stood watching. As I walked down the path from the West Road, I'd also noticed the same thing happening at Beryl's loft. Billy was looking through Rat Face's gate watching the men. Rat Face knew he was there and was enjoying his moment of glory.

"Mind, you'll have to stop that fuckin noise when the birds are due," said Billy.

Rat Face turned and snarled at him.

"Billy piss off and mind your own business."

As I walked past Billy I overheard the conversation and was delighted that Rat Face was moving further away from us. Billy ran after me.

"Hey youngin, fuckin tell Sammy he'll have to fuckin stop that noise when the fuckin birds are coming," he said as he passed me.

I ignored Billy, entered the garden, and was surprised to find Pincher sitting on the bench with granda. Both of them seemed very pleased with themselves.

"It's a good day kid," Pincher said when I opened the gate; "your granda and I are going into business, Rat Face is moving he'll not compete in any more races this year and the sun is shining."

I laughed at his comments. I had wondered how Rat Face and Beryl would continue to race their birds when their lofts were being moved, and Pincher had just confirmed what I'd thought. Rat Face wouldn't be able to race his birds. He'd have to settle his birds into a new loft and it was the wrong time of the year to move lofts. The young birds were due to start racing in five weeks time but typically Rat Face had gone straight ahead, I thought, just to impress everyone.

"Aye that'll be him and Beryl finished with the racing this season," said granda, "he's too keen to build the new loft. He'll have to settle his birds and typical of him he's even been talking about buying pigeons."

Both men were smiling.

"It's just a pity he doesn't know what he's doing," said Pincher grinning.

However, the cheerfulness was short lived. I sat down beside granda and was looking at the loft when, suddenly something black shot across the garden. I saw the movement from the corner of my eye and jumped. Granda and Pincher also jumped.

"Rats," Pincher shouted.

He was right; three other small grey animals, running across the garden, followed the first black streak. Granda jumped onto the gantry and closed the loft doors.

"Bloody Rat Face they'll have come from under his loft. The lads moving it must have disturbed them," he said.

Rats and cats were hated on the gardens. The rats would build nests under the lofts and eat any corn that was left lying on the gantries or fell through cracks in the floor. We had sealed around the front, back and sides of our loft with planks of wood, but occasionally a rat or mouse would tunnel its way under. Every year granda removed the planks and cleaned the area under the loft. He never put rat poison down fearing that somehow the pigeons might get to it and eat it. We had never had a rat problem and this was due to granda's diligence.

"That bloody Rat Face, everything he does causes problems for everyone else," shouted granda as he jumped off the gantry brandishing his sweeping brush.

Pincher had moved even quicker and was now standing on the bench seat outside the shed.

"I hate rats Sammy, dirty, unhealthy things, keep them away from me," he cried.

I wasn't afraid of the rats and was quite amused at Pincher perched on the bench. Granda rushed into the shed and came out with a large square piece of wood.

"Here son grab this and corner them," he shouted at me as he pushed the wood into my hands.

Whilst I wasn't afraid of rats, I wasn't too pleased to be trying to trap them. The rats had all disappeared into the rhubarb patch and the big leaves offered them good protection. Cautiously I moved forward stamping my feet and kicking out under the leaves. One rat made a break for it and luckily I managed to push it against the fence with the wood. Granda was straight in with his brush. He pounded away at the animal and Pincher, still standing on the bench, cheered him on.

The shouting was drawing a crowd and Billy stuck his head around the garden gate. Donkey Smith who had the loft next to ours had climbed onto the fence and was peeping over it watching us. I could never work out how he'd got the nickname Donkey and granda always just shook his head when I asked him.

"Go on Sammy," he shouted.

The rat was dead and granda bent down, picked it up and held it by its tail.

"Ah it's only a baby," shouted Donkey.

"Get the rest," shouted Pincher.

Once again, kicking out and stamping my feet, I moved amongst the rhubarb leaves. Suddenly one rat shot out, raced toward the fence and climb over. Donkey was still peeping over the fence and the rat chose that exact spot as its escape route. Donkey taken completely by surprise screamed and fell off the fence. Billy started laughing and Pincher started screaming.

"There they go," he yelled.

The other two rats now made their break for freedom. Billy, shouted, "fuck this," and slammed the gate. I jumped back, overbalanced, and fell into the rhubarb. Granda stood his ground and swung his broom. The rats made it; how they escaped, I don't know. We searched all over the garden but never found them. They had obviously escaped from the garden and deep down I was pleased. I don't like rats but when I saw granda holding that dead baby I realised I'd contributed to its death and it upset me.

Cats on the gardens were also a problem and a number of the neighbouring houses had complained that their cats had gone missing. Of course, we always denied ever harming a cat. However, some of the members would not have thought twice about disposing of a cat and burying it in their garden. A cat in the loft would cause havoc and each loft had a cat trap fitted. Granda had built ours. It was fitted in one of the doors of the loft. It consisted of a hinged flap of wood, screwed to the front of the door, covering a hole in the door. The hole was large enough to allow a pigeon access. A wire was attached to the back of the flap then pushed through the hole. At the other end of the wire, at the back of the door, a lead weight was attached. The weight was heavy enough to take the weight of a pigeon, about 14 to 16 ounces, but not the weight of a cat. The flap was left open, dropped forward, when pigeons had not returned home. If a cat jumped onto the flap the cat's weight tipped the flap forward tipping the cat off. However, that Saturday the worry was not cats it definitely was rats and the word soon spread that there were rats on the gardens.

On that Saturday afternoon, whilst we waited for our pigeons to return, granda mentioned Pincher's proposal to father. My father was never a businessman and our families past involvement with the pigeons had been purely for sport.

"How many orders does Pincher think he can get?" he asked.

"He's already got twenty orders for eggs at twenty pounds each and others are willing to pay up to fifty pounds a young bird. That, mind you, is only on these gardens, once the word gets out we could be looking at a lot more and perhaps even higher prices," replied granda.

"It means Huwey will never race again but with young birds and eggs we could probably make about two hundred pounds a year each and that's only using those two birds. That of course is if we're honest about it and only sell genuine eggs."

The last comment granda made with a smile on his face and my father looked horrified.

"You're not suggesting we use other bird's eggs are you?" he replied.

Granda continued to smile.

"No son, I'd like to keep it straight. I hate dishonesty but we do have other pigeons with good records. The blue hen always flies well from Selby and Pincher has some real good birds. He's willing to look at pairing up past winners with us then selling eggs and youngins. Also, remember, I retire in December and I will have time on my hands, I'll also have to live on the old age pension. I'll probably spend most of my time in the garden with the birds. I could run the breeding programme, sell the eggs, record sales and keep records of the bloodstocks. We could do it all professionally and people would trust us more than George Clarke and his friends," he replied.

There was little doubt that father was interested. The money we won each year, from the races, was always poured back into the pigeons. It paid for food, sand, tonics, entrance and pool money for races.

"I like keeping the paper work straight for the club so keeping breeding records and sales will be easy. It'll give me an additional interest and more importantly it'll give us an income," granda smiled and sat down.

I was sure he'd been thinking about Pincher's proposition all Friday night and they must have been discussing it when I'd arrived that morning.

"Have you said yes to Pincher?" asked father.

"No son, this loft is registered as Baker and Son, so anything that goes on here has to be discussed and both of us have to agree to it."

Father looked amused; this was a new approach to the loft and the pigeons. Previously granda had done whatever he liked; mother's outburst on Tuesday night had obviously registered with him.

"Then I say we give it a go," replied father.

I believe that weekend was an awakening for the club members and for granda. The first five pigeons home, from the Redford race, all came from the three new lofts. Club members who in the past had been happy to race their pigeons and gain one or two places over the year were no longer being placed. The lofts, which in the past had been successful, like grandas, Pinchers, Mattie Walkers and a few others were still getting places but all the time the new lofts were catching them up, and murmurs of discontent were beginning to circulate on the gardens.

"Perhaps, at the AGM, Sammy was right? Perhaps this mob flying is going to kill off all the small lofts?"

I heard these comments when I went to fill the watering cans at the water tap. Earlier when I had passed the clubhouse men standing outside had also been discussing the success of the new lofts and as I'd passed, I'd heard the words "mob flying."

We weren't placed in that Redford race, George Clarke won Malcolm Ash was second and third and Tommy Tippins was fourth and fifth. Blanco's pigeons were late coming home and we all sighed with relief. Perhaps granda's intervention had worked and perhaps Blanco had learned his lesson, all we could do was watch and wait.

Chapter Twenty-Two

The old bird season continued with races from Ashford about 340 miles, Grantham 160 miles. Then two races from Hitchin 250 miles and one more channel race from Le Bourget 550 miles. We didn't enter Huwey for the channel race; granda said he'd done enough. Whether the new proposed breeding programme with Huwey and Pincher's hen swayed his judgement, I don't know. In that old bird season, we didn't win any more races. Pincher did, he won the Grantham race but the three new lofts won and dominated all the other races. Thankfully, Blanco continued on his losing streak and we were beginning to feel confident that he had seen sense and stopped his cheating.

The young bird season started and once again, our hopes were high. Of course, everyone was interested to see how the young birds from the new lofts would perform. On the first Friday night of the season, even without Rat Face and Beryl's pigeons, there were more pigeons waiting to be race basketed than usual. A crowd had gathered at the clubhouse door and as the loft managers from the new lofts brought their baskets, everyone tried to see the birds.

"They're bloody big," someone said.

"Too big," a voice replied, "they'll have started pairing up and they'll be going through the moult. Stick with tradition our birds are as good as them."

As usual, granda and I had gone to watch the basketing. Blanco was still on the basketing committee and earlier we had seen him putting his birds into Billy's basket to be taken to the clubhouse.

"He'll not try it again," granda said, "he knows we know what he was doing, he'd be a fool to swap pigeons again." Granda had tried to convince me but I wasn't certain. Since that Saturday when we had caught him out he'd never spoken to any of us. He avoided us and we tried to avoid him. During that basketing session, I watched Blanco and when it came to Billy's basket, and his pigeons, I scrutinised his every move. It was unnecessary, because as if to make a point, hands in raincoat pockets, Blanco moved away from the baskets and swapped places with Mattie. He was now working the ringing machine. Dixie smiled at granda.

"See Sammy, I've taken on board what you said and no one handles their own birds," he said proudly.

Additionally, as if to stress the point, as his birds were the next out, Billy now swapped places with Mattie. Blanco knew granda and I were watching him and when Billy and his birds' were race basketed, he returned to his own position and his handling of the birds never changed. Even then, when the birds were in the race basket granda and I went over, counted the birds, and checked they all had race rings fitted. Donkey Smith had replaced Jack Morris on the basketing committee.

"All this shuffling around it's like a bloody barn dance Sammy, you're a tight old buggar, trust no one eh?" Donkey said and winked at granda.

Granda didn't see the joke and ignored the comment.

"Really it is difficult Sammy, all of us have pigeons in the race and we have to keep swapping over but that's the rule and we'll stick by it," said Dixie as we left the clubhouse.

"Well?" asked granda.

"Looked alright to me," I replied.

However, I still had doubts. Blanco, despite his silence, was still too confident. He hadn't smiled but there had been something about him and he seemed to be laughing at us.

"We can do no more; we've watched and seen nothing, let's just wait and see what happens," said granda.

The first young bird races were always mad events and this Selby race was no different. On the Saturday morning, eager to see the new stock in action, I was up early. We had some good birds and we fancied our chances. We were also keen to see how the new lofts performed and we were expecting a cavalry charge of birds. At the start of the season, the first old bird Selby had been a cavalry charge and there were even more birds entered for this race.

It was a dull day with low cloud and the birds were liberated on time. They were due back at two o'clock and every club member was primed for their return. On the gardens, there was no noise, corn tins were placed on the gantries and the air of anticipation was overwhelming. We scanned the Tyne valley and the sky over the church. We knew they would turn up en mass so we were all looking for a large flock of birds. Then Pincher's voice suddenly rang out.

"One bird over the church."

We all turned and stared, sure enough flying very low over the rooftops of the houses alongside the church was a single bird.

"It's blue," shouted Pincher.

"So is the sea," someone shouted back.

"It's knackered," continued Pincher, "but it's for the gardens," and as usual he was right. The bird, a scraggy looking blue pigeon, flew very low along the front row of lofts and dropped straight into Blanco's. Shock and disappointment could be felt coming from every loft.

"It's a stray, it can't be from the race," said father.

"Is that bird from the race Blanco?" someone at the back shouted.

Blanco never replied he was obviously timing the bird in.

A few minutes passed and the question was repeated.

"A yes it's a little blue a hen, she a tired out," Blanco replied.

I glanced at granda and father; both of them were struck dumb.

"This cannot be right granda," I said, "surely one young bird couldn't get away by itself from Selby."

"Depends on the bird," replied granda.

"Here they come," shouted Pincher, "in the valley, flock of about fifty, all for the gardens."

We turned and looked into the valley and Pincher was right. A flock of pigeons flying very low and fast was approaching the gardens. Everyone started shouting and rattling corn tins. The arriving birds overwhelmed the gardens and pigeons shot everywhere. A bird would be just about to drop into a loft, when another bird would nearly collide with it and both birds would circle. Granda was on the gantry shouting and rattling his tin. We were unsure which, if any of the birds, were ours. Young birds are always hard to identify, and on occasions such as this, you shouted and rattled the tin hoping one of the birds was yours.

"That's ours, that chequered bird just going over," shouted father.

Young birds love to fly and whilst this hadn't been an easy race, they certainly weren't tired out.

"Mad buggar," granda mumbled, "come on, in you come, how way."

The bird must have heard him as it nervously dropped onto the top of the loft. Very slowly, granda moved forward throwing a handful of corn onto the gantry.

"Come on son, come on," he said soothingly.

The bird cocked its head, dropped onto the gantry, and walked into the loft.

A steady stream of birds continued to arrive and for about fifteen minutes the sky was full of young pigeons darting about. It is important to get young pigeons to drop into the loft as quickly as possible. One thing that fanciers don't want is a pigeon that wouldn't drop. So this race and the trapping of the birds was a good training ground. I had been watching the arriving birds and had noted that most of the first batch of birds had headed for the rear of the gardens. They had circled for a while but had dropped fairly quickly and I thought that the winners would be in the new lofts. Coming out of the shed, I told granda what I had seen.

"The winner is in Blanco's loft," he said and I remembered the tired, scraggy bird arriving long before any of the other pigeons.

We waited until all of our birds had arrived home, then we made our way round to the clubhouse. There was an air of disbelief about the race and as we arrived a number of the members made comments.

"Something's wrong here Sammy," said Topper Brown, "Blanco's bird, puffing and blowing arrives like an old man, way out in front of the rest. How could it get away on it's own like that? It's ganna win by aboot ten minutes and it's fully nominated. These are young birds, they're untried, never raced, unproven, how can he be fully nominating the winner."

Topper had just expressed everyone's doubts and Blanco standing by the door had heard his comments.

"It's a good a pigeon, I a train my a birds to fly on their own. There's a nothing a wrong with my a bird it's a winner."

As he spoke Blanco pulled back his shoulders and pulled himself up to his full height and suddenly he became a very threatening figure.

"Oh hey nee offence Blanco but it's bloody funny that your bird broke away on its own and the rest didn't," replied Topper.

Once again Topper was expressing everyone's doubts about the race. Granda disappeared inside the clubhouse and closed the door behind him. Father and I knew he didn't want to be followed so, along with the other members, we waited outside. The exchange between Blanco and Topper had quietened everyone and we all stood, for what seemed an age, just waiting. Blanco maintained his stance on the outskirts of the men and I found him very intimidating.

Eventually the clubhouse door swung open and granda appeared holding a piece of paper. He opened the notice board and pinned the paper inside. Immediately everyone started to read it.

"Blanco first, George Clarke second and third, Tommy Tippins fourth, Ash Fifth and sixth, Pincher seventh Baker eighth, the names were read off.

"So you're happy with Blanco's win Sammy?" someone shouted.

"Blanco won fair and square," granda replied, "you all watched his bird arrive. The ring was in the clock and it was timed in six minutes before the second bird."

There was silence.

"What do you want me to say?" granda said, "we've checked everything and can find nothing wrong. Blanco won and that's an end to it."

"Thank a you a Sammy," Blanco shouted from the back and everyone jumped.

Of course it wasn't the end of it, granda knew it and so did father and I. When we returned to our loft, we sat on the bench seat and granda shook his head.

"It's not right son that bird should never have been that far in front, not from Selby and not on a day like today. Blanco's definitely up to something again but I don't know what."

I think the most disappointing thing, for me, was what had been a great sport, in which anyone could participate, was now being abused. Years of hard work had been put into producing the pigeons, and fanciers had spent money and time training their birds. They cared for, and looked after the birds like children and now someone, a newcomer, was abusing them. The atmosphere in our garden was subdued but there was nothing we could do. As granda said, "the best we can do is to keep going to the basketing and keep on watching Blanco; somehow he must be fixing the birds."

We discovered where the rats had found sanctuary. Monday night when granda went to feed the birds two council officials were waiting for him. He told us the story the following Friday night when we went to basket for the next race.

"The council's been to see me," he said, "last Saturday when Rat Face and Beryl's lofts were moved they must have disturbed a number of nests. All the houses in the next street have been complaining. Seemingly, rats were in their coalhouses and netties. Not just small rats, according to the council men these were massive fat rats. They've had to lay poison all over the street and in the back yards. They've identified that they came from Rat Face and Beryl's gardens and they're not happy. Now, they want to inspect under all the lofts and lay poison and they've seen the muck mountain at the end of the row."

I was slightly confused then I realised he was talking about the droppings hill. I had noticed that since the gardeners had stopped removing it the pile had grown considerably but I hadn't given it much thought.

"Believe me they're not at all happy with the state of that hill," said granda, "and thinking about it, I can't blame them. They've given us a week to get rid of it. They say if it isn't shifted they'll stop anyone coming onto the gardens, they reckon it's a health hazard."

"So what have you done?" asked father.

"George Clarke's going to help us sort it out. He has a friend, a farmer and he will allow us to dump the muck on his land. Tomorrow early morning one of George's lorries will be here and it'll take it away. George reckons it'll probably take about three lorry loads. Problem is we'll have to load the lorry ourselves; I've put up notices for everyone to be on the gardens at six in the morning. I've seen a few of the lads and they've agreed to turn up and I'll catch the rest of the lads at the basketing tonight."

"So fuckin Saturday is a fuckin shit-fuckin-shovelling day."

Not my words but the words of wisdom uttered from Billy Bucket Head's mouth.

We were all standing outside the clubhouse and granda had just made an announcement about moving the muck hill.

"That's right," granda answered, "and I expect you all to be here."

"I'll fuckin be there," replied Billy, "but what about that lazy fucker Rat Face; will he be fuckin gracing us with his fuckin presence?"

It was funny how whenever there was a problem Rat Face's name came up.

"After fuckin all," continued Billy, "he fuckin disturbed the fuckin rats, he stopped the fuckin gardeners taking the fuckin shite and he's caused the whole fuckin problem."

For Billy this was quite profound reasoning and no one disagreed with him. However, granda looked, despondently, at Billy.

"Billy, Billy please try and stop swearing. The lad's here you know," he said nodding towards me. Then turning to the rest of the members he said, "you lads know Roger better than me; it's up to you to see that he gets here and gets his hands dirty. I've done as much as I can."

Secretly I was quite looking forward to filling the lorry with muck. It was a small adventure and when I looked at the hill, I realised what an eyesore it was.

Once again, throughout the basketing of the pigeons, we stood silently at the back of the clubhouse. I watched Blanco as he worked basketing the birds, then when his pigeons were being handled, he moved onto the ringing machine. I scrutinised his every move and could see nothing wrong. He smiled confidently throughout the procedure, which annoyed me even more.

"Nothing son, did you see anything?" granda asked as we left the clubhouse and were walking back to our loft.

I just shook my head; I have to admit that I was sick of watching the pigeons being race rung and basketed.

"Look granda," I said, "if we know Blanco is cheating why don't we just tell Dixie and have him thrown off the basketing committee?"

Granda stopped and turned to face me.

"Son, we have no proof that Blanco is cheating, he may be winning those races genuinely. What if we accuse him and he continues to win? How would you feel if someone made false accusations against you? but it's not only about Blanco. If he is cheating then it's important that we find out how. The club members must have faith in the honesty of the system. If we make accusations and we're wrong we'll damage the club, believe me this isn't only about Blanco it's also about the system."

Frustrated granda turned and walked back to our loft and I followed.

Without my brother, we were at the muck hill for six o'clock, he had told father he had a game of football and couldn't help. I knew he didn't but didn't want to argue with him. Father had given up a days work to help and granda was waiting for us when we arrived. There was a good turnout. All the new ten loft areas at the very rear of the gardens had been taken. Rat face had rented two of the sites joined them together to make one large garden and a further eight members had joined the club. Six of the new members turned up with their shovels and wheelbarrows and I think granda was pleased. There were still four unoccupied single sites alongside the three big lofts in the now second back row. For some reason new members seemed reluctant to set up their lofts alongside these lofts. Shortly after us, Blanco arrived and set to work tying old sacking around his sandshoes. Everyone nudged each other and laughed but no one said anything to him. The lorry arrived and after a rather hectic reversing manoeuvre, during which everyone joined in giving instructions, it parked alongside the hill.

We organised ourselves into diggers and lifters. The diggers started at one end of the hill filling the wheelbarrows. Then when they were full, they were wheeled over to the lorry and the lifters lifted them and tipped the contents into the back of the lorry. Blanco because of his size was a lifter. He could lift one wheelbarrow by himself, which impressed everyone, but it frightened me. Very soon a rhythm was established and the wheelbarrows moved back and forward to the lorry. It wasn't a pleasant job and as soon as we'd removed the fresh muck from the top of the hill, the smell was released. Nevertheless, we worked well and after an hour the lorry was full and set off to the farm to dump its load. This was break time and we all sat round telling stories and joking about the smell and the pigeons. I was really enjoying myself.

After half an hour, the lorry returned and once again, we set off shovelling. The mood was good and the mountain of muck was going down. At eleven o'clock Rat Face arrived. He was dressed in his suit, was accompanied by Beryl in her best and tightest dress and she was pushing the baby in a new pram. His arrival was unexpected and unwelcome.

"You haven't done much," he said, "sorry I can't help; have to go into the shop."

Everyone stopped working and looked at him.

"You're a lazy bastard Rat Face," someone shouted.

"Here, here," replied Rat Face indignantly, "just hold on, George Clarke, Tippins and Ash aren't here. We professional men have to keep our businesses running, be fair."

A clod of pigeon muck caught him on the side of the face. Beryl screamed, turned the pram and ran back up the path.

"I'll remember that," said Rat Face as he turned and ran after her.

I was delighted, the muck had stuck to his face and as he walked away, he was picking pieces of it out of his ear.

That week's race was the second young bird Selby race and once again, at two o'clock, the birds returned. Only this time Blanco's bird wasn't amongst them. It was a repeat performance for the rest of us. A flock of about fifty birds arrived all together and all hell broke out. Once again, Pincher's and our birds were in the bunch. Only this time when the results were displayed on the notice board the three new lofts had taken the first six places. George Clarke was in third place and surprisingly Malcolm Ash had the first and second pigeons. I was pleased that Blanco's name did not appear on the list.

It took six full lorry loads to remove the muck mountain and we worked all day. We only stopped when the pigeons were due then we resumed and worked until five o'clock. The end result was worth all the effort. A new flat space was created and it opened up the fronts of the gardens.

"Good job," said granda.

He was pleased with the work and I think whilst the club members had complained, they had enjoyed the camaraderie of working together. I had enjoyed it, the jokes as we had worked had made me laugh and once again I felt like part of the club.

"What happens now Sammy?" someone asked.

"We all dispose of our own pigeon's droppings and the scrapings from the lofts," granda replied.

I knew, for us, this wasn't a problem. We had already started collecting the scrapings from our loft and passed them through the secret gate to Uncle Peter. He was very pleased to have them and, in the corner of his allotment, he had started his own manure heap.

Granda had it all planned and that Saturday night, before we left, he placed a notice on the notice board.

AS FROM TODAY, NO ONE IS TO DUMP
PIGEON MUCK OR RUBBISH ON THE LAND
IN FRONT OF THE LOFTS. ALL MEMBERS MUST DISPOSE
OF THEIR OWN MUCK.

It had been a good day but for the older members the race had been a disappointment. Now even more of them were expressing concern about the new lofts and how they were dominating the winning places.

As we were curious about Rat Face's new loft, we decided to leave the gardens by the top gate and walk round to see how the building work was going. We leaned on the fence in the doorway and admired the new framework and gantry.

"It's a good job," said granda and father agreed.

"Mind the builder lads are doing it as a fiddle," said father, "they're only working when they can fit him in, weekends and nights mostly. I know two of the lads, I've worked with them and it's all cash in hand and they mean in hand, they get it before they start work. They've heard about Rat Face and they don't trust him anymore than we do."

Granda smiled.

"Did you hear that arrogant bastard this morning? Poor old Jack he worked his heart out in that shop. Rat Face takes it over and has the audacity to call himself a professional man."

"I did and bye the way it was a good shot this morning, who ever threw that muck has a good eye," father replied.

"I always had," said granda laughing, "comes from the trenches and firing rifles."

The council arranged to inspect under each loft and for the next two weeks, their inspectors were kept busy. Surprisingly they didn't find many more rats. Billy had a nest under his loft and received a nasty letter from the council. I don't know if he ever read it, probably he rolled it into a telescope and watched the birds through it, but it certainly didn't seem to bother him. Nothing seemed to bother Billy.

Whilst Blanco wasn't placed in the second Selby young bird race, we still had serious doubts about him cheating. We could not understand the distressed condition of his bird when it had arrived home, or the gap it had opened up between itself and the following flock and I don't think we were the only ones who were suspicious. To me it was a challenge, it nagged at me and I spent hours trying to think out how he could be fixing the system.

Chapter Twenty-Three

The doubts that the three new lofts were creating about the old systems of breeding and racing were causing the other fanciers to look at their methods. This wasn't a bad thing granda argued.

"We must progress, new ideas should always be considered and tried," he said and his comments surprised me.

We were sitting in the front room of his house and I had been allowed to sit in on a discussion between him and father. I was quite pleased at being treated like one of the team and tried to make constructive comments. They were discussing the future of the loft and the birds.

"There are ways, which fanciers are trying to make the birds return home faster," granda explained. "I've seen them used on the gardens, for instance introducing jealousy for the cock birds. It needs organising but some people think it works. We pair the birds up, allow them to raise their first set of youngins then we split them. The cock birds are kept separated. Then just before they're sent to a race, a spare cock bird is put into the nesting box with the hen. We have to make sure that the race bird sees the other cock bird with his hen then we basket him. They say it gives him the incentive to get back to sort out his hen and the spare cock bird, I don't know if it works."

I was still thinking about what he had said when he continued.

"Alternatively we can keep the cocks and hens apart and only allow the cock bird to tread the hen when he returns from a chuck or a race. He knows then that whenever he returns, he can tread his hen and this gives him the incentive to get home fast. On the other hand, we can introduce him to the hen just before we basket him for the race. Then he knows what he's missing and this gives him the incentive to hurry back."

This one interested me. I was now twelve years old and was beginning to realise that the thing between my legs was used for other things than peeing. Quite what for and when was still a mystery. It appeared to me that the damn thing had also developed a mind of its own. On buses and sometimes in school it had placed me in very embarrassing situations. Nevertheless, I was having quite nice new experiences and had found new things to do with it. No one had discussed anything about babies or sex with me, and my brother's comments only confused me.

"Hens," granda continued, "just before we basket them, we can take eggs or youngins away from them. That certainly brings out the motherly instinct and certainly gives them the desire to return to the loft. Just look at the way they fight when I remove the youngins to ring them."

Father and I were listening intently.

"I hate cruelty," he said, "all of this widowhood, jealousy, taking eggs and youngins it all seems unnatural and cruel to me. We have always flown natural and we've had good results. I think our system works, but out of all these new ideas, I think the idea with the biggest impact is early breeding. Get the youngins well developed for racing, get the old birds well past feeding youngins, and fully recovered before they race. I think that's what we should be developing."

I had listened intently and really I had nothing to contribute but I did have something I wanted to say. I had spent hours thinking through the Blanco problem and, I thought, I knew what he was doing. However, I was waiting for the right time to discuss it.

"To breed off Huwey and Pincher's hen we're going to have to extend the loft and build a new section," father was talking. "And to get as many youngins and eggs as possible we must have heating into the loft and start our programme early. I think that, at the same time, in the same section, we should also start four or five of the other pairs off breeding. Then we'll start the rest of the loft off as usual. This way we'll be able to compare the results when the birds start racing."

The two men sat thinking.

"Okay son sounds reasonable to me," said granda, "as soon as the racing season is finished we'll start building a new breeding section on the side of the loft. Only, remember one thing tell nobody what we are doing. Pincher has agreed not to mention that the birds will be breeding in our loft and the less people who know the better."

I was delighted with their decision. To be involved in extending the loft and introducing a new breeding programme would be exciting and interesting.

The conversation had stopped so I introduced my new theory on Blanco.

"I think I know what Blanco is doing," I said.

They both looked at me.

"Go on son," said granda.

I was pleased with my new theory; I saw it as a real piece of detective work and it had come to me when I was at school. The rubber race rings, which father had given me on Boxing Day, had remained in my trouser pocket until mother, going to wash my trousers, had removed them and left them on the small table at the side of my bed. I had remembered what granda had said about Blanco using them as rubbers on the ends of pencils and had installed them on my pencils. It was a poor idea; the rubber was too soft and wouldn't rub anything out. At school, in the middle of an English lesson, I was pondering the problem when I suddenly realised Blanco must have lots of the rings. However, my pondering was rudely interrupted when the teacher Mr Ratcliffe, smacked me around the head.

"You Baker," he shouted, "you want to get your priorities sorted out or you'll finish up like your brother."

I knew he was right and I set to thinking about the Blanco problem. I listed the important elements of a pigeon race. Then visualising each one and remembering Blanco's capabilities as a magician, one by one, I eliminated them and that is when it hit me.

No doubt George Dixon, on a Saturday night on the telly, would have worked it out quicker, but I was still excited with my theory. Dixon of Dock Green was one of my favourite programmes. I had watched George many times telling Andy Crawford, his son in law and a detective, his theories on crimes. Now I started to lay my theory out in the same way.

"What is the most important thing in a race?" I posed the question.

Granda replied, "the pigeons son now go on, we're getting hungry."

This wasn't the type of reaction George usually got from Andy on the telly.

"No granda," I replied shaking my head and dramatising my response.

"For god's sake son, get on with it will you," granda said.

I knew he definitely wouldn't have said that if George Dixon had been telling the tale.

"The race ring granda," I said and paused for effect. Both men stared at me. I was pleased; I had their attention so I continued.

"The race ring is the only thing that is placed in the thimble and timed in. It goes into the clock, not the pigeon. When we watched the basketing for the first Selby race, when Blanco's birds came out, Blanco moved over to race ring the birds. He didn't touch the birds but he did touch the race rings. All he had to do was pocket the race ring then clock it in on the Saturday."

I was pleased with my theory and I stopped and smiled at them.

"Son the bird has to have a race ring; you saw it go onto the bird's leg. They read out the race ring number and it's recorded, if it didn't have a race ring it wouldn't go into the race basket," said father slightly annoyed.

Granda chipped in, "the race rings are all different colours for different races and all have their own individual numbers. What's the point of him putting one in his pocket?"

Just like Andy in Dixon of Dock Green, they hadn't seen the logic of the crime and now, just like George, I would enlighten them.

"The race rings are the same colours every year, not necessarily for the same races. However, the same coloured rings are used. You know

Blanco collects all the spare rings that are left lying around in the clubhouse. It's easy for him to see what colour rings are being used for a race; Dixie always has the box open. All Blanco has to do is carry a few different coloured rings in his coat pocket. Then when his birds are to be race rung, he reads out the number on the legitimate race ring but then he hides it and places an old race ring, from last year but the same colour, on the bird's leg."

I sat back and sniffed just like George did on the telly. Both of them, wide eyed, looked at me.

"Sounds feasible," said father "if Blanco can hide a pigeon up his sleeve he can certainly palm a race ring." "Come on," said granda, "this is all a bit Dixon of Dock Green to me."

I didn't know whether to be pleased at his deduction or disappointed at his ridicule.

"It's true granda, I've worked it out," I said defensively, "I saw Blanco doing his magician's act. I know he can make things disappear and it's the only way he can be winning. His mother still throws a pigeon up from their flat, and that's the pigeon we see arriving. We all watch that bird land in his loft so how can we possibly argue. Blanco doesn't time the bird in, he times in the real race ring, which he has hidden in his pocket but he doesn't cheat every race. He only does it occasionally but then when he does win, he wins all the nomination and prize money for that race. At the end of the season he can sell the bird and," I said with great emphasis, "all of his birds are roughly the same colour and when he's flying youngins, even Pincher cannot identify them."

The room was silent, I was sure I was right.

"Difficulty is proving it," said father.

"Oh I can prove it," replied granda, "the next race when the birds are in the race basket we'll check Blanco's birds, that'll prove or disprove it. Trouble is, if he's not doing it every race, to catch him, we have to pick the right race and I'll have to be discreet. It is a good theory but it's a bit way out. We've accused Blanco once before and he's beaten us and I don't want to be embarrassed again."

Granda sat back in his chair and at that moment I thought he looked a lot like Dixon of Dock Green. I half expected him to raise his hand in salute and say, "that's all for now, I'll be seeing you."

The acceptance of my theory was a great relief to me. I knew it was the only way Blanco could be cheating the system but now I knew I had to prove it. Night and day, I had thought about it and I was convinced it was the answer. Granda agreed that we would continue watching the basketing for the rest of the racing season and now I was determined to prove I was right.

The next race was a young bird race from Doncaster, 110 miles, and on the Friday night we positioned ourselves in the clubhouse. I stood as near to the ringing machine as possible and granda stood alongside me. I had lost interest in the pigeons. I didn't mind if we didn't win. I only wanted one thing, that was to prove what Blanco was doing, and that night I failed. I watched when Blanco changed places and took up his position behind the ringing machine. Hardly breathing I stared as Billy removed Blanco's pigeons from the basket and offered their legs to the machine. Blanco had entered four pigeons and I watched as the first one was race rung. Dixie took a slip of paper, with the race ring on it, out of the box; he removed the rubber ring and passed it to Blanco. Blanco took it between his thumb and forefinger, read out the number 412 and then using both hands, he stretched the ring over the pointed jaws of the machine. I could still see the number 4 and as Blanco turned the handle and the jaws opened, I could see the number stretch. As he reversed the handle, I watched as the ring slid off the jaws and onto the pigeon's leg. I could still see the number 412. The ring was the same, I was sure of it. I watched carefully as the next three pigeons were rung and I was able to see the correct rings on the birds as they were placed in the basket. Granda had also been watching and now he glanced at me, I shook my head.

That Doncaster race was a disaster. The conveyors liberated the birds early. They had been told that the weather would deteriorate and they had taken a chance. Unfortunately, their gamble did not pay off. As soon as the birds were liberated the weather closed in. It rained, and then thundered and lightning lit up the gardens. We sheltered in the loft watching the rain fall.

"Nothing will fly in that," granda said.

The estimated time for their return home arrived and passed. Then the clouds started to part and slowly the sun appeared. Steam rose from the gardens and along with the steam our spirits rose. There was no cavalry charge, after a further half an hour Pincher's voice rang out, "one bird over the church."

My heart nearly stopped. This was the usual approach for Blanco's winning birds. Surely, I thought, this can't be a bird for Blanco, if it was my theory was wrong and we had wasted our time. Granda looked at me and raised his eyebrows I shrugged my shoulders.

"It's for the gardens," shouted Pincher.

We watched as the bird approached. I suppose I wasn't watching to see if it was our bird more praying that it wasn't Blanco's.

The bird was obviously well flown down and wet and it struggled towards the gardens.

"It's for the front row," shouted Pincher.

Oh no please don't let it be for Blanco's loft, I prayed.

It passed Pincher's loft and struggled on. At Blanco's loft, it turned its head and for a second I thought it was going to drop but it flew past. It was just passing the space where Rat Face's loft had been when granda shouted.

"It's ours, it's that young chequered cock, and it's one of Huwey's youngins."

It took us all by surprise, I think granda and father had also been expecting the bird to drop into Blanco's loft. Granda rattled the tin but the bird didn't need any coaxing down, it was exhausted and dropped straight into our loft.

We were delighted, a young bird flying like that through bad weather proved it was independent and had stamina.

"That's one for the future," said granda triumphantly as he came out of the loft.

We won by ten minutes then we watched as slowly, bedraggled, worn out pigeons started to return. We never saw if Blanco got his birds, I only know he wasn't in the first ten and I was happy. However, the next nine birds all flew over the three front rows of lofts and made their way to the three new lofts at the back.

"I don't know how that chequered cock did it," said granda, "those pigeons from the back are bigger and stronger. I would have thought that on a day like today they would have beaten him. He's a chip off the old block alright, just shows the bloodstreams the thing."

For me the delight of winning the race was improved by granda's words.

Just before we took the clock to the clubhouse, we had a visitor. George Clarke knocked then entered the garden.

"Hello Sammy, if possible a word with you" It wasn't so much a question as a demand and he beckoned with his finger for granda to come forward.

The three of us stood and looked at him. He was smoking a big cigar and every time he drew on it the gold sovereign ring on his finger shone in the sunlight. He obviously saw the surprised looks on our faces. We weren't used to people entering the garden and dictating what we did.

"Little bit of business Sammy, no offence, just wanted to keep things private, you know how it is." George must have noticed our looks and toned his voice down.

I was sure granda didn't know how it was but father butted in.

"Okay dad we'll take the clock round, you see what George wants."

I was disappointed, I wanted to know what George wanted but, dutifully, I followed father out of the gate and around to the clubhouse. Our young chequered cock bird had caused quite a stir.

"Some fuckin bird that," Billy said, "be a good fuckin channel bird I wish I fuckin had him."

Blanco was there he said nothing but nodded at us. We handed the clock in and stood, outside the clubhouse, with the rest of the men discussing the race.

"The big lofts are winning all the time," Topper Brown said.

"Aye only Sammy's giving them a race," replied Mattie Walker, "be interesting next season when all the other new members are racing. I'm going to have to buy some new stock birds."

Pincher arrived and pulled us to one side.

"Your father's agreed," he said smiling and rubbing his hands together, "next year we'll make some money, just see how keen the lads are for new, good stock."

When we arrived back at our garden we found granda deep in thought.

"What did George want?" father asked.

"Offered me five hundred pounds for Huwey and the young chequered cock."

My father's jaw dropped and granda seemed to be in a daze.

"What did you say?" asked father.

"Told him I'd think about it, I've never had five hundred pounds in my life. I could nearly buy you and Peter houses."

The silence that ensued impressed upon me the dilemma that granda was now facing.

"We could sell dad," said father, "with that type of money we could buy three or four good pigeons and still have money left over. Five hundred pounds is a lot of money."

From the excitement in his voice, I knew he was in favour of the sale.

"Aye but we'll never be able to buy another Huwey son," replied granda.

I said nothing; somehow, I knew it wasn't my place to enter the conversation. I knew both men were wrestling with their thoughts so I went into the loft. Inside I crossed into the old bird loft and looked at Huwey; to me he looked pretty much like the average pigeon.

That night they didn't reach a decision and they decided to sleep on it. As we left the gardens, and were out of sight of granda, making our way home, father pulled me to one side.

"Now son," he said looking me straight in the eye, "I'm trusting you, this offer for Huwey is great but one thing you cannot do is tell your mother. You've got to promise me you'll say nothing."

He held his hand out to me and I shook it like an adult.

"I'll keep my mouth shut," I said.

Chapter Twenty-Four

It was difficult keeping the secret. It was such a lot of money and I couldn't stop thinking about it, and about what we could buy with it. Nevertheless, and even though mother did ask why we looked so happy, I did manage to keep my mouth shut. Father put her off by telling her about Huwey's son winning the race. She didn't seem very impressed just 'tutted'. Blanco was also on my mind. I knew there were another six races before the end of the season, and I knew that if we were going to catch him we would have to go to all the basketing. However, I was still convinced that my theory was correct.

The decision, not to sell, was taken by granda. The next day, when we arrived at the garden, he was waiting for us.

"I can't sell Huwey son, he's the best pigeon I've ever bred. He's like a son to me," he said, "I cannot allow him to fall into the hands of George Clarke; he's not a pigeon man, he's not like us. Huwey would have no life, he'd be a prisoner never allowed out and only used for breeding."

As he was speaking I could see a look of disappointment appearing on father's face, and eventually he said,

"It's your decision dad. I feel the same but the money would have been marvellous it would have been like a pools win."

Later granda walked round to George Clarke's loft to break the news. He was away a long time and we were beginning to worry about him. When he did return he was puffing and out of breath.

"Quick come and see this," he shouted, as he stuck his head round the gate.

We both dashed out after him.

"What is it?" asked father.

"Just follow me," wheezed granda as he set off along in front of the lofts.

We followed him; he turned up the path passed the clubhouse and just about ran to the very back row where the new lofts were being built.

"I'd just told George that we weren't selling. He wasn't very happy, called me a silly old get. Anyway, I was making my way back to the garden when I heard hammering, I thought I'd just have a look to see how Rat Face's loft was getting on and when I looked over the fence I saw this, come here," he whispered.

He had stopped at the fence surrounding Rat Face and Beryl's new loft and was peeping over the top.

"Come here," he repeated and we crept forward and peeped over the fence.

Two men with big hammers were knocking down the newly assembled framework and were stacking the wood in a pile at the bottom of the garden.

"They're taking it down," whispered granda.

"I know that lad with the hammer," said father, "it's Johnny I've worked with him."

"Ask him what they're doing," whispered granda.

"Johnny," father shouted.

The man stopped, shouldered the hammer and strolled over to us.

"How you doing?" asked father.

"Canny, yee know how it gans, yourself?"

"I'm well Johnny, what are you doing to Rat Face's loft?"

"Oh he's stopped paying, run out of money he says, still owes us forty pounds so we're taking the wood back."

"Never," replied father, he seemed quite shocked. "He's just come into a lot of money, Beryl and him inherited all Jack Morris's money."

"Had nowt," replied Johnny, "they spent all the money that was in his wallet, then when they went to the bank, they found out he owed hundreds."

"Never," father replied, once again he seemed quite shocked.

Johnny continued he seemed to know a lot about Rat Face and Beryl's business.

"Oh aye it's right, they're moving back into a flat on the West Road, putting the house and business up for sale. The lads reckon that the money will just about cover the debt, but he can't pay us, so we're getting in first and getting the timber back."

"Don't blame you," granda said.

I was delighted, what a weekend this had turned out to be. We had won the race, been offered five hundred pounds for Huwey and Rat face's loft was being demolished.

"Are you putting his old loft back up?" granda asked.

"Are you a comedian?" Johnny replied, "we're not a charity, if he wants the old loft back up he'll have to do it himself."

I couldn't believe it; it just got better and better.

Billy had seen us peeping over the fence and had sneaked alongside us. In silence, with a smile on his face, he had listened to the whole conversation. We had been enthralled by the story and by watching Johnny's mate continuing to demolish the framework and we hadn't noticed Billy. It was just what Billy wanted, some good gossip, and as soon as Johnny went back to work, Billy ran off.

Watching the demolition of Rat Face's loft we had forgotten about George Clarke's offer and it wasn't until we returned to the garden that father asked.

"George was disappointed then?"

"He's not pleased at all," replied granda, "his results with the young birds this season have been nowhere near what he expected. I told him it was only the third young bird race of the season but he's disappointed at not having won. I think he thought we couldn't refuse his offer and he really thinks Huwey is something special. I think Malcolm Ash beating him in the second Selby race has really upset him."

Over the next week, the news about Rat Face spread rapidly across the gardens. To the majority of the members it was a huge joke, although a few of his friends did not see the funny side.

"They've been getting free drinks off him for the past two weeks and now it's stopped, that's what's upset them," said Pincher.

Once again it was Friday night, Pincher had come to talk to granda about the breeding programme, and father and I left them in the garden. We had half an hour before granda had to set the clocks and we had decided to have a look at all the new lofts that were now being built on the back row.

Earlier, the birds had been basketed to go to the second Doncaster race. Granda and I had watched the basketing and again I had shook my head when Blanco's birds were ringed and placed in the race baskets. Since granda had accused him of cheating, Blanco had been ignoring us and we hadn't visited his loft. As Father and I, on our way to see the new lofts, passed his loft we noticed that he wasn't there but his birds were out. We peeped through a crack in the fence and watched the birds on the gantry.

"They look half starved," father said, "they certainly don't look in top condition."

I peered in and had to agree. The birds actually looked scrawny.

"I suppose if he keeps them hungry they'll always return from short distances and drop as quickly as possible," said father.

"Here what's a you a doing," a voice sounded from along the path.

We looked up and there was Blanco running towards us.

"It's a my a garden you no a lookee through my a fence."

"Alright Blanco, just calm down, we were doing no harm, just looking at the birds," replied father.

"My birds are a my birds you a leave them alone."

We didn't want to argue and just walked past him but as we turned into the path to pass the clubhouse father said, "you know son the more I see of Blanco's birds the more I think you're right."

I didn't need his reassurance I was already convinced I was right and I knew that one night I would see him changing the race rings.

The second Doncaster young bird's race once again was a procession for the three big lofts. Huwey's offspring the chequered cock was still recovering from last week's race so we didn't send him. Again, Malcolm Ash won, Tommy Tippins was second and George Clarke was third. Billy was fourth, which shocked everyone and then the three lofts took fifth sixth and seventh places. Pincher was eighth and Topper Brown was ninth. Of course, all the pooled nomination money went to the first pigeons. The old members received nothing and we were disappointed with tenth place.

The obvious was now dawning on all the members. The three new lofts, entering large numbers of good birds, all fully nominated, were going to win most of the races and all of the money. To improve their chances all the members had to improve their pigeon stocks. This worked in our favour and Pincher had a book full of orders for eggs and youngins. These orders were not only for eggs from Huwey and his channel hen but also for eggs from other pairs of birds from Pincher's and our loft. Our pedigree was impeccable. Granda had a name for honesty and good pigeons and I think the members preferred to deal with him rather that George Clarke and his friends. The future looked good for us and I was looking forward to next year to see the breeding programme working. However, the atmosphere of the club had changed dramatically. The races had become highly competitive and the members had become secretive. The prize money was now all that counted and quite often arguments broke out on the gardens.

The following Saturday was the first Leicester young bird race about 180 miles and, once again on the Friday night, granda and I positioned ourselves in the clubhouse. I was convinced that Blanco would cheat again. I knew that he wasn't racing for the sport and that he was only racing for the money and it appeared to me that he would do anything to get it. I knew that this season his winnings were small and I thought that he would try to cheat again. He did not have much time left and I realised to have a good young bird to sell he needed a bird which had won a number of races. If he achieved this, he could then sell the bird to George Clarke, Malcolm Ash or Tommy Tippins. However, the only way he could do this was for one of his youngins to have won a few races. As there were only five young bird races left, I knew that Blanco would have to put the little blue hen, which had won the first Selby young bird race, back into a race and ensure it won. Therefore, I knew I had to watch for this bird being entered. The problem was, prior to the race ringing, we did not know which birds individual club members were entering. Therefore, I knew I had to watch as each of Blanco's birds were being race rung and decide if it was the winning blue hen. This I knew would be difficult because most of his birds were blue.

As the committee set to work, race ringing the pigeons, the atmosphere in the clubhouse was jovial.

"You and your boy are becoming regulars," Dixie said.

Granda smiled. "Aye for some reason the boy enjoys watching you lads at work," he replied.

"Don't blame him, we make a good team," replied Dixie,

He was right; watching the four men at work was a pleasure. It was like a conveyor belt and the pigeons moved through their hands quickly and professionally. I watched as two baskets were emptied and the birds race rung then Billy's basket was placed in front of him.

"BBBBBlanco's fuckin birds," Billy called out and everyone laughed.

Blanco moved to one side and changed positions with Mattie and I leaned forward.

"Many you putting in Blanco?" said Dixie trying to make conversation.

"A four," replied Blanco.

"Little blue hen in," Dixie continued.

"Yes, a she's a in a bery bery good nick," replied Blanco reluctantly.

Obviously, the question had taken him by surprise and his reply was hesitant. I knew then that this was the race. I knew then that he was going to try to cheat and I glanced at granda, he acknowledged me with a smile.

Billy removed the first of Blanco's pigeons from the basket. He read out the metal ring number and offered the bird's left leg to the ringing machine. Blanco accepted the rubber race ring from Dixie, called out the number 111 and stretched the ring onto the jaws of the machine. Then, quickly, he turned the handle opening the jaws and stretching the ring. Billy moved the bird's leg in between the jaws. Blanco turned the handle in the opposite direction and the jaws started to close, silently the race ring slid off the silvered jaws onto the bird's leg. I had listened to Blanco shout out the race ring number and could still see the number 111 on the ring, which was now on the bird's leg. The whole procedure had only taken seconds and I concentrated even harder. Billy removed a second bird and as he did so I noticed Blanco's right hand go into his raincoat pocket. I nearly shouted out but just managed to stop myself. Blanco removed a handkerchief and wiped his brow.

"Too fast for you Blanco, getting a sweat on?" said Mattie laughing.

Once again, Blanco wiped his brow and smiled.

The second bird's leg was now offered to the machine and Blanco took the race ring from Dixie. He called out 112 then stretched the ring over the jaws. At least I thought he did but I couldn't see the number and I noticed that, whilst the ring was red, like all the others, it was ever so slightly faded. Mattie had obviously noticed nothing and he was still smiling over his joke with Blanco. He just routinely accepted the bird from Billy, and placed it in the race basket.

"It's bloody hard work turning that handle," Mattie said, "Sammy; there must be an easier way to ring these birds."

He had distracted granda and I just stood there dumbstruck. Had Blanco done it? had he palmed the race ring? Granda had said nothing and really, I had not seen a switch take place.

Inside the clubhouse, to everyone else, it was routine, as far as they knew nothing had happened. Blanco's four birds were race rung and he moved back to the race basket, Mattie replaced him on the machine, and still I said nothing. I was unsure what to do. The race basket was full; Donkey sealed the basket and carried it to the door. What could I do? I was shaking with frustration.

"You alright son," asked Dixie, "looks a bit peaky to me Sammy, best take him outside; fresh air will do him some good."

Granda looked at me, I nodded at him and we walked to the door. Outside the wind was blowing and I did feel better.

"He did it granda," I said.

Granda stared at me.

"Are you sure? I saw nothing," he replied.

I wasn't sure and it must have shown.

"Son I can't go back in there, open baskets and make accusations if you're not sure."

"There was something different with the second bird, his blue hen, the ring was slightly different and I couldn't see the number," I replied.

Granda sighed.

"Okay, we'll chance it but you say nothing. I'm not accusing anyone mind, just let me do what I have to do."

As we re-entered the clubhouse my heart was beating and again I started to sweat.

We went back into the clubhouse, it was warm inside and the four men were still working away.

"You alright son," asked Dixie.

I nodded.

"Don't say much do you?" continued Dixie.

I glanced at Blanco, he was staring at me and I knew, he knew, that I had seen what he had done. His stare gave me confidence and I knew I was right.

Granda was examining the race baskets.

"There's no seal on the flap of this basket," he said.

Everyone stopped and looked at him.

"What?" asked Dixie.

"A seal is missing from this basket," repeated granda.

"Can't be, we seal everyone," replied Dixie getting up from his seat and walking round the desk to the baskets.

"By gum Sammy lad you're right," he said as he looked at the basket, "I'll get the seals and seal it."

"Birds will have to be checked again," said granda.

There were gasps and grunts of disapproval and everyone gathered at the basket and stared at the drop down flap at the front of the basket where the seal should have been.

"No need for that Sammy," said Dixie, "obviously the seal has just missed the holes in the basket and fallen off, see there it is on the floor."

Sure enough lying alongside the basket was a broken seal. I knew what granda had done; he had broken the seal and pulled it off the basket.

"No Dixie it's got to be done right, it'll only take a minute. Here I'll handle the birds, I'll call out the ring numbers and you check them in the book."

Everyone looked surprised.

"Is a this a necessary?" interrupted Blanco.

"Rules are rules," said granda, "basket seals have to be in position before the baskets are stacked for collection."

Dixie was obviously annoyed and exhaled loudly.

"Okay Sammy let's get it done then," he said as he made his way back to the desk.

Granda pulled the basket forward in front of the door and lifted the small top trap door. Then he pulled an empty race basket alongside it and opened its trap door.

"Okay, here we go," he said and removed one bird.

"Race number 111 blue cock, Union number 5426."

"Correct Blanco's bird," called out Dixie.

Blanco had been staring into the race basket but now he moved towards the clubhouse door and opened it wide.

"I'm a sweating in a here," he said, "I'll a give you a hand a Sammy."

Before granda could reply, Blanco plunged his hand into the basket and removed a pigeon.

"No stop," shouted granda but it was too late; Blanco had a pigeon in his hand and, as if to read the ring number, was turning it. Granda pushed the bird he was holding into the empty race basket and went to take the bird off Blanco. What happened next I don't know but one minute Blanco was passing it to Granda then the bird was flying around the clubhouse.

"It's a my a blue hen, catch her," Blanco shouted waving his arms.

The bird settled on a window ledge but then, distressed by Blanco's waving, darted for the open door and disappeared into the night. We all stood in the clubhouse, transfixed, just staring at the open door.

That was the first time in the history of the club that a pigeon had escaped whilst being rung for a race. Blanco was the first to come to his senses and charged off after the bird shouting he would catch her and bring her back. He never reappeared and, disgusted, I watched as granda finished off helping to race ring the rest of the birds. The jovial atmosphere had disappeared and the remaining birds were rung in silence. Dixie took the incident personally and never spoke to us. We waited then watched as the baskets were loaded onto the transporter, and then we made our way back to our loft. I was deeply disappointed and had said nothing to granda. I knew from his face that he was also disappointed but I also knew that now he believed me.

Chapter Twenty-Five

The three new lofts were first, second and third in that, Leicester race and won all the prize money. Pincher kept his end up and one of his young birds was fourth. Blanco turned up on the day of the race. He didn't speak to anyone and left as soon as the first pigeons were clocked in. That night as we were leaving the gardens, as we passed his loft, we noticed that his three pigeons from the race were still sitting on the gantry. I had already asked granda what we could do about Blanco. He'd just shrugged his shoulders and said,

"I don't know, I suppose we just wait and see what happens, it is a problem. Dixie's annoyed and soon he's going to object to us watching the basketing. He thinks we're spying on him."

The story of the bird's escape spread throughout the gardens. It was impossible to keep a secret like that from anyone. Many of the men blamed granda and sympathised with Blanco. Some praised granda saying he was right, "the rules of the club had to be followed." George Clarke and his friends did not enter into the debate. They were happy enough that Blanco's bird hadn't competed. However, the story about the bird did benefit Blanco. By the time the story had been circulating for a week, Blanco's bird had become a flying legend and according to the gossip, it would have been a certainty to win the race. Tommy Tippins offered Blanco twenty pound for the bird and he accepted. I found this out two weeks later and couldn't believe it.

On the Friday nights before the remaining four races, we went to the basketing of the birds. We didn't feel welcome but I think because of our presence, Blanco didn't try anything else. The new lofts won all these races but a few of the older members did get third and fourth places. Of course when this happened the entire prize money had gone and once again they were disappointed. These last four races were from Peterborough 200 miles, Hitchin 250 miles and finally two Hatfield races 260 miles. Blanco wasn't in any of the top ten places for the final races. He must have known that we knew what he was doing and we saw no more cheating. I wished we had caught him and I think granda regretted not confronting him that night in the clubhouse. However, what had happened had happened and granda said we had to accept it and get on with club business. For us it had been a long, eventful season and I think granda was glad when it was over. During the season, I had seen a change in him. He had aged, he was slower and was breathing heavily and I was glad he was due to retire in December; I really thought he needed the rest.

At the end of that racing season, I was twelve years old. I was big for my age and I suppose I did look older. My brother was fifteen. He was even bigger and dressed in his suit with his hair greased, combed back then pulled forward at the front he looked eighteen. He was due to leave school the following summer and he had lost all interest in schoolwork. His hobbies were music, football and girls. Dressed in his suit he looked like one of the new pop stars that occasionally appeared on the telly. Granda had decided that, providing we didn't drink, we could go to the presentation night at the Co-op. My brother said he wasn't bothered but I was delighted. My mother, whilst hating the pigeons, loved the presentation night. It was the one occasion when she went out for a meal and she and father insisted that my brother accompany us.

We had heard so much about these presentation nights that my expectations were very high. Smartly dressed we caught the bus on the

West Road and it stopped outside the Co-operative Society or the Co-op, the name everyone called it. Granda arrived shortly after us in a taxi. This was his night and he always made the most of it. Everyone looked smart. My granny and my mother had on new dresses, bought especially from the Co-op, and father had even bought me a suit. I felt very grown up and adult. Uncle Peter had refused to come to the function. Ever since Rat Face had upset the allotment holders Peter had refused to support the Pigeon Men.

"The Co-op always makes a good job of it," my father said, and when I entered the ballroom, I had to agree with him. The tables were laid out with balloons and paper hats on them, and our names, on pieces of folded paper, indicated our seats. Father ordered the drinks, a pint for him, a port and lemon for my mother and shandy for my brother and me. My brother was disgusted and disappeared from the table. Granny and granda Baker were on the top table alongside the Lord Mayor and Lady Mayoress. I was impressed by the Mayor's chain of office. Somehow, the gold chains made the occasion seem very high class and dignified.

The tables were set out in long rows leading off the top table. On the very end table of the first row bottles of whisky, rum, brandy, sherry and mixer drinks had been placed. We had none of this and our shandies and father's pint looked rather penny-pinching in comparison.
"Why ain't we got bottles of booze?" my brother asked when he returned to the table carrying a pint.
"Oh that's George Clarke and his cronies table," answered father, "they're making a real night of it."
He never mentioned the pint of beer, my brother was holding, I think father had given up on him.
Suddenly my brother wolf whistled, and said, "hey look at this," he was pointing at the door.
Just entering the room were three of the most beautiful women I had ever seen. They were dressed in low cut evening gowns, which put to shame granny and mothers Co-op dresses. In addition, they were all wearing necklaces, which put to shame the Lord Mayor's chain of office. My brother was staring and mother chastised him.

"Sit down and shut up will you, and you shouldn't be drinking beer," she said glaring at father.

My brother sat down but turned in his seat and continued to stare at the women. He wasn't the only one. The room had gone silent and everyone was staring at the three women. I glanced over at granda and noticed him talking to the Lord Mayor. However, both of them kept glancing towards the door and it was obvious that they were finding it very difficult not to stare at the women.

"Bloody fur coats and nee knickers," said mother and we all looked at her.

George Clarke, Tommy Tippins and Malcolm Ash followed the women into the room. I say followed that is wrong they took over the room. All three men were dressed in evening suits with bow ties and were smoking big cigars. They swaggered into the room in a cloud of cigar smoke and, once again, the room went silent. George obviously knew the Lord Mayor as when he entered the room he roared out.

"Jack lad nice to see you, how you doing?"

The Lord Mayor obviously knew George and he smiled broadly, stood up, and held out his hand. Unfortunately, as he did so he knocked over granny Baker's port and lemon, and the drink splashed all over her dress. I watched, I could see the looks of disappointment on her and granda's faces and suddenly I felt very sorry for both of them.

Despite the spilt drink, it was a good night. Granda gave a good speech and welcomed the Lord Mayor. Dixie Dean mumbled a few words and the Lord Mayor talked about the city, the river, the new swimming baths, the library, the police and finally about pigeons. Then he presented the prizes. Behind the top table, another table had been set out with all the cups, plaques, certificates and envelopes' containing the prize money and the table was full. There were trophies for the club races and Federation trophies for the fanciers who had won Fed prizes. Then there were trophies for the lofts with the best results in the young and old bird races. In addition, a trophy for the loft with the best-combined results, the list seemed endless. Granda's moment of glory came when he was presented with the Federation cup for winning the Lillers channel race and we all cheered and clapped.

Blanco did not attend the presentation evening. He had told Billy that his mother wasn't well and he'd asked Billy to collect his prize money, which he did. The most regular visitors collecting their prizes from the top table were George Clarke, Malcolm Ash and Tommy Tippins. At the end of the night their table was groaning under the weight of silver cups and bottles of spirits. After the speeches, the tables were re-arranged around the room and a dance band played music.

The Lord Mayor and Lady Mayoress immediately moved onto George Clarke's table and there was loud laugher and shouting from the table.

"Enjoyed it?" said granda when he and granny Baker came to join our table.

"Been lovely," said mother.

Father had gone to the bar and I noticed him talking to Tommy Wright, George Clarke's loft manager. When he returned to our table, he was bursting with news. Pincher Martin, Dixie Dean and Billy had also joined our table and we all sat squashed together. When they had arrived, I noticed granda whispering in Billy's ear and I knew he was telling him not to swear in front of the ladies.

"You'll never guess what," father said looking at granda, "George has just sacked Tommy. Just finished him tonight, told him he wants results not promises. Seemingly George is going abroad to buy new pigeons and he's getting a younger man in as loft manager. He's employing some young lad that's been making a name for himself in Walker club; he's won six or seven races Tommy says. Seemingly George has made the lad an offer he can't refuse, good pay and full time work in the loft."

"Fu," Billy interrupted but granda, just in time, glared at Billy.

"Tommy says George is going to Belgium to buy blues, then to Malta to look at other pigeons," continued father. "He says the Maltese fanciers race their pigeons from Rome in Italy. It's about five hundred miles, most of it over the sea; any bird with that type of homing instinct has to be good."

"Doesn't have much choice," said Pincher, "if they stopped for a rest they'd drown."

Father was full of information and it was obvious that, because Tommy had been sacked, he was telling all George's secrets. The five men and I were like conspirators huddled together, leaving granny Baker and mother to talk. My brother had disappeared and I had noticed the dirty looks that mother was giving father. She was annoyed at his disappearance but father just ignored her.

"Tommy's been telling me that George and him have been experimenting with jealousy, widowhood, removing eggs and young birds, Infact every type of breeding and incentive system you can think of," said father. He was full of information and he knew he had a receptive audience.

"Been pulling more strokes than Oxford and Cambridge put together," said Pincher.

Billy, obviously puzzled, looked at Pincher it was clear that he didn't understand Pincher's attempt at a joke.

"It's only the start," said granda.

"They'll never beat Huwey and my channel hen's youngins," piped in Pincher.

"I think we'll see big changes next season," continued granda, "all the new lofts are finished and we'll have eight new members racing. Rat Face has started re-building his old loft and there are men interested in Beryl's garden and the spare sites alongside the three big lofts. We have forty members at present, and including Beryl's garden, there are seven plots left. It's turning into a big club. The more members we get, the bigger the prize money and the more interest it creates. The old members will have to grow up and realise it's no longer just a part-time hobby. If they want to survive and win then they must start breeding good birds."

For a while, granda's words dampened the evening.

The men continued to drink and discuss pigeons and every now and then one of the other club members would approach the table and present granda with a whisky.

"Great night Sammy," they would say and granda would smile. Granny Baker and mother continued talking. However, mother was continuing to give father her dirty looks and eventually I was sent to find my brother. I had enjoyed the night and quite enjoyed scouring the room looking for him. Some of the members shouted a greeting to me and I waved back at them. There was a big table in a corner, which Rat Face, Beryl and their friends had taken over. They saw me but ignored me, which pleased me. Finally, I found my brother; he was in a small bar at the side of the ballroom, talking to Malcolm Ash. He was drunk but he and Malcolm seemed to be the best of friends.

To get home father had ordered a taxi, for me it was the perfect end to the night. I never travelled in motorcars and to be driven home in that black cab was an adventure on its own. During the journey, all my brother could talk about was his new friend Malcolm.
Mother told him straight,
"You stay away from that man, he's a rogue."
Father was drunk and just smiled.

Chapter Twenty-Six

The weekend after the presentation evening, we started to build the extension to the loft. Uncle Peter helped granda and father and once again, I was labourer. This time, as I had three men giving me orders, it was more difficult than before. However, it was a privilege to watch them at work. They were craftsmen, proud of their trade and even though it was only an extension to a loft, granda insisted on the very highest standards. We added an eight-foot long extension to the side of the loft. The new wooden walls were double skinned and filled with insulation and the new window had removable blinds fitted. Alongside it, we built a small corrugated iron shed. It took two days to complete the work. Granda had asked one of the plumbers from work to give him a hand with the heating system and on the Sunday afternoon, he turned up with piping, two metal tanks and a bag full of tools. It was cramped inside the small metal shed and I think the plumber wasn't too pleased about the working conditions. It was definitely a challenge for him and as he worked, he kept shaking his head and saying.

"Sammy I don't know if this will work."

Granda had bought a large paraffin heater and, directly above the hot air vents, the plumber fixed his first metal tank. He had already attached screwed fittings to the top and bottom of the tank and he ran pipe work under the loft extension. Uncle Peter and father secured the pipe work in place. It crossed and re-crossed under the floor of the extension. Then the plumber connected one end of the pipe to the top fitting and the other end to the bottom fitting on the tank. On the top of the tank, onto a third screwed fitting, he attached the smaller tank.

"Right Sammy," he said, "get the boy to get some water."

I dutifully left the garden and returned with two watering cans full of water. The plumber took one can and started to fill the tanks. I was surprised at how much water went into the system then finally when he'd emptied one and a half watering cans he said,

"Okay Sammy, the top tank is the header tank and hopefully an expansion chamber. The paraffin heater should warm the water. The hot water should rise and leave the tank through the top pipe, then as it travels around the pipes it should cool and re-enter the tank at the bottom fitting."

As far as I was concerned, it was a wonderful system. We lit the paraffin heater and, with fingers crossed, stood well back. Uncle Peter was lying under the extension feeling the pipes.

"It's working," he cried, "the bloody pipes are getting warm."

We were delighted.

"Sammy," the plumber said with a big smile on his face. "To seal the pipes in you'll have to fit boards around the bottom of the loft. It's not a great system and you cannot allow the wind to blow under the extension. The heat has to be allowed to rise and any drafts will just cool the pipes."

That Sunday night we left the garden feeling very pleased with ourselves. The extension was finished, the heating system would work, and we would start our breeding programme early next year.

Rat Face had also been rebuilding his loft, and much to my disappointment, he returned to his original sight three lofts along from ours. He had given up the idea of building on the two new sites in the back row and had given the sites back to the council. This meant that there were now seven vacant sites on the gardens. Rat Face's friends had been helping him and they had made a reasonable job of re-installing the loft. The word on the gardens was that Beryl and him had sold the business and the house. However, all the money had been used to pay off debts and the mortgage. So Rat Face was back to where he'd started; only now Beryl couldn't rely on Jack for money and Rat Face had to support the two of them and the baby. I was pleased that Rat Face had been brought down but was disappointed that his loft was back on the front row beside us. In an attempt to raise money, Rat Face had sold all Beryl's pigeons to one of the new members in the back row. Granda seemed pleased about this.

"At least old Jack's bird's will get a decent home," he said when he heard the news.

Pincher was delighted when he inspected our new extension.
"Marvellous Sammy, Bloody marvellous," was all he said.
The two men decided to start the breeding programme in late January. The breeding birds were not to be raced so their recovery for racing wasn't too important. They agreed they would breed off six pairs. Of course, the pride of the programme was Huwey and Pincher's channel hen but the other pairs all had good pedigrees. Pincher had taken control of orders and had a book full of names. Of course, demand had outstripped supply and he even had orders for next year. He had calculated that they should receive two hundred and fifty pounds each from their sales. It was a new venture and granda rose to the occasion. I think the project revived him as for a while the old spring in his step returned. However, I was slightly disillusioned when, one day, I overheard him and father talking about pairing the other birds up.

"No son," granda said, "Huwey will still pair up with his old hen. They are a great pair; in the past, they have produced top class youngins. There's nothing to say that Huwey can't have two hens. We will start those two off when we start the rest off. Pincher's hen's youngins will be big by then and Huwey can spend a few days with his old hen. She's a good old bird and she'll be able to rear his youngins on her own. We have to be careful, despite what Pincher says, putting two channel winners together doesn't necessarily mean you'll produce more winners."

Christmas came and once again, we spent it, as a family, in our flat. We enjoyed it and on Boxing Day, as we had done the previous year, we went to granny Baker's house. The atmosphere was good. Granda had retired from work on Christmas Eve and he seemed pleased about it.

Father had promised mother that he would stay away from the pigeons and he stuck to his promise. Granda now seemed to understand the situation between my mother and father and never mentioned pigeons during our visit. I was growing up and had started to take more interest in the paper work that granda completed for the club and the Federation. The cupboard in the living room at his house was full of files and books and it was only now I realised how much work he did for the sport and how committed he was to it.

On Boxing Day as we were about to leave granda pulled my father to one side and showed him a letter.

"AGM in February," he said, "it'll be on the first Sunday morning in February, read this."

Father took the letter and glanced through it. I could tell by his face that it was bad news.

"Rat Face and his friends are proposing George Clarke as chairman and Tommy Tippins as treasurer. Surely they must realise how much work Dixie and Pincher have done for the club, this is a real stab in the back," he said.

Granda looked at him.

"I wonder why no one is standing against me," he said.

"You know why dad, you do too much work, they know they cannot manage without you," replied father.

As we walked home that night father never, spoke. I think he was upset and was realising that the pigeon club, which he had grown up with had gone and would never be the same again. Telly on a Boxing Day night always seemed to be rubbish. As soon as we got home, my brother turned it on and sat in the armchair. Father was taking his overcoat off when he pulled something from his pocket and placed it on the table.

"It's from dad, he gave it to me as we were leaving," he said looking at mother.

Mother picked up the envelope and tore it open, inside I glimpsed five-pound notes and mother started counting them.

"Two hundred pounds," she said.

"He tried to keep his word," father said.

The second week in January was quite warm and granda tried out the heating system. It wasn't great, but it definitely heated the extension. Granda was pleased with it and, for quite some time, he and Pincher stood in the loft admiring it. In the third week in January Pincher brought his birds along to our loft and we paired them up and locked them in their nest boxes. The pairing was all right the six pairs seemed to get on well and there was no fighting. The heating system ran well and granda checked the paraffin daily and topped it up when necessary. It heated the extension and actually also warmed the rest of the loft. Huwey and Pincher's hen hit it off straight away and very soon, she was down on eggs. Pincher was the most excited; he was like a child with a new toy and would stand watching the birds like a mother watches her children.

Granda had told Pincher and Dixie about the letter and the nominations he had received for their positions. They weren't surprised.

"We knew it was coming Sammy," Dixie said, "they know they cannot replace you, you know too much and work too hard. But, they can control you and by God, if he gets to be chairman, that's what George Clarke will do."

However, despite their disappointment at having men standing against them they both agreed to being nominated for their positions.

"We'll give them a fight," said Pincher, "we're better than they are."

Chapter Twenty-Seven

That year, 1959, we knew the AGM of the club would be different. We certainly were not expecting the old Sunday morning pre-pub and drinks social meeting. The eight new members from the back row of lofts would be attending and as there were nominations for chairman and treasurer there would have to be a proper vote. There was a definite air of change on the gardens, the atmosphere was strained, and the club had split into different groups. It was raining as father and I made our way to the clubhouse and this only added to the feeling of gloom. Inside the clubhouse, it was hot and steamy and cigarette smoke hung heavy in the air.

As we entered granda, Dixie and Pincher were sitting behind a table on the small raised area at the end of the room and they all nodded at us. At eleven o'clock Dixie called the packed room to order. Everyone stopped talking, started coughing and shuffling in their seats.

"We've a lot to get through," said Dixie, "so let's make a start."

"Mister Chairman," George Clarke interrupted, "mister Chairman, I believe that today we will probably be voting and I would ask the secretary to clarify who is entitled to vote."

Granda, taken by surprise, just looked at him.

"You're all entitled to vote, every member has a vote," replied granda.

"Is that every loft or everyone here?" asked George.

Granda hesitated; as this was the first time the question had been asked it was obvious to everyone that a trap was being laid. Last year was the first time that a vote on anything had been taken.

"The reason I ask," continued George in a smug voice, "is that your loft mister secretary is registered as Baker and son. Now, are you entitled to one or two votes?"

"One," shouted Rat Face.

Granda had obviously thought through the question and had an answer.

"George," he replied, "you know the answer. Your loft is registered under your business as Clarke and company. You really don't expect everybody in your company to have a vote do you?"

The room burst into laughter.

"And," continued granda, "we all know you pay rent on two garden sites but you only have one loft. One vote per loft is the answer to your question and just to clarify it, my son will be voting for our loft."

It was a great answer and I think the members appreciated it, but George had put his cards on the table and the mood of the meeting was set. However, in my mind there was a little doubt that father and granda had both come to the meeting expecting to vote.

"Now if you don't mind George we'll move on," said Dixie, "minutes of last meeting, you've all had copies will someone propose them as a true record."

Billy was just about to open his mouth when granda glared at him and he stopped. Then having second thoughts he said, "fuck it I will Sammy."

The old members had all been anticipating Billy's, "I never received them," answer, and once again they burst into laughter. Glancing round the room I noticed the only people not laughing were George Clarke and his friends and their seriousness disturbed me.

There were no matters arising from the minutes and the financial report was the next item on the agenda. This year Pincher had detailed everything. Every penny was accounted for and even a receipt for three shillings was included from Rat Face for the glass for the notice board. No one questioned it.

Next item was the election of officials, and everyone shuffled nervously.

"Election of officials," announced Dixie, "for this item I'll stand down and ask the secretary to take over."

"He hasn't been elected," shouted Rat Face.

Dixie bit at the remark.

"Now listen here," he said jumping out of his chair, "I've had enough of this stupidity. No one has stood against Sammy and we will accept that he is re-elected. We have a club to run and you are acting like a spoilt child. I'm still chairman here and until someone else is elected the dam meeting will be run my way."

Everyone was stunned it was the most passionate speech Dixie had ever made. A number of men clapped and someone shouted, "tell him Dixie."

Rat Face stared at George Clarke as if looking for support but George ignored him.

Dixie and Pincher left the raised area and took seats in the front row. Granda stood and announced that there were two nominations for chairman and then he asked if there were any more. The room remained silent.

"Would anyone like to say anything about the nominations or would the nominated men like to say anything?" asked granda.

The silence continued both George Clarke and Dixie shook their heads.

"I fuckin vote for Dixie," said Billy.

"Not yet," replied granda.

Before the meeting, granda had approached Malcolm Ash and asked him if he would assist in counting the votes and now Malcolm came to the front of the room. I wouldn't have trusted Malcolm but it had nothing to do with me.

"I know every loft and every member," said granda, "there are forty lofts so only forty votes will be allowed. Malcolm and I will count the votes, one per loft any questions?"

There were no questions and the mood of anticipation intensified.

"Okay first nomination for chairman is George Clarke; all those in favour raise their hands."

A large number of hands at the back of the room were raised and Billy sitting in the front slowly raised his. Very slowly and looking directly at Billy granda said,

"those members who want George Clarke elected as chairman raise their hands now."

Billy glanced round and dropped his hand.

"Fuckin Sorry Sammy not fuckin yet eh!" he said.

Granda walked to the back of the room and counted hands. He noted the numbers on a piece of paper then returned to the table and Malcolm joined him.

"Okay, now all those who want Dixie Dean as chairman, raise their hands."

Billy's hand was the first one up. Once again, granda walked up one side of the room counting hands and Malcolm, on the other side of the room, did the same. Then both of them returned to the table.

"Abstentions," granda said and three hands went up. I glanced around the room and was amazed; one of the hands raised belonged to Blanco.

Granda totalled up his count and Malcolm nodded in agreement.

"Okay," granda said reading off his piece of paper. "George Clarke received nineteen votes, Dixie Dean received eighteen votes and there were three abstentions. George Clarke is elected."

The men at the back of the room cheered and Dixie's head dropped.

Granda shouted over the noise, "okay, there are two nominations for the position of Treasurer, Tommy Tippins and Pincher Martin. The voting will be the same and Malcolm and I will count the votes. All those in favour of Tommy Tippins as treasurer raise your hands."

Once again, hands shot up at the back of the room and granda and Malcolm walked up the room counting them.

"All those in favour of Pincher Martin," granda said, and hands shot up at the front of the room. Granda and Malcolm stood together and counted the hands.

"Abstentions."

Once again, three hands were raised and again I looked and saw Blanco with his hand in the air. My hatred of him was now complete, he wasn't just a cheat he was a back stabber.

"Result of vote," announced granda, Tommy Tippins nineteen votes, Pincher Martin eighteen votes and three abstentions, Tommy Tippins is elected treasurer."

Again, the men at the back of the room cheered and George Clarke stood up and walked to the front of the room.

It was strange seeing George and Tommy sitting alongside granda at the head of the room. However, George seemed to know what he was doing and he did have an air of authority about him. The other items on the agenda were an anticlimax and the meeting progressed very quickly. After the meeting, Pincher and Dixie walked back to our garden with us. Inside the garden Dixie asked the question I was wondering about.

"Why did Blanco abstain from voting?" he said.

"I asked him," replied Pincher, "he said he didn't understand the procedure but by God he understood the procedure when George and Tommy were buying his birds off him."

Pincher's words were bitter.

"If he had voted for us we'd have had a draw, what would we have done then Sammy?" Dixie asked.

Granda smiled, "I suppose you as chairman would have had a casting vote. That's the way I've always understood the system and that's what I would have said."

"The other two new lads, who didn't vote, said they didn't know any of the officials and as the vote was so close they didn't like to vote," piped in Pincher. "You know Sammy I thought you might have threatened to resign if Dixie and I were voted out, that might have changed some of their minds."

Unhappily, granda looked at him.

"I know that Pincher, but it might not have. I have worked in this club for forty years. It has become my life, I've watched it grow and get established. My missus is involved and my life revolves around it. If I had resigned what would I have achieved? I would be cutting my nose off to spite my face. Surely, it's better for me to stay and fight from within the committee than come out and let them just have their own way. Now I'm retired, if I didn't have the club to run, what would I do with myself?"

Granda's speech killed any further conversation and very quickly, the two men left the garden.

We stayed and cleaned the loft then we checked on the breeding pairs. They were all doing well, the eggs had hatched and the youngins were growing.

"You know son," granda said as we looked at the birds, "I really regret the way I've dealt with Blanco. I should have exposed him as a cheat but I had no proof. I wish now, on that first occasion when he was swapping birds, I had believed you. It was then that we really could have caught him out, now, unfortunately, we're stuck with him."

It had been a sad Sunday morning. The usual feelings of anticipation following an AGM were not there. The loss of Dixie and Pincher as officials was depressing and granda's speech about Blanco hadn't cheered me. As I stood on the gantry, looking at the grey garden and watching the drizzle fall I suddenly thought that there must be more to life than this.

Chapter Twenty-Eight

During the weeks leading up to the start of the racing season, and during the breeding season, my disillusionment with the club and the pigeons continued and I seldom visited the gardens. Father kept me updated on the sale of the youngins and the eggs and from what he said granda and Pincher were doing very well. Granda had also paired up our old birds and we had a good kit of new youngins. My absence wasn't totally due to my disillusionment I had found another interest. Like my brother, I had developed an interest in girls and I actually had a girlfriend. She was my first girlfriend and regularly, much to my brother's amusement, we went for walks on the moor near our flat. He had moved on from the catholic youth club and, unbeknown to my parents, was frequenting the workingmens clubs. Fay was my girlfriends name; she was in my class at school and she was a quiet girl. She had a nice figure and for her age she had well-developed breasts, just being with her excited me.

My brother was due to leave school in the summer and now he acted as if he owned the house. Mother and father didn't seem to notice but it annoyed me.

"Are you shagging Fay yet?" he asked one night.

I was disgusted with his comment. Fay was above all crude things like that; just to kiss her was sufficient for me. I knew nothing about girls and Fay's body fascinated me. I was curious to find things out; but the right time and place never seemed to arise.

The new racing season was about to start and the weekend of the first, old bird, Selby race arrived. On the Friday night, out of curiosity, I went to the gardens expecting to watch the basketing. The same basketing committee were operating but granda said we couldn't watch. George Clarke had introduced a new committee rule. Now only one extra official was allowed in the clubhouse, and George Clarke, eager to see how everything worked, had told granda he was going to watch the basketing. Next week George had told Tommy Tippins, as he was the new treasurer, to watch the procedure. George, granda explained, had made the rule to ensure that all the officials knew everything about the running of the club. He went on to say that, he thought George was ensuring that if he ever resigned they would be capable of running the club.

"But what about Blanco?" I asked.

Granda just shrugged his shoulders.

Just being on the gardens, listening to the talk and experiencing the old sounds and smells brought some of the old excitement back, and I started to look forward to Saturday and the race. I left the gardens before the basketing started; I had a date and I had to meet Fay. Granda walked with me to the clubhouse and smiled when I left him, somehow he seemed to know where I was going.

Unfortunately, Fay had decided that Saturday afternoons were the best times for our walks on the moor. It was a hard decision to make and Fay wasn't too pleased, when I met her and told her I was going to the garden on Saturday.

"Bloody pigeons, that's all you ever think about, what about me?" she said.

It all sounded very familiar and I began to understand how father felt.

That Selby race was a classic. All forty members had entered birds and it was the biggest race ever on the gardens. Nine hundred and eighty birds were entered. The three big lofts had nominated just about every bird they had entered and the prize money was high. I needn't have worried about the basketing; there were so many birds, granda and two other members were co-opted onto the basketing committee to help out. Later he told me they had three ringing machines going and they were so busy Blanco couldn't have cheated if he'd wanted to. This was also the first race for the other eight new club members. They were keen, and the other members were keen to see what their birds could do. Everyone on the gardens was excited and that Saturday morning as I entered the gardens the old feelings of anticipation hit me.

Granda had entered the little blue hen, which Rat Face had obstructed two years earlier and last year had won the race. He was more than ready, the corn tin was placed on the gantry. The two old birds, his droppers, were flopping about in front of the loft and even he looked younger.

"Start of a new season," he said rubbing his hands together, "clean slate, birds are due at two o'clock, now we'll see what these new lads are made of."

He was bursting with enthusiasm.

Father arrived at a quarter to two and the three of us stood in the garden scanning the sky.

"Here they come," Pincher's voice boomed out.

It was just like the old times and as usual, Pincher was right, out of the valley, spread out in a line across the sky, was a huge flock of pigeons.

"Bloody hell," said father.

Granda grabbed the corn tin and along with all the other fanciers started rattling. The sky was suddenly filled with pigeons. Birds crisscrossed the lofts, men swore and the noise was deafening. To see who won was impossible and we knew that once again seconds would count, it was down to the members trapping and timing in.

Later, at the clubhouse, as we waited for the official result, Pincher appeared and seemed very pleased with himself.

"I think I got it," he said.

We also were optimistic. Our blue hen had been amongst the flock, but so had most of the other club members' birds. However, when the clock committee had opened the clocks and placed the official result on the notice board Pincher was right, he had won and his bird was fully nominated. Pincher was delighted. George Clarke and his two friends had taken the next five positions also with fully nominated birds, and our blue hen was in sixth place. Killer Kilpatrick one of the new members who had bought Beryl's birds was in seventh place, and we were pleased.

"It's a good incentive for the new members," granda said.

Having read the results and still basking in his glory, Pincher hung around the clubhouse. He was still hanging around, revelling in his win, when Tommy Tippins came to read the results. Pincher crept up behind him and as Tommy, standing in front of the notice board, was reading the results, he whispered in his ear,

"Take my job Tommy but you'll never beat my pigeons."

Tommy was taken by surprise, he jumped back and Pincher laughed.

When George Clarke came to the notice board, Pincher was still there.

"You might be the chairman George but you're a loser. I've just won all your nomination money and we're selling more birds and eggs than you ever will," he said.

George just ignored him.

When Rat Face turned up Pincher sneered at him, "thought you were a business man Rat Face, well your birds are rubbish and you've got nothing. You're not even half the man Jack Morris was; his birds are still beating you."

Father had gone back to the loft to start cleaning out but granda and I, sensing trouble, had stayed at the clubhouse. Granda had tried to persuade Pincher to return to his loft and now, as Rat Face stared angrily at Pincher, once again, granda stepped forward and tried to get him to move. Pincher would have none of it, the loss of his position as treasurer had left him a very bitter man. This harsh, outspokenness was a new side of Pincher, which I had never seen before. Usually he got on well with everyone and certainly never upset anyone. When granda told him to go back to his garden he was annoyed and said, "Stuff them Sammy, why worry about them. They don't care about us but we'll show them what pigeon racing and breeding is all about. We're already beating them selling birds and eggs and we'll beat them in all the races."

Unfortunately, his voice was loud and everyone at the clubhouse heard him. I saw George and Tommy turn and like Rat Face stare at him, Pincher, defiantly, stared back.

"Come on Pincher we don't have to brag, we're bigger than that," said granda.

Pincher smiling replied, "Sammy I love it, we're rubbing their noses in it and to me it feels nice. We have been too quiet, we've let these people walk all over us and it's time we spoke up. They're trying to take over the club and they think they can win all the races, well I'll show them they can't."

Once again, his words were loud enough for everyone to hear. George and Tommy just smiled and walked away; Rat Face appeared flabbergasted and like a lap dog ran after them.

Whilst we didn't win that first Selby race, we were happy with our sixths place and we did have another pigeon in that first flock. The dropping and clocking in speeds had won the race and it proved to us that we had pigeons that could keep up with the rest. This did inspire us and I found myself once again looking forward to the next race.

On my return home, my brother was waiting for me.
"Seen the gorgeous Fay today?" he asked.
I didn't reply.
"I have," he said mockingly, "seen her on the moor with that fat kid from your class."
I still didn't reply but he knew his comments were hurting me.
"Finished is it? didn't take her long to get fixed up, did it?" he continued.
I was supposed to meet Fay later that night but after my brother's comments, I didn't go to meet her. Infact all the following day, Sunday, I stayed in the house. Fay had let me down and the feelings of despair,

loss and betrayal, I was now experiencing, were new and unpleasant. In the evening father decided to walk down to granda's house.

"Come on son, you need some air," he said.

I thought that mother and him had planned it. My brother had, of course, been talking about the lovely Fay in front of them and had totally embarrassed me. However, it was unusual for father to go to granda's on a Sunday evening, and I accompanied him.

Granny, I suppose like all grandmothers had a peculiar way of knowing when something was wrong. She just seemed to know when I needed comforting, and she knew the best way to do it. Chip sandwiches made with best butter were just the right pick me up. Sitting at the living room table, with butter running down my cheeks, I sat and listened to father and granda talking.

"He's going a bit over the top," said granda.

"It's only natural dad," father replied, "he was treasurer for a long time and did a first class job of it."

"Yes son but he's letting himself down by shouting the odds at George Clarke and everyone. They couldn't care less about what he says. They're businessmen; they've heard it all before. They didn't get their money by feeling sorry for other people or taking notice of snide remarks. Remember they've spent a lot of money on birds. George actually bought two birds from Malta and three Belgium Blues; he's determined to be the best on the gardens."

A knock on the front door interrupted granda and he climbed out of his chair and disappeared along the passage.

Sitting at the table, I could hear what was taking place at the front door and I heard granda's surprised voice as he opened the door.

"Officer is something wrong?" he asked.

It was obvious that father and granny had also heard as the room went silent and we all strained to hear the conversation.

"Sorry to bother you sir but we have you listed as the contact for the Banwell Pigeon Club. Sammy Baker, is that correct?"

Granda must have nodded as the policeman continued.

"There's been a fire on the gardens and one of the lofts has burned down. We really want to know who owns the loft and wondered if you can give us the owner's name and address."

Father was out of his chair and rushing along the passageway and I was right behind him.

"We'll come with you," said father.

As granda got his coat, father asked the policeman which loft had been on fire. I was terrified in case he described ours.

"Very end loft on the front row, east end of the gardens, next to the path, lovely garden very well kept."

I knew at once that it was Pinchers.

"Is it bad?" father asked.

"Best see for yourself," replied the policeman, "if you intend to bring the lad, he might be upset, it's a mess and some of the birds have been slaughtered."

I had seen dead pigeons before so the policeman's comments didn't bother me. Father knew this and allowed me to accompany the three of them to the gardens.

As we hurried along Elwick Road to the gardens, it was getting dark and as we approached the gate, I could see there was light, grey steam coming from the end of the garden site. We used Uncle Peter's shortcut through the allotments, I hung back and let granda, and the policeman lead the way. The path leading to Pincher's loft, where the firemen had run their hoses, had been turned to mud. One fire engine was still parked on the path and a number of firemen stood at the back of it smoking cigarettes.

Granda stopped at the gate leading into Pincher's garden and stared up at the fencing. I followed his stare and gasped in disbelief. Pigeon's heads were impaled on the points at the top of the fencing. The scene was horrific. The sightless eyes of the pigeons stared out over the Tyne valley and I caught my breath. I couldn't turn away and the three of us stood staring at the sight.

"Told you it wasn't too nice," the policeman said.

No one answered.

"No pigeon fancier would ever do this," said granda, "those birds never hurt anyone, only a mad man would stick their heads around the garden like that."

"Must have broken in, slaughtered the birds then set the loft on fire," said the policeman, "now can you tell me who owns this loft?"

"John Martin, he lives with his mother at 34 Beaumont Street off Elwick Road," replied granda.

"Will you stay here till I bring him?" asked the policeman.

Granda nodded.

The firemen returned to the garden and started making up their equipment.

"Nothing we could do," one of them said, "the garden gate and the loft doors had been forced, and the loft was well alight when we got here, sorry mate."

To check that everything was alright at our garden, father had gone to our loft and now he returned with a sack.

"Best get them heads down before Pincher gets here," he said.

The two of them, father and granda, moved slowly along the fencing removing the bloodied heads from the points. I stood silently and watched. Then I looked at the loft, there was nothing left of it. The original framework was still standing although the timbers were badly scorched and would have to be replaced. The rest of the loft and the pigeons were just piles of black, smoking charcoal. The whole thing was like a horror movie. Hammer House of Horrors could not have put up a better set. By the time that father and granda had removed all the heads the sack was red with blood then Pincher arrived.

I had never seen a grown man cry before and to spare Pincher embarrassment I moved out of the garden. I also knew Pincher's tears would affect me and I did not want them to see me crying. What do you say to someone who has lost everything? I didn't know, so I listened outside the gate but heard nothing, just Pincher sobbing.

"Why Sammy why?" suddenly Pincher's words, choking in his throat, broke the silence, "I knew everyone of those birds and they all knew me, they all had names Sammy. They trusted me they were my family. I never had time to meet women; I never married, I always put the pigeons first.

I raised every one of those birds myself they were like children to me and now they're dead, murdered."

"Has to be a mad man Pincher, no pigeon man would do this," replied granda.

"Sammy you're still living in the past," sobbed Pincher "this is no longer a sport its business. There are men on these gardens that are not pigeon men they're only here for the money. They know I'm better than them and always will be and this is the only way they can stop me."

"We can rebuild Pincher, I've still got your channel hen and your other birds that we're using for breeding. We'll not sell any more youngins and you can have them. In two months we can build a new loft, start the birds breeding and next season you'll be back racing again."

Granda sounded optimistic.

"Then what?" sobbed Pincher, "they'll just burn me out again."

"No, no Pincher, I can't believe any of the club members would have anything to do with this. Believe me this is the work of someone not right in the head," granda replied.

The policeman had been standing at the bottom of the garden listening and suddenly he interrupted them.

"We do have somebody in custody; one of the firemen caught him hiding behind the clubhouse. He's a young lad, had a packet of cigarettes and some matches in his pocket, smelt of smoke and was very frightened, says his name is David. We're just getting his parents down to the station now."

"David," Pincher sobbed, "no way, David could not have done this. He wouldn't know how to break into a loft pull the birds' heads off, stick them on the fencing then set the place on fire. David isn't like that, there's not a malicious bone in the boy's body."

I was still outside the garden, listening, and was shocked by what the policeman had said. I agreed with Pincher I couldn't see David carrying out such a barbarous act but from what the policeman had said he certainly seemed to be a suspect.

We stayed with Pincher for another hour then father and I made our way home.

"Granda will stay with him and walk him home," said father, "this has been a terrible night; I hope I never see that type of thing again."

I couldn't reply, I agreed totally with his sentiments.

When we arrived home, Mother was waiting for us. Obviously, she didn't know what had happened and didn't realise how distressed we were. She had a big smile on her face and before we could say anything, excitedly, she said, "you've had a visitor young man; a nice young lady called Fay came to see you."

I really hadn't thought the night could get much worse but it just had.

Chapter Twenty-Nine

During the following week, I didn't visit the gardens. On the Monday night father went straight from work and did not return home until very late. I never saw him but lying in bed I did hear him and mother arguing. Their voices echoed through the small flat, and lying awake, I could hear every word they said.

"A gun! You're buying a gun; you've gone bloody mad there are no guns coming into this house," Mother's words jolted me wide-awake. "And sleeping in the shed in the pigeon garden, have you gone mad? You cannot sleep in a cold shed then go to work. How are you going to get your meals? I'm certainly not carrying meals down to the gardens." As her words continued so, my interest grew.

A gun and living in the pigeon garden, this wasn't unlike one of the westerns on the telly. However, they usually finished with the family watching the masked man ride off and asking.

"Who was that man in the mask?"

Only here in Newcastle I knew there was no man in a mask, only my father. Moreover, I knew he had never fired a gun and I knew he didn't have a mask.

"David's not to blame," as I lay listening to his words father's voice was emotional, "the police have got it all wrong. The poor kid has been taken away from his parents and sent to a home. David never set fire to Pincher's loft. Who ever did it was a pigeon man. Unless you can really handle pigeons, you cannot catch and neck thirty birds in a matter of minutes. No way, the person that did it is still on the gardens and he's laughing at us. Believe me we are in line for the same treatment. Some of the members are getting together to start patrolling but nothing will happen when they're there. It's in the early hours when he'll strike again."

Now mother's voice was nearly hysterical.

"I don't care, you're not getting a gun," she shouted, "you'll probably shoot yourself or your bloody father, and then where will we be? Why should anyone burn your loft? You haven't upset anyone. You told me Pincher had ridiculed some of the men, perhaps he deserved it."

The silence that followed said it all. I remembered Pincher's face and the shell of his loft with the birds' heads stuck on the railings, and I knew no one deserved that.

"I can't believe you just said that," father answered quietly, "anyway it doesn't matter, I've had my dinner and I'm going back to the garden. I've no gun but I'm taking the boy's cricket bat and I'll kill anybody that comes near our loft."

I wanted to get out of bed and talk to them. I needed reassuring; I wanted everything to go back to how it had been. I had never experienced these feelings before. I was terrified at the feeling of dread that was running through me. The thought of father waiting in the darkness inside the shed armed with my cricket bat horrified me. What if someone entered the garden and father swung the bat and killed him? In an attempt to gain comfort, I looked across the bedroom to see if my brother was awake. He wasn't, he stunk of beer and was snoring loudly. Then I heard the front door slam and I knew that father had gone. Only the sound of my mother crying now filtered through the thin walls of the flat. Even when you are unsure what to do, sometimes, instinctively, you know what is best and I stayed in my bed, somehow, I knew mother needed to be on her own

For the remainder of the week father returned home late, ate a meal, and then went back to the garden. I never saw him but lying in my bed I waited for him, and then listened to my parents arguing. Thankfully, he hadn't attacked anyone and my fears of him turning into a murderer were beginning to subside. I had asked my mother what he was doing and she had told me about him guarding the loft.

"But don't worry son," she'd said, "your father wouldn't hurt a fly. His presence should be enough to put anyone off and he's fitted new locks and bolts on the gate and on the loft. They've even fixed barbed wire around the fencing." This did worry me; barbed wire had never been used on the gardens. I knew that a pigeon flying into this type of wire would cut itself to pieces. So on the Friday night before the second old bird race from Doncaster, I walked to the gardens not knowing what I would find.

The gardens had changed. I realised this as soon as I turned off the West Road and approached the entrance. I saw that the two main gates, now closed, blocked the path. There was a chain wrapped around them and a padlock secured it in place. Normally the gates were left wide open and anyone could just walk in. In addition, the gates had been heightened and barbed wire had been secured along the tops of them. On the Pathe News at the cinema, I had recently seen pictures of a concentration camp and the gates now reminded me of it. I inspected the new padlock and realised that I didn't have a key. I stood looking at the lock and wondering what to do. I hadn't seen father all week and it hadn't occurred to me that I wouldn't be able to get in. Now standing looking at the lock, I thought it was a sensible step to take. However, it was also stopping me from entering. I inspected the new barbed wire and realised there was no way I could climb over the gates. I was just about to leave to walk round to the Elwick Road entrance, when a voice from behind me said,

"What do yee want?"

I turned and Rat Face stood menacingly behind me.

"No none members allowed on the gardens," he said as he pushed me to one side and unlocked the padlock.

"I'm going to granda's," I replied rather childishly.

"Are you deaf? No none members allowed on the gardens," he repeated.

As he spoke, he pushed his face into mine and I could smell the familiar stink of stale beer. It was obvious that he was enjoying what he was doing. The two gates were heavy and as Rat Face removed the chain both gates swung open. He staggered and tried to catch the gates but failed leaving the path wide open, I swerved to one side and raced past him.

"Little get," he screamed after me, "you shouldn't be in here."

I didn't stop; I raced down the path, past the clubhouse turned right and sped along to our garden.

As I ran, I noticed there was also a new sound, a barking dog. Dogs had never been allowed on the gardens. The very sight of a dog running around in a garden would have scared the pigeons, so there had always been an unwritten rule that no dogs were allowed. As I ran towards our garden, I realised that the barking of the dog was coming from two lofts along from ours, Billy's loft, and by the sound of it, the dog was not a terrier like Tiny. To me the dog sounded more like the hound of the Baskervilles. I crashed into our garden gate and realised it was bolted shut. The gate and the fence rattled and the noise startled me, it also startled the dog and it started barking even louder.

Panicking I shouted, "granda it's me, let me in."

"That bloody dog," said granda as he opened the gate. "Bloody Billy bought it off Malcolm Ash it's one of his guard dogs from the scrap business. Bloody things mental, here climb on the gantry and take a look over the fences you'll see it."

I did as I was told and sure enough in Billy's garden there was the biggest, scruffiest, meanest looking Alsatian dog that I had ever seen. The dog saw me and bounded towards the fence. It jumped at the fence and its head and two front paws appeared over the top. The fence shook and rocked and for a minute I thought it would collapse.

"Billy's terrified of it," said granda, "keeps it locked in the shed but somehow it's escaped. He'll have to lock it up when he gets here."

With all of the excitement, I had not looked around our garden and it was only now, when I turned, I realised that barbed wire was stretched along the top of the fencing.

"What about the birds granda will they not cut themselves on the wire," I asked.

"They've been alright so far son, seem to know it's there and always miss it. I don't like it but at the moment, it's necessary. Hopefully we'll catch who ever fired Pincher's loft then we'll be able to take it down."

It was Friday night and despite all the new security measures and the feelings of fear there was still work to be done. The birds we were entering for the race had to be taken to the clubhouse and we had just finished basketing them when father arrived.

"Seen my new home?" he asked.

I had seen it; granda had shown it to me. A mattress on top of two bales of hay and an old armchair all pushed into my shed; to me it did not constitute a home.

"Either I stay or, like Billy, we get a dog," said father laughing, "but hopefully it shouldn't be for long."

We carried our basket and made our way to the clubhouse. We walked along the path and at the corner we passed Pincher's loft, I looked at the burned out shell. I felt so sorry for Pincher and I knew that the gardens would never be the same without him.

We handed the basket in at the clubhouse and granda paid Dixie for his nominations. Dixie was very subdued and took the money without a word.

"Many birds being entered?" granda asked.

"Not as many as last week," Dixie mumbled.

"So you'll not need a hand then?" granda replied.

"No," Dixie replied.

It was obvious that Dixie did not want to talk and we turned to leave. Tommy Tippins stood in the corner watching the proceedings and he nodded at granda. Blanco, dressed in his raincoat stood, in his usual position, putting pigeons into the race baskets. I glanced at him and he smiled back at me. Somehow, the smile told me that he intended to do something. Something in his smug smile said, "you can't catch me and you can't stop me."

"Blanco's fixing the race again," I said to granda as soon as we left the clubhouse.

"I've spoken to him," said granda, "I've told him I know what he's been doing but he denies everything. I have told him that if I suspect him again I will call the police in. He was very upset, said he thought I was his friend. Said he has never cheated and was hurt that I even suspected him. I can only hope that my talk will have scared him off but we still cannot prove anything. All we can do is wait and see what happens."

It was not the answer I had hoped for but I realised granda was tired and worried and the continuous barking of Billy's dog wasn't helping. I knew granda had a lot on his mind, so I said no more. As I had arranged to meet Fay at the bottom of our street, and I didn't want to be late, I left the gardens early. Billy's dog was still barking when granda walked with me to the gates.

"If you're coming to the race tomorrow I'll meet you at the gates at one o'clock," he said.

I agreed I certainly didn't want to be relying on Rat Face to let me in again.

I was late and Fay was waiting for me. When she'd called at my house on Sunday, my mother had invited her in and talked to her. She had even given her a glass of dandelion and burdock to drink and now Fay seemed to think she was one of the family. At school on Monday morning, Fay had been waiting for me and since then I had been unable to get rid of her. She admitted she had walked across the moor with Fatty Turner but she said he wasn't her boyfriend. I didn't believe her and tonight I had decided I would tell her I didn't want to see her again. I never got the chance. As soon as I approached her, she kissed me and slipped her hand into mine. I was horrified; one thing I did not want was to be seen at the bottom of my street holding hands with a girl. So as quickly as I could I walked with her towards the moor. As we walked, I tried to think of a way of telling her gently, so as not to hurt her feelings, that we were finished but the opportunity never arose. She talked all the time and I just listened. Cautiously, taking care not to stand in cow pats, we crossed the moor. Fay seemed to know exactly where she was going then near the centre, she suddenly decided to sit down.

"Sit beside me," she said patting the grass and I obeyed.

The thing in my trousers with a mind of its own was, once again, beginning to misbehave and I turned attempting to hide the bulge from her.

"You can kiss me if you want," she said lying back on the grass.

The smell of Fay, the warmth of her body and the taste of her lips dispelled any ideas that I had of finishing with her. I kissed her, placed my hand on top of her cardigan, and felt the small lump that I thought was her breast. It didn't do a lot for me. I removed my hand and slowly slid it up inside her jumper. She didn't move, struggle or say anything and I thought this was all too easy. I was now confronted with a new problem. Fay was wearing a bra and it seemed impossible to get my hand underneath it. I decided to try and come in from the top but, nearly dislocating my wrist, decided this was not the best approach. Fay didn't offer any help and I went back to sliding my hand under the tight elastic. When, eventually, I negotiated a way underneath and actually felt her breast I was thrilled. Trouble was so was the thing between my legs and the bulge in my trousers was most uncomfortable. Then just as I was feeling very embarrassed and trying to decide where next to explore Fay pushed me away and stood up.

"You are naughty and very forward," she said, "now you really are my boyfriend."

I was still in a state of discomfort and had to sit for a while waiting for my embarrassment to fade. Fay didn't seem to notice anything and was eager to walk home.

Walking home, Fay clung onto my hand and never stopped talking. I was confused, whilst I had felt her breast it did not appear to have been a big deal for her. I wasn't sure what I was supposed to do or say. She never mentioned it and I remained silent. For me it had been a nice, new experience and had eased my curiosity but it hadn't been such a big deal and I felt as if I'd been manipulated and trapped. By the time we reached my street, I was confused. Her incessant talking and my uncertainty had given me a headache and, to get rid of her, I would have agreed to anything. At the bottom of my street I did just that, I agreed to meet her again the next night.

Chapter Thirty

On Saturday as I walked to the gardens I was still confused, although I had made a decision. I had liked the idea of having a girlfriend but Fay seemed to be taking the whole thing too seriously. I felt that she'd trapped me and I'd decided that I would finish with her.

At one o'clock granda was waiting at the West Road gates, he unlocked them and let me in. On Friday night, he had told me that each loft had been issued with one key, to open the padlock, and that Father had already had a copy of the key made for his use. However, he'd explained, the gate to the allotments off Elwick Road still remained unlocked and he always used that gate. Then he went through the gate in the fence in Uncle Peter's allotment. In our family, this little gate was now known as Saint Peter's gate. So really, the new security measures were not causing granda any real difficulty.

When he opened the gates granda looked serious and said,
"Pincher's in the garden son, just be careful what you say. He seems alright but if you can, try not to mention his loft. I don't know how long he'll stay but let's be nice to him."
Granda didn't have to tell me to be nice to Pincher. I knew how much he was suffering and the last thing in the world I would have done was

upset him. We walked down the path and I noticed that the gardens were quiet, no dog barking.

"What's happened to Billy's dog?" I asked.

"Locked up in the shed," replied granda, "for an hour last night Billy tried to entice it into the shed. Eventually Blanco went in, calmed it down, and locked it up. I think this whole security thing is getting out of hand."

He glanced at me as we walked, then he placed his hand on my shoulder and stopped me.

"You're a young man just about the same age as David. Do you think David could have set fire to Pincher's loft? Some of the new members believe he did and the problem has now gone away. They're saying that all this security is unnecessary. The council have put David in a home you know. His parents are very upset and they came to see me. They said he would never have killed the pigeons. They said he loved the gardens and he thought he had lots of friends here."

I was quite flattered to be asked for my opinion on such an important matter. I had thought about David and what he could, and could not, have done. Every way I had looked at it I just couldn't see him breaking into Pincher's loft, killing the birds and setting fire to it. I suppose that like granda I also felt very sorry for him.

"I don't think David did it," I said.

"Who do you think did it then?" asked granda.

We had reached the corner of the path, and had stopped outside the remains of Pincher's loft. We should have turned right to go to our loft instead granda had suddenly stopped and was looking at me. In my opinion, two or three people were capable of doing it. However, I knew my knowledge of the gardens and the members of the club was insignificant compared to granda's and I wondered why he was asking me.

"Well Pincher did shout at George Clarke and Tommy Tippins," I said, "and he told Rat Face what he thought of him. Pincher was also flying some of the best pigeons on the gardens and other people might have been jealous of him. If David had done it, I don't think he would have stuck the birds' heads on the fence."

It was the best answer I could come up with, granda smiled and we set off for our garden.

When we entered, Pincher was sitting on the bench watching granda's droppers.

"Hello son," he said cheerfully, "good day for the race. Not much wind, they'll be back right on time."

His behaviour and attitude seemed completely normal; it was as if nothing had happened. I just smiled and realised I really didn't know what to say to him.

"Seen Billy's dog?" Pincher asked.

I nodded.

"Keep well away from it son, that Malcolm Ash saw Billy coming when he sold him that dog, it's out of control," he smiled as he spoke.

It really was as if nothing had happened and it was the same old Pincher.

I started helping granda to clean out the loft. We spread dry sand on the floor. Pincher climbed onto the gantry and as we worked, occasionally, he made comments.

"Sand's getting expensive Sammy. Feeding beans Sammy? That bird's blooming Sammy looks in good condition."

Granda chatted away with him but it was obvious it was only small talk and Pincher didn't really want to make conversation. Eventually he opened the loft door, entered the loft and went through into the new extension. He stood for a while watching the pigeons then he caught his channel hen. Gently he held her in his hands and talked to her. He kissed and caressed the bird and I noticed the tears in his eyes.

"She's a lovely bird Sammy," he said softly, "best bird I've ever bred. I call her Brenda you know. I've never told anyone that before, always seemed stupid giving the birds' people's names."

Pincher wasn't talking to us. He was talking to himself and it was obvious, in his mind, he was back in his own loft.

"She is a lovely bird Pinch," granda said affectionately. "Soon we'll be breeding your new bloodstock off her. I've had a word with my old boss and he's willing to give us enough wood to rebuild your loft. My two boys are going to pitch in and with you and the lad there helping, I reckon we can rebuild in a week."

I don't know if Pincher heard him, he never replied, he just continued smoothing the pigeon's feathers.

Granda and I, having finished cleaning out the loft, left Pincher with his bird. We sat on the bench alongside the shed silently staring at the sky; there was nothing more to say.

"Time to go Sammy," Pincher's voice startled me, "birds are due back, best get back to the loft," he said.

I looked at granda.

"Stay here Pincher, watch the birds come in if you like," granda replied.

"No no Sammy I don't like strangers in my garden during a race and I'll not abuse your hospitality."

Pincher didn't wait to hear granda's reply he jumped off the gantry and walked down the garden path and out through the gate. In silence, granda and I stood and watched him go.

Just before the pigeons were due back father arrived. He'd been working and when he entered the garden he closed and bolted the gate behind him.

"Just seen Pincher, he's in his usual position on the lookout from his gantry. He seems fine, just waved at me as I passed," he said.

"I suppose old habits die hard," said granda.

Abruptly all thoughts of Pincher were driven out of our heads as Billy's dog started barking.

"Sounds like it's loose," said father.

"Bloody well better not be," replied granda, "no pigeon will land with that beast tearing around."

Suddenly there was a banging on the gate.

"Sammy, Sammy fuckin help me, it's fuckin me Billy, the fuckin dog's loose. I fuckin forgot about it, went to get my fuckin clock and the bloody, fuckin thing jumped me," Billy's voice was panicky.

"We don't need this," said granda.

"Pigeon over the church clock tower," Pincher's voice rang out loud and clear.

"You'll have to wait Billy," granda shouted.

Once again, Pincher's unbroken voice boomed out across the gardens, "blue cock bird could be one of Sammy's or Blanco's."

Donkey Smith who had the loft between Billy's loft and ours suddenly joined in.

"Billy will you piss off with that dog, my droppers have just been scared up and the bloody things trying to climb over the fence."

We didn't know where to look. Granda was glancing towards the clock tower then at the garden gate, which Billy was still shaking, then at his droppers.

"Billy be quiet, wait till this bird drops," he shouted.

From the other side of the gate Billy called back, "fuck it Sammy it might be one of mine."

"No chance Billy," someone from the next row of lofts shouted.

Suddenly there were screams from Donkey's garden, "Help, help the dogs over the fence," screamed Donkey.

"Donkey get out of the garden," shouted granda.

"Definitely Blanco's blue cock," Pincher called out.

Terrified screams and shouting were now coming from Donkey's garden.

"Billy go and help Donkey," shouted granda.

The whole place was in chaos, I didn't know whether to laugh or cry.

Billy's conscience must have pricked him as the banging on our gate stopped and we heard him opening Donkey's gate. Just behind the gate, the dog must have been waiting as vicious snarling and barking erupted.

"Fuckin help," once again, Billy's voice rang out; only this time the sound was moving and fast.

"Blanco, Blanco the fuckin dogs got out and it's fuckin after me," he cried.

"It's a my a bird Billy, you a no come in a here," Blanco's frightened voice replied.

His order must have come too late as we heard Blanco's gate crash open then slam shut. Blanco's white droppers, both startled, shot into the air. The blue cock bird was just arriving at Blanco's loft and it joined the two white droppers, it veered off, clapped its wings and circled. Billy's dog was now jumping at Blanco's gate snarling and barking.

"Bunch of about fifty coming out of the valley," it was Pincher he was still on the lookout and everyone turned to look into the valley.

"Shut that fucking dog up," someone shouted.

The voice was hardly audible above the rattling of corn tins.

"They're all for the gardens, good luck everybody." Pincher's tone of voice reminded me of the RAF war films when the wing commander directs his spitfire pilots onto the enemy bombers. I half expected him to finish off with 'tally ho.'

All hell broke loose. The pigeons were all for the gardens and there were about fifty of them. Men shouted, corn tins rattled, Billy's dog snarled and barked. Blanco was distraught and was shouting at Billy, his voice could be heard above everything else.

Get a out a my a fuckin garden," he shouted.

I was quite surprised this was the first time I had ever heard Blanco swear.

"The fuckin dog Blanco, the fuckin dog it's fuckin outside it'll fuckin eat me," Billy cried.

"I a hope it a fuckin does," Blanco replied.

Everything seemed to be happening at once and I didn't know where to look. We clocked in two pigeons and one of them was the little blue hen. We knew we were amongst the winners but once again, it was impossible to see who had won. The majority of the pigeons had flown to the back of the gardens and I knew that the three big lofts would also be amongst the winners. It took about fifteen minutes for sanity to be restored. The steady clunk of clocks, being struck, had told us that everyone was timing in and slowly the birds dropped and disappeared from the sky. Blanco's bird had dropped. I didn't see it but it was no longer flying, so I was unable to say whether it had been placed. With all the excitement, I had forgotten about Blanco and the look he had given me last night, but now the memory came back.

The gardens had returned to relative quiet. The dog had calmed slightly but had positioned itself outside Blanco's garden gate. Billy, still inside Blanco's garden, with his back pressed against the gate keeping it shut, was on the other side of the gate. Blanco must have also calmed down as his voice had returned to normal and we heard him speaking to Billy.

"I a will a get a the dog. You a open the gate a slowly, then you a open your a garden and a your shed. We a Lock the dog in the shed, you can do this?"

Billy must have nodded as we heard the creak of Blanco's gate as it opened. The dog barked a couple of times then whined and silence was restored. I climbed onto our gantry and looked over the fence. In the next garden Donkey was sitting on a chair with a hanky wrapped around his hand. I looked past him and saw Blanco leading the dog into Billy's garden. Billy had run ahead and had the shed door open. Blanco, confidently holding the dog's collar, guided it into the shed and closed the door.

"Look at my hand, look at the bloody fence, I'll kill that bloody dog," Donkey shouted.

Chapter Thirty-One

Something had to be done about Billy's dog. When we handed our clock in at the clubhouse everyone was discussing it. Back in our garden, we were still discussing it when Frankie Lane, George Clarke's new loft manager, knocked on the gate.

"Sorry to bother you Mr Baker," he said very respectfully, "Mr Clarke wants a meeting of the club officials, now, in his garden."

His emphasises on the word 'now' sounded as if granda was one of George's employees and was being summoned.

"What about?" asked granda.

"He's spitting blood Sammy," Frankie had resorted to broad Geordie, "what with that dog, Blanco, Pincher's loft and this morning he couldn't get in through the main gates. Lost his key or something, tore his suit pants climbing over the gates. He's putting a lot of money into the club and reckons the club's being run like the Boy's Brigade."

Granda was smiling.

"Well the Boy's Brigade's being going for some time now and it seems to run pretty well to me," he said, "tell him I'll be along."

Father was fuming.

"Who does he think he is?" he stormed when Frankie had gone. "Only been chairman for a couple of months and starts telling you to report to his office, bloody cheek of the man."

"Calm down son," granda replied, "the man's right, the club has hit a rough patch. There have been too many changes, too many new faces on the gardens, too much money and a lot of bad feelings. I'm pleased after all he is the chairman and he has every right to call a meeting. He can obviously see the problems and is taking his position seriously. Dixie was chairman for nearly thirty years and during all that time he never called a meeting."

Father and I, both intrigued, waited in the garden whilst granda went to his meeting.

"Go home if you want son," father said.

There was no way I was leaving; it had been too much of an exciting day to leave now. It was a long wait and it was beginning to get dark when granda returned.

"Well?" asked father.

"The man's on the ball son," granda said, "you'd be surprised at how good he is."

"Firstly, the dog's got to go. He and Malcolm Ash are going to Billy's garden tonight to collect it. If Billy won't give it up, George is going to the council to get Billy thrown off the gardens. Bit extreme but Billy wants to get rid of it anyway, so he won't object. I doubt whether Malcolm will give him his money back though. Mind to be fair George has given Malcolm a right bollocking for selling Billy the dog."

We listened; George Clarke seemed to be taking his position seriously.

"The one good thing about it," father said, "is that he's going to do it. Usually you get stuck with all the dirty work."

"True," said granda, "now I'll tell you the rest but it's confidential and you mustn't repeat it."

We both looked at each other, this sounded really intriguing and like conspirators, we leaned forward and nodded in agreement.

"They're onto Blanco," granda hesitated; I think his hesitation was mainly for effect. However, he was clearly relieved that someone else was taking on some of his problems.

"What?" replied father.

"Yes, remember the birds Blanco sold to them. George bought that winning blue hen and Tommy Tippins bought the blue hen bird, the one that got out of the basket. Well they reckon they're rubbish. Inbred skemmies they called them. They can't understand how Blanco's birds are winning, or how they always arrive from the same direction."

"Or how they're always on their own and well ahead of the rest," interrupted father.

Granda looked at him as if to chastise him for butting in and spoiling his story, then he continued.

"Today's race has put the cap on it. Blanco obviously didn't win, Billy saw to that, but if Billy's dog hadn't been there he would have. They know Blanco's fiddling, they just don't know how."

"Did you enlighten them?" father asked.

"Son," said granda, sitting back and scratching his nose, "they say knowledge is power and sometimes it pays to just play your cards near to your chest. When the time is right, I'll tell them but not just yet. I did mention getting the police in, but that's a non-starter. To them police is a dirty word. They work in their own way and they say they'll sort it out. The club is changing and I suppose we must change with the times. Really I feel a little sorry and frightened for Blanco."

Granda took a rest and eager to hear the rest of the story of the meeting father and I waited.

"Did you take any minutes of the meeting?" asked father.

Granda laughed, "are you joking, nothing George says goes on paper. He wanted nothing of what was said recorded. Said the meeting was an unofficial, extraordinary business meeting and who am I to disagree with him."

"What about Pincher's loft," I asked.

"Well, I was quite impressed," replied granda, "whilst George doesn't like the police he knows a lot of them, same club or something. Anyway, he's been talking to them and they reckon they've got the right lad. They say that David's admitted setting fire to the loft and killing the birds.

Seemingly Pincher had caught him smoking and told him off for playing with matches and they seem convinced David did it."

I was surprised but pleased at the relief in granda's voice. However, no matter how many times I heard people accuse David, I just could not bring myself to believe that he had slaughtered the birds and set the loft on fire.

"Tomorrow," granda continued, "the barbed wire's coming off the main gates and the chain and lock will only be used at night. They're confident that no more lofts will be set alight. George says he's put the word out that no more lofts will catch fire, and he means it."

"What do you think dad? Do you think it will stop and should I get back to my own bed now?" said father laughing.

"Be a good idea son, that wife of yours has put up with enough. Might even get me out of her bad books," replied granda.

The atmosphere had changed for the better and despite not believing the story about David; I was pleased to accept granda's reassurance.

"Okay, it's getting late," he said, "let's get finished here. You son," he said nodding at me, "get some fresh water. We'll feed and water them, then we'll go and look at the results before we all go home."

The thought of father coming home pleased me and I picked up the two watering cans and headed off to the tap. It was a lovely evening and, as I walked to the tap, I felt happier. Suddenly something in my head told me I had forgotten something and I remembered Fay. I had arranged to meet her at seven o'clock and now it was well past seven. It had been such an eventful day that Fay, my girlfriend, had gone completely out of my head. It was now too late to do anything about it so, enjoying the evening, I walked slowly to the tap.

Pincher's burned out loft was three gardens down from the water tap and as I filled the cans, I glanced at the burned out framework. The fading sun was glinting on the charcoal and I realised there was something strange about it, something new was hanging from the blackened timbers. At first, I couldn't decide what it was and I was intrigued. I left the watering cans beside the tap and walked to Pincher's garden gate. It was unlocked; I pushed it open and went in. How I wished I hadn't, the sight before me shocked me. Swinging, very slowly, in the evening breeze was Pincher. One end of a rope was attached to the blackened framework. The other end of the rope was tied tightly in a hangman's noose, which was around Pincher's neck, and Pincher's feet, moving slowly in the breeze, hung just above the gantry. Recently I had seen a cowboy film and in it, the ranchers had hung a cowhand. They had left the body, hanging just like Pincher's, silhouetted in the evening sunset. The image then had frightened me, now this was a replay, only this was not a film, it was not pretending, this was for real.

I tried to scream but nothing came out. Around me, the evening breeze ruffled the grass and slowly Pincher's body turned towards me and I looked into his face. I couldn't look away; I was frozen to the spot and I stared at his blackened face. His eyes were wide open and bulging but the funny thing was he seemed to be smiling. I turned and, as fast as I could, ran back to our garden. I didn't have to say anything; my shocked state must have said it all because granda didn't need an explanation. However, father asked,

"What is it son?"

"Come on," said granda, he knew what it was, "Pincher?" he said as he passed me.

I, still shaking, just nodded.

Pincher was dead; in my mind, there was no doubt about it. This was the first time I had seen a dead person but the blue faced figure lying on the ground, where father and granda had laid him, certainly showed no signs of life. The rope, now cut, but still around his neck also gave it away.

"Telephone for the police," granda shouted and father ran out of the garden, "pass me that coat and that sacking," granda instructed and I obeyed.

One of the great things about granda was his ability to take control of a situation, he covered Pincher with the coat and the sacking and the two of us sat on the gantry.

"Sorry son I should have kept you out of this, are you alright?" asked granda.

I was alright, the shock of finding Pincher had worn off and the activity of cutting him down and laying him on the ground had moved my mind on. However, granda's voice was breaking with emotion.

"I should have stopped Pincher leaving our garden this afternoon. I thought he might do something stupid but not this."

For a while, we sat in silence then I left granda with Pincher's body and I walked back to our garden. Somehow, I knew he wanted to be alone with his friend.

The police arrived and organised everything. After a while, a black van from the Co-op funeral department arrived and removed Pincher's body. I was interviewed and, being the one who had found the body, was suddenly a very important person. It was sad and as the news spread different members of the club appeared. George Clarke arrived and seemed genuinely shocked at the news.

"That bloody kid David's got a lot to answer for," he said.

We won that Doncaster race. The little blue hen did it again. It was the only good thing about the day. However, Pincher's death completely spoiled our win. As we walked home father said, "we'll dedicate that win to Pincher; I only hope he's somewhere where he knows we won. He'll be pleased that none of the big boys won."

It was late when father and I returned home and mother was waiting for us, she looked upset. I was tired, Pincher's death was now having an effect upon me, and I went straight to bed. My brother, oddly, was already in bed, however, as usual, he was stinking of beer and snoring. I didn't disturb him and crept into my bed. Just before I fell asleep, I heard my mother crying. Whether her tears were for Pincher, or for joy that my father had returned home I did not know.

Chapter Thirty-Two

The next morning I found out that my mother's tears were not for any of the reasons I had suspected. Last night my brother had been arrested for under age drinking and drunkenness. A policeman had called at the flat and told mother she had to go to the police station to collect him. In the police station, the on-duty sergeant had given her a real telling off for not controlling her son. He had asked her where the boy's father was and when mother told him he was at the pigeon garden, the sergeant had shook his head and said he was a disgrace. Only because the sergeant had said he would let my brother go, without charging him if he thought he had responsible parents, had my mother put up with the humiliation. Mother didn't seem too bothered about my brother's drunkenness. Her real distress was at the suggestion that she was a bad parent. I sat smiling, quietly enjoying the ear bashing that my brother and father were getting.

However, having harangued my brother and father she then turned her attention to me.

"And you," she screamed, "what have you been up to?"

In her usual manner mother folded her arms across her chest, which meant, I am waiting for an answer. I just looked at her wondering what she was on about and I shrugged my shoulders.

"Don't you shrug your shoulders at me boy," she screamed, "just let me remind you. Fay and her mother also came to see me yesterday. Fay's mother is a foul mouthed, very unpleasant person," she stopped talking and tapped her foot.

This was supposed to be the signal for me to tell all, but I still didn't know what she wanted to hear.

"Fay's mother found grass stains on Fay's skirt, and would you believe it, also on her 'brassiere'," mother nearly choked on the word.

My brother started to laugh and father hit him on the back of the head.

"Yes her bra young man, her bra," mother shouted and pushed her face into mine, "Fay's mother is very upset, even talked about going to the police. Thankfully she's agreed that I'll deal with it."

Until then I hadn't been too worried but the mention of the police put the whole thing in a different light. I didn't think I had broken the law but I was starting to worry.

"Fay told her mother some story about you and another boy, Fatty Turner, feeling her breasts. I'm disgusted with you, what are you, some kind of pervert?"

My brother was now rocking with laughter but for me it wasn't funny. I could see nothing wrong in what I had done, it was only curiosity that had driven me but it did appear that I had broken some law.

"Your father will now start acting like a father and he will deal with both of you. I just despair for the lot of you," this was her final outburst and with that she sat down, crossed her arms, and glared at father.

It was obvious that the outcome of her crying last night was that father had to discipline us and really sort us out. We, in her opinion, were guilty of the worst types of crimes, drunkenness and sex attacks. To me it seemed that of the two crimes my brother was getting off lightly. The police sergeant had told mother that this time they would take no further action but next time they would be charging him and his parents would have to take him to court. Father really was appalled and laid the law down to both of us.

I sat quietly, listening whilst my brother received his judgement. He was told to start looking for a job, stop drinking and, every night, he had to be home before nine o'clock. Nonchalantly, he accepted his punishment and was allowed to leave the room. However, I knew he would be smirking behind the living room door listening to my fate. Then father started on me. I was subjected to a half hour lecture on the birds and bees; I would have preferred looking for a job and stopping drinking. Father talked about the pollen and how the bees transferred it. Then he talked about the pigeons treading each other and how they only did it when they were paired up.

"Just like a couple when they're married," he said.

I knew this wasn't always true, I'd seen the spare cock birds treading different hens and I told him so.

Mother raised her eyes to the ceiling.

"Well they shouldn't have been," father said angrily.

What all of this had to do with me feeling Fay I don't know. However, the worst thing for me was that mother had told me, about Fay's accusations, in front of my brother. I knew that at every opportunity he would now remind me of it and make fun of me.

That afternoon having nothing to do, and definitely not wanting to see Fay or her mother, I accompanied father to the garden. The main gates were unlocked but there was an air of gloom about the place and men only nodded as we passed. No words were spoken then quietly one of them said, "bad news about Pincher."

Father just nodded.

Granda was at the garden and told us that, that morning he had visited Pincher's mother.

"She's in a terrible state," he said, "Pincher was all she had, no other relatives. She has asked me to organise the funeral says we were the only family Pincher had and wants all of us to go to the funeral. She has even given me money to buy beer for the lads on the gardens to be drunk on the night of his funeral. She also wants us to burn the remains of the loft, even told me to keep Pincher's birds and says she wants nothing more to do with them."

"That channel hen's worth a lot of money, we should sell it and give her the money," answered father.

"I told her that but she wouldn't hear of it, said Pincher would only want us to have his birds. She says she's no need for money, rather the bird has a good home."

"It's a real nice thing to do," said father, "that hen is really worth having."

I was tired of hearing about Pincher and decided to take a walk around the gardens. Really, I just wanted some peace and quiet and I wanted to see Pincher's garden. I did not want to remember it as I had seen it last night. I wanted to remember it without Pincher hanging there. No one disagreed so I set off along the front row of lofts to Pincher's garden, sadly, I couldn't get in. I was disappointed, the gate to his garden had been nailed shut so I turned the corner and continued along the other rows of lofts just looking at them. I spent a lot of time looking at the top row, the new lofts. They were well built and they all looked clean. On my way back, just outside the clubhouse, I came across Billy.

"Youngin tell Sammy the fuckin dog's gone, George and Malcolm fucked off with it last night. I made sure it's gone to a fuckin good home," he said.

I nodded and left Billy reading the result of yesterday's race, which were still pinned to the notice board.

When I arrived back at our loft, father and granda were inside the loft and I could hear both of them laughing. I thought, because of Pincher's death, this was unusual and it was obvious that they had not heard me enter the garden.

"Aye feeling her bloody titties," father said laughing.

Granda was giggling, "and she had grass stains on her skirt," he giggled, "the lad's a real Romeo but don't tell your mother or she'll be washing his mouth out with soap and water."

Both of them roared with laughter. It was nice to hear them laugh but I was annoyed that they were laughing at my expense.

I hung around in the garden until they came out of the loft then we tidied up and made our way home.

"I'll let you know when the funeral is and I'll organise that drink for all the lads. Probably burn the remains of Pincher's loft at the same time, bit like a Viking funeral, seems like a fitting send off," said granda as we said goodnight.

Chapter Thirty-Three

Granda made all the arrangements for the funeral. He also worked out Pincher's winnings from the first Selby race and tried to give them to his mother. She wouldn't take it and insisted that granda spend the money on crates of beer for the club members. Granda agreed and during the week, some of the members helped him to pull down the remains of Pincher's loft and stack it on the site of the old muck hill. It had the potential to be quite a bonfire, a number of the fanciers took the opportunity to pile on old doors, and pieces of wood they'd had lying around their gardens. The funeral was arranged, at the crematorium, for the following Friday afternoon. This suited everyone; all of the members would be handing in their birds for the first Grantham race and usually when they'd handed their birds in they all went to the pub. The promise of free beer and a bonfire would be too much for them to miss. Pincher's mother was also insisting that our family travel, in the cars, with her to the crematorium. My mother wasn't keen on the idea but father talked her round and my brother and I were promised a day off school, so we readily agreed.

My return to school on Monday morning had been filled with trepidation. I had half expected the police to be waiting with Fay to arrest me.

However, no one was waiting and at first, no one said anything. However, as the morning past more and more kids started to point at me and laugh. It was only later in the morning that I realised that my brother must be behind the rumours that were now spreading like wild fire, throughout the school. Fay and I were in the same class but during the morning, we never spoke. Infact we never even made eye contact. When we returned from lunch Fay was missing from the class and before lessons started, the teacher took me into the corridor and told me the headmaster wanted to speak to me. As I had already realised that Fatty was missing from the class, I didn't have to guess what it was all about and slowly I made my way to the headmaster's office. Fatty Turner had beaten me there. He was standing hands in pockets waiting outside the door. Fatty wasn't one of my usual friends and we spoke very little. When he saw me, he just raised his eyes to the ceiling and grunted.

Inside the headmaster's office, the two of us lined up in front of his desk.
"Now what have you two been up to?" the headmaster asked.
Fatty looked at me and I looked at Fatty, then both together we said, "nothing sir."
"That's not what I'm hearing. There are some malicious, filthy rumours circulating about you two and a certain young lady. I have spoken to the young lady and she tells me there is no truth whatsoever in the rumours and I believe her. However, some people might say there is no smoke without fire. And I will warn you now that if I find out that you have been abusing any young ladies, I will be down on you like a ton of bricks."
Fatty started to cry.
"What are you snivelling at boy?" the headmaster shouted at him.
"I've done nothing," sobbed Fatty.
I said nothing; really, there was nothing to say.
"Now tomorrow morning in assembly I will be acting to quash these rumours but if you have any information as to who is the instigator of this maliciousness, you should tell me now," said the headmaster.
As much as I wanted to tell him that, I thought it was my brother I couldn't, so we just stood staring at him. The silence seemed to drag on for hours but eventually he scratched his nose and said,

"Alright gentlemen back to your class."

Oh, how I regretted going for that walk on the moor with Fay. As far as I was concerned, I had done nothing wrong. Bloody Fay had egged me on; she had virtually shoved my hand up her jumper. The last thing I wanted was all the trouble that was now descending upon me.

We left the office, Fatty still crying.

"If he tells my father he'll kill me," he sobbed, "that bloody Fay, I never even got a feel of her tits."

I must admit I felt like crying, I didn't know what the rumours were that were circulating but I could imagine. Re-entering the classroom took a lot of nerve. I went first and Fatty crept in behind me. The boys in the class all started laughing and the girls ignored us. Fatty and I, not looking at anyone, crept to our seats. Fay must have been upset, as she had gone home, at least, as she wasn't in the classroom I assumed she had.

The afternoon crept by and when, at four o'clock, the school bell rang I was greatly relieved. I just wanted to get home and be on my own. I raced through the school gates and ran along Windsor Road. At the end of Windsor Road, I turned left into our back lane and ran straight into Fay.

"I've been waiting for you," she said.

I was horrified and stepped away from her.

"Don't come near me," I whispered glancing round to see if any one was watching, "you've got me into real trouble, just keep away from me."

Fay started to cry and I started to panic.

"I'm sorry," she sobbed, "on Friday night when I got home my mother started collecting my clothes for the wash and found grass marks on my skirt and dirty marks on my bra. She locked me in the coalhouse and wouldn't let me out until I told her where I'd been and who I'd been with. She kept me locked in the dark for hours. I only told her your name because you're nice and I thought she wouldn't think badly of you."

I remembered my mother saying that Fay's mother was a very unpleasant woman. My parents would never have locked me in the coalhouse so I began to feel sorry for Fay. However, she was still crying and I was terrified that someone would walk past and ask her what was wrong. The only thing I could think of was to walk with her across the moor. At least on the moor we would be out of sight. I took Fay's hand and, as quickly as possible, praying no one would see us, I walked with her onto the moor.

In the middle of the moor, there was a small seat and we sat down. Fay had stopped crying and tried to explain what had happened. She told me again that her mother had locked her in the coalhouse. She had only been dressed in her nightie and her mother had left her there. Poor Fay hadn't known what to do; she'd been cold and frightened and, she said, would have done anything to get out. Eventually, just to get out, she had told her mother that she'd been walking with me. She told her mother nothing had happened and she often walked on the moor with boys, Fatty Turner being one of them. Her mother had gone berserk and hit her with a slipper. Fay showed me the marks on her legs. As my parents rarely hit me, I found it difficult to understand this type of brutality.

"What did your dad say?" I asked.

"Haven't got one," replied Fay, "just another five younger brothers and sisters."

The Fay that was telling me the story was not the same girl that had been on the moor on Friday night. She was frightened, vulnerable and needed someone.

"I really wanted to be your girlfriend," she said and started to cry again. "I know I talked too much and shouldn't have led you on but I thought that if I let you feel me, you'd be my boyfriend. All of the other girls have boyfriends and I thought there was something wrong with me. Honestly I never wanted to get you into trouble."

With that, she flung her arms around my neck and sobbed on my shoulder.

What could I do? I felt so sorry for her. She was so unhappy and needed someone to talk to, so I kissed her. Her mouth was salty and she pulled me closer, then we sat for a long time just holding each other, eventually she asked,

"Will you still be my boyfriend?" and I replied, "yes."

On Tuesday morning, at school, in assembly it was a smiling Fay that sat in the next row to me. The headmaster, true to his word, started assembly by telling everyone that some malicious, sick, evil person had been spreading vile rumours about other children. Everyone knew who he was talking about and a number of heads turned in my direction. I actually thought that his description of my brother was quite accurate. The headmaster went on to say that, there was no truth in any of the rumours and anyone heard discussing or starting further rumours would be dealt with most severely. I was pleased with the way he handled it and felt relieved.

Chapter Thirty-Four

On Friday afternoon the Baker family, all dressed in their best clothes, assembled at Pincher Martin's house. Pincher's mother was a very old woman and she had to be helped out of the house into the black Daimler car. She sat in the back seat and the six Baker family members filled the rest of the car. It was the first time I had ridden in a luxury car and I thoroughly enjoyed the experience. The black hearse travelled in front of us and as we entered the gates of the crematorium, all I could see was pigeon club members lined up. As the hearse passed them as a sign of respect, they removed their trilby hats and caps and stood to attention. As we passed, I was unsure what to do, smile, wave or just continue to look glum, as I had done throughout the journey. We had to sit in the front pews of the small church with Mrs Martin and she cried throughout the service. I felt very sorry for her. The vicar seemed confused and kept referring to us as Pincher's loving family. Then when the vicar had finished he asked granda if he would like to say a few words and granda obliged. Granda spoke about Pincher his friend and how he had bred and raced the best pigeons on the gardens. Moreover, how he knew every member's pigeons and could spot them from miles away. It was an emotional speech but I quite enjoyed it. When he finished there were grunts of approval from the club members. However, I was pleased when the curtains closed around the coffin and I realised that was the end of the service.

When we were leaving the small church, and were just about to get back into the car, Mrs Martin announced she wanted Pincher's ashes. She said she wanted granda to spread them on the gardens. I think this was news to granda. However, he returned to the church and after a long wait, we saw him emerge from a side door holding what looked like an earthenware urn. As he got into the car, granda passed the urn to my brother. The journey back to Mrs Martin's house was a lot quicker than the one coming and I smiled and waved as we passed people waiting at the bus stops. Typically, my brother had opened the urn and when no one was looking, he was flicking ash at me. At her house we all disembarked from the car and helped Pincher's mother back inside. She was very nice, shook all our hands, and said, "I want you boys to enjoy that beer tonight in honour of John."

Granda, father and I had intended to go straight to the gardens. The pigeons needed basketing for Saturday's race from Grantham and it was getting late. I don't think my brother had intended to accompany us to the gardens, but now hearing the words free beer he suddenly developed a new interest in the pigeons.

Mother decided to walk with granny to her house and the four Baker men made their way to the gardens. We walked together along Elwick Road then we slipped through Saint Peter's gate into the pigeon gardens. The remains of Pincher's loft, and the extra scrap wood, stood magnificently on the old muck hill site. I looked into Pincher's garden it was now completely empty. The soil on the site, where his loft had been, had been raked completely flat. His small lawn and vegetable patch, whilst slightly trodden by the firemen, were recovering and if I hadn't known better I might have thought a loft had never stood there.

"So much for thirty odd years of pigeon racing I thought."

There was a general air of excitement on the gardens. The race this week was from Grantham, about 160 miles, and men were already taking their birds to the clubhouse for basketing. The clock committee was assembling ready to go to granda's so we had to hurry. Earlier granda had explained that Malcolm Ash, the scrap man, was organising the beer. Malcolm had told granda he had some good contacts and could get crates of Newcastle Brown Ale at a knocked down price. He hadn't enlightened granda as to where he was getting it from and granda hadn't pushed him for an answer. He had also agreed to provide something to eat. The word had soon spread around the gardens and everyone was looking forward to free beer and a feed.

My mother's parting words, when we left her on Elwick road, were "no beer for those two."

I wasn't expecting any but dejectedly my brother had looked at her and said,

"Come on mam just one or two bottles won't hurt, I'll not get drunk."

Mother had flown at him.

"No, you're not old enough, remember what that policeman said."

We basketed our birds and took them round to the clubhouse. I was disappointed to see Blanco still race basketing the birds but decided to ignore him. Since the new members had started racing their pigeons, the number of clocks needing to be checked had increased. A further two men had been co-opted onto the clock committee and now the club also had transport of their own. George Clarke had provided a van to transport them from the gardens to granda's house, and back again.

"It's a sign of the times," granda said quite proudly, "everyone is getting transport and the club is modernising."

I really thought he just liked riding in the front of the van.

We waited for the clock committee to return and to fill the time father and I cleaned out the loft. My brother had carried Pincher's ashes to the gardens and he had placed the urn on the gantry. As we worked in the loft he, imitating Pincher's voice, and standing on the gantry called out, "One over the church, blue cock, Sammy's bird, we'll not be hanging around here for long."

Actually, he did quite a good impression of Pincher and I laughed. Father didn't see the funny side, he went out onto the gantry, and clipped him one.

When father was away getting fresh water, Billy entered the garden.

"Where's fuckin Sammy," he asked, I think he was really just being nosey.

The urn must have caught his attention as he walked up to the gantry and stood looking at it. Then without receiving an answer, he removed the top of the urn, looked in, and smelt it.

"What the fucks this?" he asked.

My brother turning away from him replied.

"New conditioner, put it in the birds' drinking water but, don't touch it, it's expensive we've only just bought it from Belgium."

Having said his piece my brother, deliberately, turned his back on Billy and winked at me. I was inside the loft, peeping out, and I watched as Billy put his hand into the urn, removed a handful of ashes and put them into his jacket pocket. When father returned, very quickly and looking rather guilty, Billy left the garden.

"What's wrong with him?" father asked.

I didn't tell him what had happened; I knew he'd be furious.

At seven o'clock, the clock committee returned. All the birds were in the race baskets and had been loaded onto the transporters and everyone assembled around the bonfire. Some of the men brought seats and small tables and the feeling of expectation was mounting. Malcolm Ash arrived in one of his scrap lorries and piled on the back were crates of Newcastle Brown Ale.

"Let's get at it," shouted Rat Face.

"Just a minute," shouted granda, "let's just remember why we're doing this."

The sun was setting and it was getting dark. Granda's words halted everyone, the proceedings took on a sombre note, and all the men stood and waited.

"Get the ashes," father said.

My brother ran back to the garden and returned with the urn and granda gathered all the men together in a circle.

"Let's just spend a minute remembering Pincher," granda said and everyone went silent.

After about a minute granda announced, "we'll now spread Pincher's ashes."

My brother had climbed onto the back of Malcolm's lorry. He had removed the top of the urn and now he jerked the urn upwards throwing Pincher's ashes into the air. Unfortunately, there was a strong South-Westerly wind blowing and everyone, with the exception of my brother, was covered in ash.

The crates were unloaded from Malcolm's lorry and the 'Psst' sound of bottle tops being flicked off echoed over the gardens. I was given the honour of lighting the bonfire and, very warily, I approached it with a burning piece of paper. However, someone, unbeknown to us, had thrown petrol over it and the whole thing lit with a sudden 'whoosh,' and I was thrown backwards. My caution had paid off and although slightly shaken I wasn't hurt. Soon the pile of wood was well alight and someone called out.

"How-way Mashy where's the grub."

Malcolm climbed onto the back of the lorry and removed two blankets revealing two tin baths full of tripe.

"Tripe, bloody hell Malcolm you could have got pies or pasties," the same voice shouted.

"Nowt wrong with tripe," Malcolm replied, "I boiled it in milk this afternoon in the yard, and it's bloody lovely. It'll line your stomach for the beer."

The men sat, or stood around the bonfire and the atmosphere was good. They joked and laughed and I joined in. Blanco and Billy had placed two empty crates on their sides and they sat on them a little apart from the other men. They had placed another crate between them on which stood bottles of beer and they were chewing away their hands full of tripe. Slightly away from the other men, George Clarke, Tommy Tippins and Malcolm also sat around a small card table. They were drinking whisky and smoking cigars. The time passed and the pile of crates was getting smaller. As it did, the men became more boisterous and their laughter became louder. I hadn't seen my brother or my granda for a while and was beginning to wonder where they were when suddenly I heard granda's voice.

"Blanco's loft, quick Blanco's loft's on fire."

At first, no one reacted then a few men turned to look in the direction of Blanco's loft.

"Bloody hell," shouted Jimmy the labourer, "someone call the fire brigade."

Blanco was now standing by Malcolm's lorry and he started to shout.

"My a loft it's a burning."

I had been sitting behind the lorry and couldn't see the loft so I dashed round to the front and sure enough wisps of light grey smoke were drifting out from under the roof of Blanco's loft. Granda must have been walking past Blanco's garden when he saw the fire. I saw him run into the garden and he must have opened the loft doors as all of a sudden Blanco's pigeons shot out of the smoke. Everyone started dashing about. Men ran trying to find hosepipes and buckets and others dashed into Blanco's garden.

Rat Face whose loft was next to Blanco's was screaming, "get some water."

"Keep back," granda shouted, "it's going up."

The smoke coming from the loft had turned from grey to black and suddenly orange tongues of flame appeared in the smoke.

"My a loft," Blanco cried.

His voice was drowned out as the black smoke turned into flames and the whole loft was engulfed. Now there was no smoke just bright yellow and orange flame, the heat was intense, and it drove everyone out of Blanco's garden.

"Forget Blanco's; protect the other lofts," granda shouted. The men formed bucket chains from the water tap and started throwing water onto the two lofts alongside Blanco's.

The clanging of a bell announced the arrival of the fire brigade but there really wasn't much they could do. The firemen ran out two hoses and continued protecting the lofts alongside Blanco's. As the firemen had taken over from the club members they now returned to their drinking. The firemen and Blanco's burning loft provided them with first class entertainment.

"Who organised the entertainment," Malcolm Ash asked and some of the men started laughing.

When they'd been released Blanco's birds had flown for a few minutes then, because of the darkness, they'd dropped anywhere. Now they all sat, forlornly, on fences all over the gardens.

"At least your birds are alright Blanco," someone shouted.

Blanco, standing alone, with his overcoat buttoned to his neck had watched his loft burn. He didn't seem too impressed.

By the time the local beat policeman had arrived the club members had eaten all the tripe. It was the same policeman that had called at granda's on the night Pincher's loft had burned.

"How did it start?" he asked granda.

"Must have been a spark from the bonfire," he replied, "I was just passing when I saw smoke coming out of the loft so I opened the doors and let the birds out."

George Clarke smoking a big cigar approached them.

"Hello John," he said offering his hand, which the policeman shook, "good to see you. Sammy here is right must have been a spark from the bonfire. We were just saying goodbye to Pincher, you know the man that hanged himself. Then, the next minute the lofts well alight. I've had a word with Clive the fire officer, you'll probably know him, and he agrees it must have been a spark. We'll clean it all up and rebuild the loft for Blanco, his birds are alright and he doesn't seem too upset."

That was an understatement Blanco was distraught. He was wandering round the gardens throwing his arms in the air and swearing in some foreign language.

"Seems straight forward Mr Clarke," the policeman said, "if there's no real damage, I'll put it down as an accident and leave it at that."

I had mixed feelings about Blanco's loft burning down. I suppose, in some way, I felt sorry for him but I was also pleased that his cheating might have stopped. However, I had really enjoyed the night. I had listened to all the members' joking; I had helped the fireman with their hoses and had drunk two bottles of beer. For me it really was a night to remember. Granda and father had joined George Clarke and Tommy Tippins and were sitting at their table on the muck hill site drinking whisky. They both seemed quite drunk. I had forgotten about my brother and it was only when the excitement was dying down that I went looking for him. Eventually I found him talking to Malcolm Ash and from the slur in his voice; I knew that he was also drunk. As I approached them, I heard Malcolm say,

"I only hope that copper doesn't ask where we got the beer and tripe from."

My brother laughed, they both seemed as thick as thieves.

On our return home, we were all in a sorry state. Father had giggled and laughed all the way home. My brother had stumbled along behind us and I had tried to steer them both in the right direction. Mother was waiting at the door,

"What in God's name have you been doing?" she screamed at father, "look at the state you're all in. what's all this mud and ash? You're drunk, stinking of smoke and they're your best clothes, they're ruined, just look at them."

She was right and we stood in front of her like three naughty schoolboys. I had never thought about how we looked and it was only then, when I looked at the state of us, I realised we were still wearing our funeral clothes. I was shocked; the three of us were covered in mud and ash and our faces were dirty from the smoke. My brother was carrying Pincher's urn and trying to be funny said,

"It's only Pincher we brought some of him home."

Mother was not amused.

Chapter Thirty-Five

Usually, Saturday morning in the Baker flat was a busy and happy time. Most Saturdays by the time my brother and I climb out of bed father had gone to work and mother would be cooking breakfast for us. Today was different, father hadn't gone to work, but my brother had. Mother wasn't cooking breakfast she was busy cleaning our clothes. I had slept through my brother's early departure and was surprised, when I awoke, to find him gone. Father followed me into the small living room. He didn't look well and all my mother said was, "serves you right."

Father ignored the comment and disappeared to the outside toilet.

"Who's this Mash you're brother's gone to work for?" mother asked me.

This was news to me and, for a long time, I had to think. Then I remembered the previous night and my brother and Malcolm plotting together.

"Oh, it must be Malcolm Ash he's a scrap merchant, has a loft on the gardens," I replied.

Mother stopped what she was doing.

"A what?" she asked.

"A scrap merchant," I replied, timidly.

"You mean a rag and bone man?" replied mother horrified.

I had never thought of Malcolm Ash as a rag and bone man. He certainly did not go around the back lanes with a horse and cart collecting rubbish usually he was smartly dressed.

"No, I think he buys old cars and things and sells parts from them," I replied.

My mother said nothing.

On his return from the toilet father looked even worse.

"I'm not well," was all he said.

However, it was sufficient to give mother the opportunity to reply.

"Not well, not bloody well, that's an understatement; you were absolutely blotto last night. I couldn't get a word of sense out of you, even had to undress you and put you to bed. What an example to set for your children."

I, by now, was feeling very uncomfortable.

"And," continued mother, "did you give permission for your eldest son to become a rag and bone man."

Father with his head in his hands just groaned.

All morning Mother hadn't stopped moaning. Everything we did was wrong, I was glad when at twelve o'clock father, and I left the house and walked to the gardens. The gardens looked like father must have felt. The hill site was covered with empty beer bottles and two empty tin baths lay upside down on the path. Billy was just starting to pick up the empty bottles.

"Is there any fuckin money on these fuckin bottles?" he asked.

Father just belched and turned away. As we passed what was left of Blanco's loft I noticed his pigeons sitting on the railings and on the gantry. It was a terrible site and I felt sorry for Blanco. When we opened our garden gate and saw granda, he looked even worse than father did.

"We've got a job," he said, as we entered, "George Clarke was here earlier and said Blanco wasn't coming back. Seemingly last night he had words with him, told him straight that he knew he was cheating. He even told him that he wasn't welcome on the gardens and told him not to come back."

Father and I looked at him in amazement.

"Well," said father, "I can't say I'm sorry but I'm surprised that he went so quietly."

"Who knows what George can do and only Blanco knows what George said to him," replied granda.

Father thought about this for a while then said,

"Do you think Blanco's loft caught fire by accident dad?"

"I know it did," replied granda, confidently, "I saw the sparks falling on the loft, it was a pure accident."

Granda seemed very sure of himself.

"Oh," he continued, "and George asked if we'd do him a favour, asked if we'd catch Blanco's birds."

Grantham was a good race point and we knew the birds would return on time. Granda knew the time of liberation and said the birds would be back at half past two. He was concerned that Blanco's birds might interfere with the returning pigeons and said we should catch them before the race birds returned. It was obvious that both he and father did not relish the prospect of chasing pigeons. However, we went to Blanco's garden and very quietly we entered. Except for a small section of framework, there was nothing left of Blanco's loft. However, the gantry was reasonably intact. The pigeons were all sitting quietly on the gantry and the fencing watching us. Granda had brought his trusty corn tin and he rattled it. This caught their attention, they cocked their heads to one side, and then the birds sitting on the fencing flew down onto the gantry.

"We need two race baskets," said granda.

Father and I went to the clubhouse and collected them. Whilst we were away, granda must have been re-assessing the situation.

"This isn't going to be easy," he said, "we'll never catch all of them on the gantry. I think we should catch the two white droppers and take them to our loft. We'll lock all our birds in the young bird section, and then try and attract Blanco's birds into our loft and catch them there."

The plan seemed reasonable so we set to work to catch the two white droppers. Fortunately, these birds were quite tame and were very hungry. Granda sat on the gantry, rattled the tin and placed corn just alongside him. We stood at the bottom of the garden holding our breath and silently watched the birds. The two white droppers were the first to take the bait and slowly they approached granda.

The other pigeons watched with interest and a few of them started to move forward to get the corn. The white cock bird was the bravest; he nipped in and pinched a piece of corn. Then he returned for a second, he was just alongside granda when granda's hand shot out and he caught the bird. The other pigeons jumped back but fortunately, they didn't take off. Father very slowly went forward and took the cock bird from granda then he returned to the bottom of the garden. The other pigeons didn't seem to miss the white cock bird and very soon, the white hen bird was within reach and was taking pieces of corn. Once again, granda's hand shot out and the hen bird was caught.

We took the two birds and the two race baskets back to our garden. Granda took the two white droppers into the loft; inside he had a ball of string. He took one bird at a time and wrapped string around them stopping them from using their wings. The birds didn't seem to mind. We locked all our pigeons in the young bird loft, opened up the main doors to the loft and placed the two white droppers on our gantry. The two birds were hungry and were quite content to run around the gantry eating corn. Next granda went back to Blanco's garden and very gently chased the birds. Fortunately, they did not take off and fly around; they all flew up onto the fencing. There were three lofts between Blanco's loft and ours. They belonged to Rat Face, Jimmy the labourer and Mattie Walker and luckily, none of these lofts were open. Father caught the white cock bird while I held the corn tin. He threw the bird into the air then, when it dropped, he caught it and I rattled the corn tin.

At first, nothing happened. Then two of Blanco's birds, sitting on the fencing, turned and watched with interest as the white cock bird appeared then disappeared over the top of our fencing.
"It's not working," said father.
I think his judgement was impaired by his hangover.
"Keep going," shouted granda and I rattled the tin even harder.
One bird took off from Blanco's fence, flew over the three lofts, and landed on our fencing. I threw a handful of corn onto the gantry and

the bird cocked its head and looked at it. A second pigeon followed and father placed the white cock bird on the gantry. It seemed quite pleased to be back safely on its feet and waddled off to enjoy the corn. The first pigeon onto the fence now flew down and joined the two white droppers. Next, a third and fourth pigeon flew over the three lofts and landed on our fence. They watched the other birds feeding. This seemed to be the signal for the remainder of Blanco's birds to fly over and land on the fencing.

I was impressed our plan was working. Granda joined us in the garden and I threw more corn onto the gantry.

"No son, start throwing it into the loft," he said, "we need them inside the loft whilst they're still hungry. If you feed them they'll just go back to Blanco's place."

I obeyed and, as quietly as possible, threw corn into the loft. The birds were obviously starving as they started fighting for the pieces of corn. At first, they were reluctant to enter the loft but the two white droppers had no fear. They charged inside the loft grabbing every piece of corn.

"Greedy beggars, that corn costs money," granda whispered.

Very slowly, with his arms outstretched, granda walked forward and ushered the birds into the loft. As soon as they were all inside he swung the loft doors shut and we all heaved a sigh of relief.

Blanco's birds were starving, and reluctantly, granda fed and watered them. It was now nearly half past two and the gardens had come to life. All the lofts were open and granda and father set to work catching the birds and stuffing them into the two race baskets. They were both sweating but I thought that the exercise was getting rid of their hangovers. Finally, all the birds were basketed and we carried the baskets to the bottom of the garden. Granda insisted on cleaning inside the loft where Blanco's birds had been.

"George Clarke was right," he said, "them birds do look like skemmies, bloody Blanco mustn't have been feeding them properly."

Throughout the whole procedure our pigeons had sat, very interested, just watching us work and now they all cooed as if showing their appreciation.

We had only just finished when someone called out, "birds in the valley."

"Pincher's not dead," someone else called out.

We were ready and it was just as well, the lead bird was our blue hen. Granda was elated.

"Come on girl," he shouted rattling the tin, "it's the blue hen again, she's in great condition," granda said excitedly.

The blue hen flew straight out of the valley and straight into our loft. Two other birds were just behind her and they flew on to the back of the gardens.

"Is it fully nominated?" father asked and granda with a huge smile on his face nodded.

"She's a good sprinter son she's always good from Selby, Doncaster or Grantham, of course she is," he replied.

Catching Blanco's birds had been good therapy for all of us. It had stopped us thinking about Pincher or Blanco. However, when we handed our clock in at the clubhouse other members started to ask granda questions. It was obvious that the word had gone round that Blanco wasn't coming back.

"Is it fuckin true Blanco's fuckin chucked it?" Billy asked. "Fuck me, if he has I might fuckin buy some of his fuckin birds," he continued.

It was obvious that Billy was the only one on the gardens who had not heard the rumours, started by George Clarke and Tommy Tippins, about the state of Blanco's birds. "They're rubbish Billy," said Rat Face meanly, "Blanco ripped off George and Tommy."

We didn't enter the debate.

"Blanco's birds are going to Walker club," a voice said, "young Frankie here knows a young lad down there; he's just starting up and is willing to buy them."

George Clarke must have overheard the conversation. He and his loft manager had walked round to the clubhouse and now Frankie, his loft manager, took their clock into the clubhouse.

"A word Sammy," George said, beckoning to granda.

Father and I made our way back to our garden and started cleaning out. As I had a date with Fay I wanted to be away early. Of course, no one else knew about my date and I wasn't intending to tell anyone. We had just about finished when granda returned.

"What did he want?" asked father.

"He wants to buy Pincher's channel hen," granda replied.

"How does he know you've got it? We've told no one that we've got the bird," replied father, he was annoyed.

"Son you'd be surprised what George Clarke knows. There's not much going on, on these gardens that he doesn't know about. I told him I couldn't sell her and he was really annoyed but I'd never forgive myself if I sold that hen. Pincher's mother gave her to me and it would be wrong of me to sell her. Tonight I'll fill in the transfer form and send it off to the Union then the hen will be officially mine."

We won that first Grantham race, the blue hen was fully nominated and our prize money for the season was steadily growing.

Chapter Thirty-Six

Fay was waiting for me by the school gate. We had decided it was safer to meet at the school rather than meeting near our homes. Since we had talked on the moor my respect for Fay had grown and I had realised how much she needed friendship and to be accepted. She had told me she had duties at home, which included cooking, cleaning, washing and looking after her brothers and sisters. These were things I knew nothing about and was full of admiration for her. I was fascinated by the life style of her family and the more we talked, the more I respected my parents and realised how lucky we were. Ever since Fay had opened up and started talking about herself, I had begun to respect her and whilst my interest in her body hadn't gone away, I didn't try anything else. However, whenever we kissed, the thing with a mind of its own was still prone to placing me in embarrassing situations.

That night we walked into town and watched the crowds queuing for the cinema.
"I've never been to the cinema," Fay announced.
I couldn't believe that anyone had never been to the cinema.
"Mother says we've got no money for such luxuries."

"I'll take you," I said, "but not tonight, we'll arrange to go next week."

Her face lit up and I felt proud of myself. It wasn't until I had kissed her goodnight and was walking home that I realised what I'd done. Taking Fay to the cinema would be very public and the last thing I wanted was her mother calling at my house again.

Before going out I had told my parents I was going to the boys club and when I arrived home, there were no questions. I soon realised that tonight I wasn't in the spotlight. However, my brother was, he had returned home from his days work covered in oil and grease, and he'd been drinking with the lads from the scrap yard. This had upset mother but when he announced he'd been offered a full time job in the scrap yard, she'd gone mad. The argument was still going on when I came into the living room. My father was trying to tell him he had a future in football or, like the rest of the Baker men, as a joiner. My brother would have none of it. It was, infact, the first time I had heard him talk logically. He was arguing that he wasn't good enough to get a place in a professional football team and he didn't want to be a joiner. He was a very good footballer but the competition for apprenticeships was intense and even if he did sign for a club, there were no guarantees that he would be taken on full time. Burnley and Newcastle football scouts had watched him play however, the clubs had not made any offers. Actually he wasn't due to finish school until July but Malcolm had said he could work part time until he left school, then he could take up the job full time. Mother was adamant that he was not going to be a rag and bone man and that he wasn't going back to Malcolm's scrap yard. I, personally, was quite impressed that he had been offered a job; I certainly wouldn't have employed him. Earlier that night as I had walked home, I had decided I would tell mother about Fay and me going to the cinema. I thought that by telling her, if we were seen, at least I wouldn't be accused of going behind her back. However, as they argued I realised that tonight was not the time for me to make my announcement.

On Sunday morning, mother was even more annoyed; my brother had gone back to work. Regular work on a Sunday was a new experience for our family. Father would only work when there was an emergency job on. Now mother saw Malcolm not only as a rag and bone man but also as an ungodly rag and bone man. I was tired of the tension in the house and decided to go to the garden. Father, still trying to console her, stayed at home. I knew he would rather have come with me but she was blaming him for all the trouble at home.

The garden gates off the West Road were open so I walked down the path and past the clubhouse. I stopped at the notice board and read the results from Saturday's race. Baker and Son were first then George Clarke was second and Tommy Tippins third. Malcolm Ash was fourth then George and Tommy were fifth and sixth. I thought back to granda's prediction that the three new lofts, mob flying, would be winning all the races and realised his prediction was coming true. I also realised that the opposition was being eliminated. Pincher, who had always flown great pigeons, had gone. Blanco, even though he had been cheating, had been a threat and now he had gone. I thought that now, the only quality opposition to the three big lofts was us.

The club had grown and the atmosphere over the past three years had changed. Before granda and Rat face had fallen out, to an extent, every one of the fanciers had been a friend. The argument had split the club and friendships in the club had changed. However, I suppose it may also have been a natural progression. The club had expanded and the new members, in the two new back rows of lofts, tended to hang around together and the old timers in the front three rows stayed together. The exceptions to this rule were Rat Face, Jimmy the labourer and two more of Rat Face's friends. Whilst they were old timers, they hung around George Clarke's loft. There was no open hostility between the groups but the old comradeship was no longer there.

Since Dixie Dean had been voted out as chairman he seldom visited our garden and we didn't see him very often. Dixie had taken a back seat in the running of the club and apart from the basketing committee; he did not get involved in any club business. Therefore, I was surprised when I entered granda's garden to find Dixie sitting on the bench. As I entered their conversation stopped, Dixie had the last words.

"So Sammy be careful, remember what I've told you," he said.

It was obvious that whatever they had been talking about it wasn't going to continue whilst I was present. However, when Dixie had gone, granda did seem concerned and he told me why Dixie had called.

"Dixie saw Blanco on Elwick Road and Blanco told him that George had threatened him, told him not to come back to the gardens. Blanco has been to the police, accused George Clarke of burning him out and threatening him. Dixie has a lot of sympathy for Blanco. He thinks we should be telling him to come back. He thinks we should be calling a club meeting to discuss the matter. Even thinks we should be discussing removing George Clarke from the gardens. I told Dixie that Blanco was cheating but I don't think he believed me. I think, he thinks we are now on George Clarke's side and I feel as if I've let him down. Trouble is son I know George didn't burn Blanco out. The fire officer and the policeman at the fire both agreed it was a spark from the bonfire that caused the fire. In addition, if George has threatened Blanco there are no witnesses. Dixie listened when I told him about how Blanco was cheating but he wouldn't accept it. Remember he is the chairman of the basketing committee; it's all he's got left, and if we were right, he would look a fool. He is also concerned that all the good lofts are disappearing and he thinks we are next. I don't agree with him. I don't think anyone would be silly enough to burn us out. David's in a home and Blanco's loft was an accident. I don't think we should worry but I am concerned about Dixie, he shouldn't be going around making accusations about George."

It was frightening to hear that Dixie shared my worries and even granda's words of reassurance didn't calm my fears.

When father arrived at the garden granda told him Dixie's story and went on to say, "Dixie also told me that the young birds we bred out of Pincher's channel hen with Huwey are in George Clarke's loft."

This information shocked me. It meant our bloodstock was returning to the gardens to race against us. Naively, I had thought that when we sold the birds we'd never see them again.

"We kept the first pair and Pincher took the second," granda continued. "They must have died in the fire but we took one more round of youngins and sold them. Well Dixie tells me that the lad from Sunderland, Boldon Colliery club, who bought the pair of youngins, did so for

George Clarke. Mind you, he paid enough for them. Dixie reckons the birds, although too young to fly this year, have been rung and will fly next year. They were rung in the Boldon club and have been registered with the Union but they've already been transferred to George."

Father sighed.

"I suppose we shouldn't be surprised," he said, "we knew the money men would be buying the best and that's all they're doing. Perhaps we were naïve to think that George and his buddies wouldn't get their hands on them. I am worried about the loft though, are you sure Blanco's loft was an accident?"

Granda nodded.

"Son I know for a fact that George Clarke had nothing to do with Blanco's loft burning. I saw sparks blow onto the roof of the loft, it was definitely an accident."

Talk of Huwey's youngins interested me and I went into the loft. The pair of youngins that Huwey and Pincher's hen had produced were progressing well. The birds had matured and granda was about to start their training. Outside our garden, we never talked about the birds although there was little doubt that everyone knew of their existence. When the young bird racing started their chances to prove themselves would come. We still had eight inland old bird races and three channel races to complete before we would see what they could do. The next race for the old birds was from Peterborough a distance of about two hundred miles. Granda had already selected the birds for the race and he and father spent most of that Sunday morning discussing them. They also discussed whether Huwey would fly the channel again. I think granda was reluctant to send him. The bird had been a good and faithful servant to the loft and it would be a disaster to lose him.

When racing, the risk of losing birds is always present. Pigeons some time just get lost and never returned home. Occasionally days after a race, flown down and in a sorry state, pigeons would return. These birds would now always carry the stigma of being unreliable and possibly would not be raced again. Sometimes, sadly, a fancier would receive a ring in an envelope through the post. Obviously, someone had found a dead bird, taken the time to remove the ring, find out who the owner was, and return it. At least when this happened the owner knew that his pigeon was dead. Quite often the birds just disappeared. Hawks took some of the pigeons. Some times pigeons returned with shotgun pellets in them and the stories of Frenchmen shooting at them seemed to have some credibility. Overhead electrical cables also claimed some pigeons. Occasionally we had pigeons return from races with terrible injuries, lost legs, crops sliced open, keel or chest bones broken, usually this was the result of the birds hitting the wires. Granda and his needle and thread could usually repair most of the damage. Of course, a bird with damage that was more serious, a broken wing, or the loss of the ring leg meant that the bird was no good to us. If they returned in that condition usually, they were killed. Quite often, if this were the case, fanciers, in an attempt to save money, would try to get the finder to dispose of the bird.

Channel races were notorious for losing birds. The channel could be a very dangerous place. The winds and squalls could force a bird off its flight path and stories were told of birds turning up in different parts of the world. Stories also appeared in the papers about birds hitching lifts on cross channel ferries and cargo ships. How true these stories were I am unsure. The local paper liked pigeon stories and once reported on a bird being found in South America. The story suggested the bird had flown there, which was rubbish. The bird had obviously landed on a cargo ship and a friendly seaman must have been feeding it. Then when they had reached South America, the bird must have taken off and landed in someone's loft. I always thought the bird was fortunate not to have been eaten.

There were also stories about certain unscrupulous fanciers who kept birds when they were lost and dropped into their lofts for water. If the bird looked like a good bird, it was possible for someone to keep the bird and breed from it. Occasionally, years after being lost, birds would return to their lofts and this would always be the fancier's explanation for its absence. Of course, those birds were of no further use for racing. If the bird had been kept in a loft and had reared youngins there was always the possibility that it might return there.

The pigeon's homing instinct, despite theories about the sun, celestial navigation and landmarks, was then and still is a mystery. It is a fact that a pigeon can be sent hundreds of miles away from home, to a new race point and it will return. Our pigeons did go missing and we were no different from any of the other fanciers. We had our fair share of losses, it didn't matter how good they were, when they were racing, there were always dangers for the birds.

That Sunday I was bored and I left our garden and went to Blanco's garden. I suppose I was just being nosey but I had never had an opportunity to explore Blanco's garden. The loft had burned out, there was nothing left of it. As I looked at the remains, I was reminded of the time when granda had helped Blanco build it and I felt quite sorry. Blanco had never kept much in the garden. He had used some of the old doors left over from the loft to build a lean-to shed against the railings. The door was open and I went in. It was obvious that someone had beaten me to it. Everything had been turned over and there was absolutely nothing of value left inside. Outside, even Blanco's small vegetable patch had been emptied; the small leeks and beetroot that he had been growing had all disappeared. This was another feature of the new culture on the gardens. Thieving had never been a problem but over the past year, fanciers had started locking their sheds and their lofts. I felt sad that the trust, that had once existed, had gone.

The deputation arrived just as we were about to leave for our lunch and they stopped us outside our garden. Granda had spotted them marching towards us and had obviously decided not to use Saint Peter's gate. Dixie had clearly been around the lofts trying to gather support and now he, Billy, Mattie, Topper Brown and Donkey Smith stood in front of us looking very stern.

"Fuck it Sammy we'd like you to call a fuckin meeting of the fuckin club," Billy said.

"What for?" granda replied.

"We fuckin think Blanco should be allowed back into the fuckin club. We can't see that he's done anything fuckin wrong and fuckin really we should help him to re-build his fuckin loft."

The others all nodded in agreement.

"There is nothing stopping Blanco coming back," said granda.

"That fuckin George fuckin Clarke has fuckin told him he can't," replied Billy.

"No he hasn't, George can't tell anyone who can and cannot become members. If Blanco wants to rebuild then he can," replied granda.

"That's right Sammy," a voice said from behind them.

George, Rat Face and Jimmy the labourer now stood behind the men.

"Let me tell you all," George said, "I have not threatened Blanco and I did not torch his loft. If Blanco wants to come back tell him to come back. I'll even get his pigeons back for him."

George sounded sympathetic and genuine.

"He's afraid of you," replied Dixie.

"I can't help that," said George, "perhaps Blanco's afraid of what we'll find out if he does come back. Just you think back to when he was flying; he won some funny races with some funny birds. You must remember that Redford race when he won by an hour and other races when his birds wouldn't drop. I can't prove anything but Blanco's birds were out of step with all the other birds on the gardens. He had only been racing a short time and was winning good races. Something was stinking, I seem to remember you lads complaining, but if you're happy, well you tell him to come back."

"I don't want him back," said Rat Face and Jimmy the labourer nodded in agreement.

The two groups of men stood facing each other and granda stepped between them. Then looking at Dixie and Billy he said, "You heard what George said, if you want Blanco to come back you ask him."

"It would be better coming from you Sammy, after all you are the secretary of the club," said Donkey.

Granda thought about it then shaking his head replied, "I'm sorry I can't do that."

"Oh fuckin aye," said Billy, "so now you're fuckin one of fuckin George's men are you Sammy?"

Granda just continued shaking his head and slowly walked away.

I knew that news of the confrontation would soon spread around the gardens. It had sickened me; I knew how Blanco had cheated and how granda did not take sides. I remembered how he had tried to warn the members about mob flying and how they had ignored his warning. I knew how much he loved the club and tried to be fair to everyone and I knew how much Billy's comments had hurt him.

Chapter Thirty-Seven

It had been a bad week for the family and the week ahead, for me, looked no better. At home, the relationship between my mother and father was once again strained. My brother wasn't speaking to anyone and after school, he went straight to work at the scrap yard. I was worried about granda, the loft, the pigeons and Fay. I really wasn't looking forward to the next race and my interest in the gardens was dying. At the same time, I wasn't looking forward to Saturday night when I would have to take Fay to the cinema. At school, the headmaster's intervention had worked and the nasty rumours about me had stopped. However, my status amongst the boys at school had risen and older boys now said hello and patted me on the back. On the other hand, to the girls I was a leper, a person they stayed away from and I didn't know whether to be pleased or not.

I suppose, that week, of all my worries the only one I could do something about was the Fay situation. During the week, I met Fay twice and we walked on the moor. On the last occasion, I asked her if her mother knew about us and she shook her head.

"When I'm meeting you, I tell her I'm meeting my friends," she said.

"Well I think I should come to your house and meet your mother," I replied.

Fay looked horrified.

"When?" she asked.

I had thought this out and decided that I was fed up with hiding. If I was going to see Fay then I would do it in public. My plan was to first meet her mother and if she threw me out then I needn't mention it to my parents.

"Tonight," I replied boldly.

At first, Fay was against the idea but as we talked, she warmed to the suggestion and eventually we changed direction and headed towards her house.

As we walked up the back lane towards her back yard Fay said, "when you meet mother let her do all the talking."

I agreed and we entered her back yard.

I had never seen so many nappies. They hung in every space in the back yard but unfortunately one of the washing lines had snapped and one string of nappies lay on the concrete yard.

"Mother will go mad, the lines are always snapping," Fay said as she picked them up.

We had entered the yard through the back door, and having negotiating our way through the wet nappies had come across the broken line.

"She needs window sash cord it's stronger," I said. I must have appeared very knowledgeable as Fay looked at me and said, "do you have any?"

It was a silly question father had a shed full of the stuff.

"Well Yes," I replied.

"Could we have some?" Fay asked, "if you put up new washing lines for her she'll be dead pleased. Go and get it and I'll wait until you come back."

I ran home and in our back yard, I went into the shed and raided father's window sash collection. One parcel of sash cord was usually enough but to be on the safe side I took two. Then I ran back to Fay's back yard.

The nappies had gone and the yard was clear. Two figures stood at the kitchen door, I hesitated then approached them. I had never seen Fay's mother before and she was a big woman. She glared at me.

"Fay tells me you can put up new washing lines for us," she said.

It wasn't quite the conversation I'd planned to have with her but so what it was progress.

"Yes," I said.

"Let's see you then," she replied.

Fay stood at her side smiling at me. I felt like Sir Lancelot come to the rescue of the fair maiden. It was nothing of a job and I quickly used up the two parcels of sash cord. Fay's mother inspected the cord and seemed impressed.

"Brand new that should last some time," she said.

Proudly I just nodded.

"Fay tells me you and her are friends and you want to take her to the cinema."

The bluntness of her statement shocked me, and blushing I answered, "yes."

"Well that's a good job you've done for us and you seem to have a nice mother so you can."

I was delighted.

"But," she said taking hold of my jumper and dragging me towards her, "you touch her tits again and I'll cut your balls off."

That night, in her back yard, I actually kissed Fay goodnight. I walked home elated, that was the hardest part over I thought. I put off telling mother about Fay until her mood seemed to have improved. On the Thursday night, when I returned from school, I found her on her own.

"I'm taking Fay to the cinema on Saturday night," I said.

"That's nice," she replied.

For me it was just another lesson in life. In future if I thought I had a problem, maybe talking it through with someone may solve it. I didn't know that Fay's mother had already been to see mother and told her about her ultimatum.

The next race was from Peterborough a distance of about 200 miles and I went to the basketing on the Friday night. As the season wore on and the flight distances increased the number of birds being sent was dropping. This meant that the race basketing was usually completed a lot quicker. We took our pigeons to the clubhouse and I waited outside. A number of members were talking about the meeting that had been called for Sunday morning. I stood by the notice board and read the official notification of the meeting.

Full Club Meeting All Members Must Attend.

Sunday 1100 hrs in clubhouse.

Agenda.
1. Blanco.
2. Wednesday racing
3. National Race

S Baker
Secretary

Granda hadn't mentioned the forthcoming meeting and when he left the clubhouse he didn't talk to any of the men outside. As we passed them one of the new members asked, "what's all this about Sammy?"

"Come to the meeting and find out," granda replied.

I knew because he hadn't mentioned the meeting granda didn't want to talk about it, so I didn't ask any questions. However, when I was leaving the garden I said,

"Is it alright if I come to the meeting on Sunday?"
Granda smiled, "of course it is son," he replied.

On Saturday, for us, the Peterborough race was a disaster we weren't in the top ten places. Surprisingly one of the new members won the race then George, Tommy and Malcolm took all the other places. We didn't clock a bird in and I left the gardens early, this suited me, as I had to meet Fay at half past six. At home, I was surprised at how much interest mother took in my appearance. She insisted I put on my best suit. She had brushed it and ironed the trousers and it had recovered well from Pincher's wake.

I called at Fay's home at exactly half past six and she was ready and waiting for me. It was just as well I called because if I had arranged to meet her I wouldn't have recognised her. Her mother had helped her with her makeup and had lent her some clothes and stockings. She looked much older and, as we set off holding hands, I felt uncomfortable. When we turned the corner and were out of her mother's sight, she said, "you'd think you were taking mother to the pictures. She has insisted on making me up and dressing me. I feel like an old woman."

"I suppose my mother did the same," I replied.

Fay loved the cinema. We only had one bad moment and that was as we approached the cinema I realised the film, that was showing, was X rated. Fortunately, the girl selling the tickets just chewed her gum and handed us the tickets. I was pleased she never questioned our ages. During the film, I put my arm around Fay and she snuggled into me. I could feel her suspender pressing into my leg and I had to concentrate on the film to stop myself getting excited. We stayed like that for the duration of the film and when it was time to leave my whole arm was numb. The cinema lights came on and we stood for the national anthem. Then as we turned to go, I noticed a small pile of dust left on my seat. Pincher was certainly being scattered all over the place I thought. It was a lovely night and once again, in the safety of her back yard I kissed Fay good night. As I walked home thoughts of her suspenders were still running through my head.

Sunday morning, father and I set off for the gardens and arrived just before the meeting was due to start. Granda had set out the clubhouse and he sat, behind a table at the front, alongside George Clarke and Tommy Tippins. The clubhouse was full and some men even stood at the back. As I wasn't a member and not wanting to encourage any embarrassment for granda, I also stood at the back. At precisely eleven o'clock George called the meeting to order. I had noticed that a new gavel and striking block had been placed on the table and George lifted the gavel and hammered on the block.

"Quiet," he said and the room went silent.

"George was obviously used to chairing meetings. His tone of voice was authoritive and his attitude was positive.

"We've called this meeting," George said, "to clear the air. There have been some malicious rumours circulating about me and it's time they stopped. Hopefully this meeting will do just that, but it's also important that everyone has their say."

He stopped talking and glared at Dixie and his friends. Then he relaxed in his chair and said, "first item on the agenda, Blanco."

Dixie and a few of the old timers shuffled in their seats and now they stared at George. I thought there was really going to be a big argument. However, granda spoke up.

"I was approached to contact Blanco to see if he was coming back to the club," granda began and the tension in the room eased. "Well, I was reluctant to do that. As secretary of the club it's not my job to chase after fully grown men to find out what they're doing."

George Clarke was nodding like a toy dog I had seen on the back window shelf of a car.

"However," continued granda, "my visiting Blanco proved to be unnecessary. On Wednesday morning the council gardens department telephoned me and said they wanted to inspect the gardens. They'd heard about the two fires and about Pincher and they wanted to see the state of the site."

Everyone was now interested, one thing about granda he could tell a good story.

"Well two council officers came on Wednesday afternoon and I showed them round. They inspected everything, the fence, the water tap,

Pincher and Blanco's gardens and all your sites. One or two of you may be getting letters about the amount of pigeon muck you have stacked in your gardens. But apart from that they were happy and they're organising for Blanco's garden to be cleared."

"What the fuck's this got to do with fuckin Blanco coming back?" Billy chirped up.

George smashed the gavel onto the block and everyone jumped.

"You," shouted George pointing the gavel threateningly at Billy, "just wait; watch your manners, and stop that bloody swearing. All items will go through the chair and if you wish to make a comment raise your hand."

This procedure was new. When Dixie had been chairman anyone, at any time, could speak up. Now Billy looked sheepishly towards Dixie for support but Dixie just shrugged his shoulders.

Granda continued, "good question Billy, well when they were leaving one of them told me that Blanco had been into the Town Hall. He had handed in his notice for his garden and told them he had sold his birds to a lad in the Walker club. He was looking for a rebate on this years rent. The council man said he'd given him a rebate and he hadn't seemed upset."

Granda sat back and George said, "well done Sammy excellent work, any questions."

The room remained silent and granda, once again, had done a great job of defusing a situation.

"Okay then, let's have no more talk of threats or burnings. Blanco can do whatever he wants and I do not threaten people," said George glaring at the old timers in the front row. "Now, next item, I know very little about this item but the secretary here has received a note from a number of members asking that it be placed on the agenda. Who wishes to speak on the item?"

No one moved and the silence was deafening. George might not verbally threaten anyone but his manner certainly did.

Once again, granda's voice broke the silence, "I know a little about the item," he said, "perhaps I can start it off."

"I'll speak on the item Sammy," said Dixie.

Very slowly, Dixie got to his feet and turned to face the club members, whether he did this for effect or not it certainly impressed everyone. When he turned his back on George, it seemed to say "and you don't matter."

"A number of the lads are fed up with not winning," Dixie began and there were grunts of agreement from the front row, "every Saturday we see the same faces taking all the places," he continued. "The three big lofts are flooding the races with birds and we small lofts haven't got a chance. We can't afford to buy foreign birds or employ loft managers. We try to improve our bloodstock but don't have the money to introduce new stock and we can only see the situation getting worse. So we want to start a Wednesday race club. We are not too interested in the money; we joined this club for the sport and as our hobby. Some of the newer club members just see races as business and for us a lot of the enjoyment has gone out of the sport."

The front row clapped but the majority of members remained silent.

I was confused, if a Wednesday club was to be formed what was to stop the three big lofts from competing.

"We don't expect the club or the Fed to organise the races, we'll do that ourselves," Dixie was speaking again. "We'll still compete on a Saturday but the Wednesday races will be confined to ten birds per loft and any betting will be between members, just side bets. Entry money will be used for prizes, cups, plaques, and transport money. Now really we don't have to ask the club's permission to do this. We could say these are Wednesday training tosses but we don't work like that. We like everything above board, honest and out in the open." With that, Dixie sat down.

The final comment was obviously aimed at George and for a minute, he said nothing. Then obviously stuck for words said, "what's your opinion mister secretary?"

Granda got to his feet and once again all eyes were on him.

"Well," he began, "first of all, the club could not provide a basketing committee or a clock committee. A number of the members are working and just wouldn't be able to give the time. Then on a Wednesday, when your birds are due back, the club could not stop anyone from letting their birds out. In addition, you would have to organise your own transport, the Fed would not go to the expense of providing a vehicle. And there are probably a few other things but if you're willing to accept them then I can see no problem."

"We agree with all you've said Sammy," Dixie replied, "however, we would ask the members, who don't race on a Wednesday, to give us a break and if possible not let their birds out when our birds are racing."

"Wait a minute," George interrupted, "what you're creating here is a second division. Lofts competing on a Wednesday would be under no obligation to compete on a Saturday."

"Lofts aren't under any obligation to compete on a Saturday anyway," granda replied, "but if they don't they don't get any of the official prize money."

"Yes but the nomination money will go down," George replied.

One of the new members, Killer Kilpatrick now spoke up. In the short time he had been a member he had gained a reputation as a sensible, responsible member and the other members listened to him carefully.

"Mister Chairman, I work during the week and would not be participating in the Wednesday league."

Everyone was listening and it was obvious that the other members were trying to think of reasons for and against the proposal.

"But providing the members," Killer continued, "don't steal any of our sponsors or affect the Saturday racing in any way, I can see nothing wrong with the proposal."

In the room there was a sigh of relief, everyone seemed pleased that someone had given them a positive lead.

George Clarke seemed relieved that someone had given a lead and went into a huddle with granda. Everybody in the room started to talk and there was an air of excitement.

George smashed the gavel down onto the striker.

"We can see nothing wrong with the proposal does anyone want to speak against it," he said. No one did and George asked, "does anyone want to object to the proposal of forming the Wednesday league?"

No one spoke and no hands were raised.

"Next item on the agenda mister secretary," George said, and once again, granda stood up.

"This year the channel race from Beauvais has been well sponsored by a brewery and the federations throughout the country want to get together and make it a national race. It will mean you will have to pay to enter your birds into the national race but the prize money and the prizes will be very good. I will be putting the rules and all the information on the notice board. The race is due in ten weeks time, third last race for the old birds and I hope you'll all think about it."

With that granda sat down, George smashed his new gavel onto the striking block and announced,

"Meeting closed."

Back in our garden, as I could see nothing wrong with it, I asked father about the Wednesday league. He explained that in his opinion it was a poor attempt to go back to the old days. Pigeons racing on a Wednesday might not be fully recovered to race on a Saturday. So perhaps the best birds would not be entered. There was no prize money so the big lofts, not wanting to risk their birds, would not be entering. Betting between individual lofts, again in his opinion, was not a good idea; it was uncontrolled and could lead to fights. Transporting the birds in vans without proper conveyors, he said, was fraught with danger and from his comments I realised we would not be taking part in the Wednesday league. His final words really made me think,

"Son the new fanciers are here to stay. It's no good trying to hang on to the past. If we want to compete then we must bring our birds up to their standard. The Wednesday league is amateurish and the club has moved out of that arena. We are now racing for big money and the new lofts are professional, to survive we have to be as good as them. At the end of the day it is good news for pigeon racing but bad news for some of the fanciers and it's no good changing the rules just because you're losing."

His words surprised me, his attitude had changed and he was beginning to sound like George Clarke.

Chapter Thirty-Eight

Granda and father were really on the horns of a dilemma, not that I knew what a dilemma was but I heard granda say it. The big question for them was not the Wednesday league but should they send Huwey to the Beauvais race. It was about five hundred and twenty miles for the bird to fly and they talked about it for hours.

The racing season continued with races from Hitchin about 250 miles distance, then Hatfield 260 miles. In both of these races, we weren't in the first three places. The three big lofts took all the places. The Wednesday league was getting itself organised and they had arranged their first race for the following week. They had found a removal company that, for a reasonable price, would transport and liberate their birds and everyone was interested to see how it went. There had been a lot of discussion amongst the lofts, which had said they would not be competing. Dixie had asked them not to exercise their birds on a Wednesday. We had agreed but the three big lofts were adamant that they would continue; they said it was part of their training programmes. Rat Face and some of his friends said they would also be flying their birds but I suspected this was just out of spite.

A week after the council officers had inspected the gardens; a few members received letters instructing them, for health reasons, to remove the pigeon muck from their gardens. I was pleased when I heard that Rat Face was one of the recipients. His solution to his problem was to go to the allotments and try to sell it. We heard this from Uncle Peter and we had a good laugh at the responses he had received from the allotment holders. Uncle Peter took most of our muck but we also spread quite a lot of it on our rhubarb patch. The other pigeon fanciers usually bagged theirs and took it to the tip. Over the next week I was delighted to see Rat Face struggling with sacks of muck making his way to the tip.

My brother was still working for Malcolm Ash. In an attempt to persuade him to sack my brother Father had spoken to Malcolm. However, Malcolm would have none of it. He seemed to respect my brother and was very complimentary about the work he did. My mother, whilst not accepting the situation, tolerated it. It was now the end of May. My brother would finish school in July, and both my parents were encouraging him to look elsewhere for employment. One night he surprised us all when he returned from school with forms for my father to sign.

"It's a job I'm applying for," he announced.

Mother's face lit up with pride, a job that required parental permission certainly sounded respectable. However, until father arrived home, my brother would not enlighten us as to what the job was. On his return home father took one look at the forms and tore them up.

"Navy, son you can work in the scrap yard, I'll never sign forms for you to join the navy," he said.

The disappointment on mother's face was measurable. I wasn't sure if my brother would have really joined the navy but the forms did get him approval for his scrap yard job. However, his success did reflect on me and I received strict lectures on my future. Father told me there was a job, as an apprentice joiner, just waiting for me with his company. Unfortunately, this information did not inspire me. Mother started talking to me about professional jobs and every day she changed her mind, a solicitor on Monday, and a policeman on Tuesday, Wednesday a council official. However, I still had two years at school before I had to make a decision and kept putting her off. I knew that her disappointment in my brother would directly affect me.

I had become a regular caller at Fay's house and as I got to know her mother, she didn't appear quite so frightening. Infact I got on quite well with her. I loved to watch Fay with her younger sisters and brothers. In the house, she was so confident and capable and yet outside she was insecure and unsure of herself. The more I saw of her the more I liked her. Her brothers and sisters now treated me like one of the family and regularly we baby-sat giving her mother time to go to bingo.

"No hanky panky," she'd say as she left the house.

There wasn't a lot of opportunity for hanky panky with five youngsters running round the house.

Granda was still unsure about sending Huwey to the Beauvais race but he had started training him up.

"We'll wait and see," he said, "but just to be on the safe side we'll make sure he's fit."

It seemed sensible enough to me. Granda was also unsure about continuing to breed from Huwey and Pincher's channel hen and the other pairs we had set up in the new stock loft. He had made quite a lot of money from selling eggs from the six breeding pairs. In addition, the men who had placed orders with Pincher for the next year were pestering granda to know if they would still get their youngins or their eggs. Father was really up for it.

"If we're not making money from racing we should be making money from selling," he said.

However, our success was not to everyone's liking. George Clarke, Malcolm and Tommy Tippins were also selling birds. Most of them were being bred through Belgium Blues and other channel winners, which they had bought. However, the local appeal of Huwey and Pincher's hen always brought the local fanciers to our loft first.

George Clarke was very interested to know if granda was entering Huwey for the Beauvais race. He pestered granda to enter the bird and one day he admitted to granda that he would be placing a bet on Huwey winning. It was the first time we had heard of side bets being taken on other fancier's pigeons. When we were discussing it granda said, "I suppose it was inevitable, their commitment to the sport is based purely on profit and making money."

The weeks continued to pass with races from Redford, about 325 miles, then the first channel race from Lillers, 440 miles. We weren't placed in the Redford race but we did have a secret weapon for the Lillers race. Granda had been training the chequered cock, one of Huwey's youngins, the bird that last year, had won the Hatfield young bird race. Of course, we had told no one. Since we'd heard about the side betting we no longer discussed our birds in public. We saw this as just another dilution of the friendship and camaraderie that use to exist on the gardens. Granda and father still had their contacts among the lorry drivers at work and they took the birds away for training chucks. Huwey and his youngin had been getting special training. They had been taken away in individual pannier baskets, and had been liberated on their own. 'One uppers' granda called these chucks. He believed it made the birds independent, made them fly on their own, and made them make their own decisions. Both of the pigeons had performed well in these chucks and we were pleased with them.

At the race basketing on the Thursday night before the Lillers race, no one noticed the chequered cock. The atmosphere in the clubhouse was cold and many of the old timers didn't enter pigeons. However, the three big lofts made up for them, each of the lofts entered ten birds.
"It's definitely quantity not quality in those lofts," father said.
Granda disagreed, "you're wrong son, those pigeons are good birds. They have been training hard don't underestimate them. The lofts need winners especially channel winners, believe me they'll be trying hard."
His words sent a shiver down my spine; the days when everyone knew the special pigeons on the gardens had gone. All the fanciers use to know the individual personalities of certain birds and the weather conditions those birds liked, and during basketing, men would always make comments. That had gone; race basketing was now carried out as quickly as possible and usually in silence. Pincher was also a big loss, his knowledge of everyone's birds and his shouting and identifying them use to keep everyone updated. Now on race days no one could identify the pigeons or their owners.

Lillers was a good race. The birds returned the same day. We didn't win; Huwey's youngin was third on the gardens. Tommy Tippins had two pigeons that beat him home. We were still pleased with the third place. Any place in the first ten, from a channel race, for a one-year-old bird was very good and we had high hopes for his future. Of course, Tommy was delighted to take first and second places it was quite an achievement. However, his success did not please the old timers, for them it was just another sign of the times.

The Wednesday league was going reasonably well but there was friction developing. Rat Face and his friends would persist in letting their birds out just as the racing birds were returning. There was no doubt that it was done on purpose and some of the members had nearly come to blows over it. Granda tried his best to keep the peace but slowly the old friendly atmosphere was going. Nevertheless, the weeks passed and eventually July arrived. My brother left school and went to work full time for Malcolm in the scrap yard, and we entered Huwey in the national race from Beauvais.

Granda had prepared him well. He'd trained him and fed him on his secret formulae. Huwey looked marvellous, his feathers were blooming, his eyes were clear and he strutted around the loft. To this day, I still believe he knew what was coming; he was like a prizefighter just before the fight. At the race basketing on the Thursday night a lot of the old atmosphere did return. The three Baker men assembled in the garden and granda caught Huwey. He held him in his hands and looked into the bird's eyes. I swear the bird smiled at him. It certainly didn't struggle, its head went up and it cooed. For the few minutes that granda held the bird father and I no longer existed, it was just granda and his friend. He kissed the bird; it waggled its tail feathers, lifted them and creamy white excreta shot out of its bottom.
"Look at that," granda said, "solid, not green or slimy, healthy shite you can't beat it."

All three of us escorted Huwey to the clubhouse and the basketing. Most of the club members had assembled outside the clubhouse and Dixie greeted us,

"Is he fit Sammy?" he asked reverently.

"As fit as he'll ever be," granda replied.

"Weather forecast suits him Sammy; it'll be a hard day," said Mattie Walker.

It was like the old days, everyone was interested. There were 150 birds entered from the gardens. All the new lofts had entered birds, which was good, and the three big lofts had entered ten birds each. Beauvais was a race of 520 miles the longest race of the season. It was a lot to ask of any pigeon and all the birds entered were treated with respect.

"Fully nominated?" George Clarke asked granda and granda nodded. "Well good luck to him Sammy," he said, "he's got a lot of my money riding on him."

I wished he hadn't said it. Somehow, for me, someone else betting on our bird and possibly making money from us diluted the integrity of the bird.

It was a great night and just like old times we stood outside the clubhouse talking. Everyone was excited and looking forward to Saturday. However, as we left the gardens, for father and me, the night was spoilt. Granda had gone through Saint Peter's gate and father and I made our way out of the top gates. As we left the gardens, we noticed some one standing in the bushes. The figure looked familiar and we saw his face as he lit a cigarette.

"That's David," father said, "someone said he was being allowed home but I thought he'd have to stay away from here."

David saw us, moved out of the bushes, and set off up the West Road walking away from us. Father pulled the gates together and fastened the padlock.

"Let's just hope he stays out of the gardens," he said. However, I was worried and I could tell he was.

"Don't tell your granda, we don't want to worry him," he said.

Then he rattled the chain checking that the gates were securely locked.

Chapter Thirty-Nine

Fay was very understanding about the pigeons and, on Saturday nights, if I was late she never objected. On the Saturday morning of the Beauvais race, father and I were talking.

"That's the type of woman you want," father said, "a good woman must be able to understand her man's hobbies. Look at your granny she helps granda and never nags him."

Mother had been listening and interrupted him, "Yes and she's never had a holiday. She never sees him; he's always at the bloody garden. He only talks about the pigeons and the club. She's spent her whole married life answering telephone calls and giving liberation times to pigeon men. She's not a wife she's a slave."

We were taken aback at the passion of her outburst.

"She's had a good life," father replied defensively, "my dad's treated her well. He's always provided well for her and for his family."

"And for his pigeons," mother shot back at him. "Just think how much money has he's wasted on them birds. They could have had holidays, bought a bigger house even a car. Once a year she goes to the presentation, apart from that she never goes out, bloody Pincher's cremation was a big event for her."

I think father realised that he wasn't going to win the argument and we left the flat as quickly as possible.

It was a clear day, a good day for a channel race although there was a North-Easterly wind blowing.

"Wind will be on their noses today," granda said when we met him at the garden, "but, it's Huwey's type of day. They're up at six o'clock, should take them about eleven hours. It's going to be a long day."

It was a long day. We cleaned the loft, scattered fresh sand, messed around in the vegetable patch, and cleaned the shed. Granda even opened his wood store and checked his fittings.

"Get some fish and chips," he said.

It was after two o'clock, we were getting hungry and fish and chips sounded great to me. Father gave me five shillings and I set off along the path back to the West Road gates. I knew there was a good chip shop there and my mouth started to water. The main gates were open so I walked through them and out of the gardens.

"Oih," a voice said.

I turned and looked towards the bushes and there stood David. I was stunned I did not want to be associated with him and was reluctant to acknowledge him.

"Oih," he repeated, beckoning me to go over to him. I looked around and there was no one else about. Deep down I suppose I was frightened of David. He was bigger than me and his disability frightened me. Slowly I walked over to him and as I approached, he twisted his face as if he was going to cry and said, "I not fire the pigeons." He seemed to be pleading with me. "I like the pigeons I never burn them," he whispered. Then he offered me a cigarette.

"I don't smoke," I said.

David nodded, pushed the cigarettes back into his pocket and moved away from me I just stood mesmerized. When he reached the corner, he turned and once again said, "I not fire the pigeons."

I knew he was telling the truth and I felt so very sorry for him. Pincher was not the only victim of whoever had fired his loft David was also suffering.

I walked to the fish shop, bought fish and chips and a bottle of cream soda then walked back to the garden. It really was a feast and sitting in the garden, we ate the food and swigged soda cream from the bottle. I didn't mention David to granda or father, there just seemed to be very little point. There was nothing they could do anyway and I believed David didn't pose a threat to the lofts. Whoever had burned Pincher out was still on the gardens and probably we would never find out who it was.

We waited, the hands on the church clock reached five o'clock and the atmosphere was rising. The gardens were silent but when I stood on the gantry and looked out over the lofts, I could see men standing on their gantries just staring into the Tyne valley. Half expecting to see Pincher in his lookout position I glanced towards his garden. There was nothing there just an open space where, for years, his loft had stood. The hands of the clock slowly crept round to half past five then six o'clock.

"Where is he Sammy?" someone shouted.

"Not far away," granda shouted back.

My stomach was turning over. I knew Huwey would never let us down but I wished he would just fly out of the valley. At half past six, granda broke the silence.

"Well it's going to be a long night," he said, "there's no birds back and I'm starting to worry."

I remembered I had arranged to meet Fay at half past seven but somehow I knew that I wouldn't make it.

"Weather must have been bad in the channel," father said.

We waited, at half past seven someone shouted,

"Bird coming out of the valley."

The gardens came to life everyone was on their gantries, straining their eyes, staring into the valley. It was still silent but I could feel the electricity in the air.

"It's for the gardens," granda said.

The black spot that everyone was watching was slowly getting bigger and I could feel my heart beating.

"Let it be Huwey, please let it be Huwey," I prayed.

"It's well flown down," father said.

And he was right; the pigeon was flying low with long wing beats.

"It's not Huwey," granda said.

I nearly started to cry.

"It's a dark chequer; it's for one of the lofts at the back."

Again, he was right.

The bird flew straight over our loft and we watched it pass us. None of the fanciers rattled a corn tin; there was a sense of reverence across the gardens. The usual rattling of corn tins and shouting just seemed disrespectful to the bird. Besides, it was unnecessary. The bird knew exactly where it was going.

"That bird's had enough," granda said and I noticed the sadness in his voice.

"Fully nominated, one for George Clarke," a voice rang out across the gardens.

"Well he'll be happy," said granda.

To me it seemed like it was all over. The important thing now was for Huwey to come home and in silence, we waited. At eight o'clock, another black dot appeared in the Tyne valley and my heart leapt, this must be Huwey I thought. Again the bird was struggling and we watched as once again it approached us then flew over our loft and landed somewhere at the back.

"That's one for Killer Kilpatrick he reckons it's knackered," the same voice rang out across the gardens and then silence returned.

"This is going to be a disaster," granda said, "I should never have sent Huwey. I was being greedy the bird didn't deserve this."

Once again, I nearly cried.

"Don't be so stupid dad," father said, "Huwey can do it easily, alright he's not won but he'll be back. Just calm down and wait."

We waited and the sky turned grey then dark grey. Then just as the sun was about to disappear a voice rang out.

"One bird over the church."

My heart leapt, this had to be Huwey it just had to be.

"It's a skemmy, it's for the church," a second voice replied.

Silently, holding the corn tin, granda stood alone on the gantry. He was staring at the church and he was silhouetted in the fading light. I felt so sorry for him, his friend and his best bird, a bird he had bred and reared was missing and there was nothing we could say. Father and I knew he didn't want to talk and we both turned away knowing there was nothing we could do.

We stayed until ten o'clock.

"Come on dad the bird's gone down for the night; he'll not fly in the dark. He'll be back first thing in the morning," father said.

"I'll just wait a little while longer son," granda replied.

"Dad, you're being silly, you know he'll be here in the morning. Go home get a nights sleep and we'll be back first thing. Huwey will be waiting for us you'll see."

"Just leave me a while son, you and the boy go home. I'll wait a little longer; I'm fine, I just want to be on my own." The tone of granda's voice told us he meant what he'd said. We both knew that he wanted us to go; he wanted to be on his own, he was mourning the loss of his bird.

Father and I walked home. When we left the gardens we checked that the gates were locked. I still didn't mention my meeting with David. At home, mother was waiting.

"You're in trouble young man," she said, "Fay called she waited for hours for you and she was upset."

I had forgotten all about Fay and now I felt guilty.

"I'll see her tomorrow night," I said and made my way to bed. It really had been a miserable end to the day, we had lost Huwey and now Fay was upset.

At six o'clock in the morning father stuck his head round the bedroom door.

"I'm leaving in five minutes, if you want to come with me you'll have to move yourself," he said.

I looked over at my brother's bed he never moved. I had not heard him come to bed but from the smell of stale beer, I knew he'd been drinking. I dressed and we left the house. Mother wasn't up and, very quietly, we closed the front door. The sun was just rising and the air was clear and fresh.

"He'll be back by now I'll bet on it," father said, as we walked along the West Road.

I enjoyed the peace and quiet of that Sunday morning but as we walked, I constantly scanned the sky looking for pigeons. At the gardens, we unlocked the gate and walked down the path. At the corner, Mattie Walker and Billy were standing talking.

"He's been here all night," Mattie said.

"Dad?" father asked.

"Aye Sammy," Mattie replied, "I left at eleven last night and returned at five. He was here when I left and still here when I returned."

Suddenly Billy pointed at the bushes opposite our loft. "What the fuck's that?" he said.

A little old woman with a pinny wrapped around her and with a parcel in her hands had suddenly appeared out of the bushes. It really was quite funny and Billy started to laugh.

"Oh no," father said, "it's my mother."

"Fuck me, where's she fuckin come from?" asked Billy.

We knew she had used Saint Peter's gate to get into the gardens.

"Don't know," replied father as we dashed off along the path to the garden.

Granny hadn't seen us and had beaten us into the garden and as we approached, we could hear her talking.

"Come on Sammy, this isn't doing you any good," her voice was breaking with emotion. "Huwey wouldn't want you to make yourself ill. If he's coming home he'll come irrespective of whether you're here or not."

"I should never have sent him," granda's voice came from behind the fence, "I got out of France unhurt but somehow I knew he wouldn't."

We pushed open the gate and entered the garden.

"Right Sammy Baker the boys are here now," granny said, "now, you're coming home with me. He's been here all night, a man of his age acting like a fool over a pigeon."

Granda just shook his head and followed her out of the garden.

All morning we stayed at the garden. We let the birds out and cleaned out the loft but all the time we were listening and watching for Huwey. Pigeons started to return and by midday, a few had found their way home. One hundred and fifty pigeons had left the gardens on the Thursday night and by midday we estimated that twenty had returned. This was when we knew that something had happened to Huwey. If twenty birds had made it Huwey, if he could, would have also made it.

"I wonder where he is," I asked father.

He just shrugged his shoulders.

We never received a ring in an envelope or a telephone call. No one ever contacted us to say they had found Huwey and after four days, we gave up hope of ever seeing him again. His loss had a dramatic effect upon granda. His interest in the birds seemed to wane, he slowed down and let father take the lead in making decisions in the loft. That week I visited the loft every night and quite often found him just staring into the valley and whilst he never said anything, I knew what he was looking for.

Fay wasn't as forgiving as granny. On that Saturday night we were supposed to be going for a walk and she had waited for two hours. Eventually she had gone to my house and spoke to mother. Mother, very kindly, had enlightened her on the facts about courting and marrying a pigeon man. Mother's stories had not impressed Fay and her understanding attitude had changed.

"If you want to be my boyfriend then you must meet me on time," that was all she said.

Funny thing was I did still want to be her boyfriend. Months earlier, I would have jumped at the opportunity to split up but now things had changed. Also months earlier she would not have given me an ultimatum; I had been telling her to be more confident and even this seemed to have backfired on me.

Chapter Forty

The loss of Huwey shocked everyone and after a few days the club members stopped asking granda if he'd returned. I suppose even they could see how much granda was hurting or perhaps George Clarke's pigeon, which had won the race, was the new hero. Which ever it was, I'm sure granda was relieved not to be constantly reminded of his loss.

Despite our loss, club life went on and there were still two races to go before the end of the old bird season. These races were from Hitchin about 250 miles and a final channel race from Lillers. The week after we lost Huwey, father started making decisions on the running of the loft. He stepped into granda's shoes and decided which pigeons would be entered for the Hitchin race and on the Friday night he basketed ten birds.

"Tens a lot," granda said.

"Hitchin's a good race point the birds are tired but they can do it," replied father.

I was quite surprised at his unsympathetic but positive attitude.

"What about Lillers?" granda asked.

"Huwey's youngin's going," replied father very abruptly. "We'll show these big lads who's got the best pigeons. Since the last Lillers race that chequered cock has been rested, now he's fit and ready to fly again. There's no point in being sentimental. We know Huwey's had an accident, someone's shot him, he's hit the wires, or he's a prisoner in a strange loft. It doesn't matter, Huwey's gone, we need a replacement and we know his son can do it."

I was surprised that granda did not object. However, I think he knew it made sense, no longer were we keeping the pigeons as pets. They were racing pigeons. Racing the birds was our sport and we needed to win. Father had decided that we would continue to sell youngins and eggs, and for our breeding programme, we needed winners and our attitudes were hardening and changing.

For us the Hitchin race was a great success and once again, the Baker loft won. A red hen father had been watching came through for us. Killer Kilpatrick was second and George Clarke was third. Once again, the Bakers name was at the top on the results sheet and our birds were gaining in reputation and credibility. On the Thursday night before the Lillers race, we took the chequered cock and two other pigeons to be race basketed. Dixie spotted the bird.

"That's Huwey's off spring," he said and we nodded. "Third in the last Lillers," he continued and once again, we nodded.

"Looks in good condition Sammy," he said as he held the bird ready to be race rung, "he'll fly Lillers no problem."

George Clarke was supervising the basketing and he never took his eyes off the bird. Rat Face was just handing in his pannier basket, containing one bird, and he also stared at the bird.

"Bloodstock's still there Sammy," Dixie continued, "old Huwey left you a great legacy, takes years to breed pigeons of that calibre."

"I wish he wouldn't talk like that in front of certain people," father said as we left the clubhouse. "It can make other people jealous. Yes we have to have winners but the way things are at the moment I don't like showing our birds off in front of certain people."

Dixie was right, the chequered cock flew Lillers no problem. He arrived back at five o'clock on the Saturday night, was the first bird on the gardens, and was first in the Federation. We were delighted but still Huwey's loss hung over us. Granda kept saying he had been greedy to send Huwey and no matter how many times he was told not to be so silly he still moped around the garden. However, father was inspired by his success and his commitment to the pigeons became even greater. On the Sunday night after the Lillers race, I walked with him to the gardens and he was full of it. He had big ideas and explained that next year we would start a proper breeding programme. We would use all Huwey's youngins and sell more birds. The business side of the sport had certainly taken hold of him. The gardens were quiet and we were surprised when we didn't find granda there. After we had cleaned out the loft, fed and watered the birds we made our way down to his house. Granny answered our knock on the door.

"Come in son," she said, "you're father's tired he's just been having a lie down."

I could see by the look on my father's face that he was worried. It was the first time I had ever heard of granda having a lie down. To me he had always appeared fit and healthy. However, after a short while granda, looking better, joined us in the living room. We had spent quite a while cleaning the loft and it was getting late. Outside it was dark and granny was busy making some supper for us. Father still bursting with pride was discussing the forth-coming young bird season with granda and I was watching the television.

The knock on the door sounded ominous and it brought silence to the house. Granda got up and walked along the passageway to the front door. Father and I, and granny, still in the kitchen, were all straining our ears to hear what was being said. We heard a male voice and the word "fire" and that was enough for all of us. Granny and father collided as they ran towards the front door. I reluctantly and full of dread followed them. I didn't want to hear bad news and I knew fine well that this was bad news.

"There's another fire on the gardens," granda said, "it could be our loft."

His words were like a blow to my stomach. Granny grasped her pinny and pulled it up to her face. Father pushed past granda and the policeman and started running down the front garden path and then along the street towards the gardens. Granda was about to follow him when granny stopped him.

"Sammy put your coat on, what's done is done. You need to look after yourself put your coat on."

Granda stopped and slowly took down his overcoat from the peg behind the door and put the coat on.

"Come on son," he said to me putting his arm around me.

We could see the glow from the fire as we hurried along Elwick Road. We cut through the allotments and slipped through Saint Peter's gate. The little gate was wide open and it was obvious that father had also used this route. We didn't try to hide the existence of the little gate and the small group of spectators watching our loft burn didn't seem surprised to see us emerge from the bushes. The fire brigade had just arrived and one of their hoses was laid along the path and into our garden. I couldn't see father and glanced back towards granda. He stood, frozen to the spot staring at the fencing and by the light of the fire; I could see the look of sheer horror on his face. I followed his gaze and when I saw the pigeon heads impaled on the points of the fencing, my eyes filled with tears. Dixie and some of the other club members were watching the fire and as they moved away from us. I think they sensed the feeling of utter despair and anger that was growing within us and realised that nothing they could say or do would ever console us.

Granda moved forward but tripped over the fire hose and fell forward into the mud. I raced forward and tried to lift him but he was too heavy for me. He didn't seem capable of helping himself and seemed to have lost the will to get up. He just lay there and panicking I pulled frantically at his overcoat.

"We'll get him son," one of the firemen said and two of them lifted him clear of the mud. They carried him along to the clubhouse and I followed. Once inside they sat him on a chair. He said nothing but instead just stared at the floor. I was at a loss; I didn't know what to do and just wished my father were there. Dixie came into the clubhouse.

"The police have got your dad," he said looking at me.

I was shocked.

"When he saw the loft on fire and the pigeons heads he went mad, charged off looking for who ever had done it. I think they're just holding him in case he hurts someone."

Dixie put his arm around me and I felt about four years old then suddenly granda's voice broke the silence.

"Did any of the birds get out?" he whispered.

Dixie just shook his head.

I know it was stupid but I had to go back to look at the loft. I really could not believe that it was all over. Years of breeding, cleaning, feeding, watering, laughing, and cheering had all gone. I could not understand the loss and as I walked towards the smouldering remains I really expected to see our loft still standing. Billy and Mattie had found a sack and started removing the pigeon's heads from the fencing. I walked passed them and stared at the loft. Only the burned out framework remained and as I looked at it, I was reminded of Pincher hanging in the sunset. Someone put a hand on my shoulder and I looked up and saw the tear stained face of my father.

"It's all over," he whispered.

That Sunday night was the worst night of my life. There was nothing left for us to salvage and after an hour we made our way back to granda's house. When we arrived granny said nothing. From our faces, she obviously knew that it was the worst possible news. Inside the three of us sat, in silence, in the living room. Eventually father spoke, "police have arrested David; they found him outside the gates with matches in his pocket. I would have killed him but they stopped me."

Granda and I looked at him.

"David never did that," said granda, "those birds were killed because they were the best. They were killed by someone who was jealous, someone who knew he could never beat us, David could never have handled those birds."

Chapter Forty-One

For the next week, thoughts of Pincher and what he had done when his loft had been burned down filled my head. However, father was quick to dispel my fears.

"Don't worry about you're granda son," he said, "Sammy Baker never gives in; he would never do anything as stupid as Pincher. Pincher had nothing left; granda has your granny and us. Believe me granda would never kill himself."

That week was the first week of the school summer holidays and I visited granda every night. He didn't say much and I knew how much he was hurting. On the Friday night, whilst I was there, the clock committee arrived to set the clocks for the first young bird race. It was from Selby and they were all excited. However, none of them mentioned granda's loss. I really think they didn't know what to say to him but as they were leaving Killer Kilpatrick said,

"We'll all help you rebuild Sammy."

"No need Killer but thanks for the offer, I appreciate it," granda replied, "the whole family's going to help. We'll start tomorrow."

This was news to me. We had discussed rebuilding but no dates had been set and granda's heart hadn't seemed to be in it. Later father arrived and granda told him of his decision. He explained that the owner of the building company where he use to work had called and told him that the company would provide all the materials needed to rebuild the loft.

"I thought as much," father replied, "he stopped me at work the other day and was asking questions about the fire. Seemingly he's in the same private club as George Clarke and they'd been talking."

Granda nodded and said, "I thought that tomorrow, if you're willing, you, Peter and the boy could start clearing the site. It'll also give us an opportunity to see the first young bird race."

That Saturday morning we started to rebuild. We cleared the site of all the charred timbers and stacked them outside the garden. Father and granda measured and discussed the size of the new loft and how many compartments it should have. Our endeavours created a lot of interest and a number of the fanciers called in. George Clarke came and shook granda's hand. "Any bird in my loft is yours Sammy," he said, "just come round, look the birds over and take your pick. I'll give you a pair to start you off. Just tell me when you're coming and I'll prepare everything for you."

"He means he'll hide Huwey's pair of youngins," granda said when George had left.

We stopped work to watch the arrival of the young birds from Selby. It was pure comedy. The young birds flooded in; men shouted and rattled their corn tins. The young birds were full of flying and obviously weren't tired. They circled the gardens and swooped along the fronts of the lofts. It was a new experience for us not to be amongst it. We waited until the birds had settled and the winners were in then, where the new loft would be constructed, we raked the ground flat. Whilst the fire had completely consumed the loft, the firemen had managed to save our sheds so we still had baskets and our clocks. Granda and father calculated the amount of wood, bricks, cement, felt and other materials we would need to complete the rebuild. Father agreed to see the owner of the company first thing on Monday morning and, quite pleased with our days work we left the gardens.

Whilst granda had worked alongside us, I knew that he was not fully committed to the work. I knew, that he knew, we could never replace what he had lost. I also thought that something else was wrong. He was slow and his breathing was heavy. However, I didn't mention it to anyone. I also did not like to mention restocking the loft. I knew that because we never sold pigeons granda's bloodstock would be difficult to re-establish. However, I was impressed with the interest and dedication father was putting into rebuilding. He was already contacting fanciers in other clubs, who at one time or another had bought pigeons from us. They were all keen for granda to visit them and look at their pigeons. It was only now that I realised the amount of respect granda had throughout the North East pigeon fancying community. Being off school, I had time on my hands and promised to accompany granda if he wished to visit any of the lofts.

The lorry delivering the building materials arrived on the Thursday afternoon. Fortunately, the driver was able to back his vehicle through the main gates off the West Road and down to our garden. Granda inspected the materials and was pleased with them. As I stacked the timber against the shed, he said, "we can do a good job with this lot. I think it should take about two weeks to get the job done."

Granda was right, the following week Uncle Peter and father were on their summer holidays and on the Monday morning, they started work. As usual, I was their labourer but I loved to watch them working. They were skilled men and they worked to a high standard. Of course, granda supervised the job. I think, for him, it was like being back at work and every morning he turned up in his overalls with his lunch box and his paper. I, as the labourer, was in great demand and spent the days carrying and fetching for the three men. The building work caused great interest amongst the other club members and we regularly had spectators. The new loft was bigger and when completed was a credit to the skills of the three men. They had incorporated many of the new ideas and we had blinds installed at the windows and insulation in the walls and roof. We had also installed our own security systems. Metal bars were fitted on the windows and the lock on the front doors was a huge metal bar, which was held in position with bolts and then secured with a padlock. I enjoyed the work but the loft never felt the same. The smells and characteristics of the old loft were missing. When it was completed, granda and father set about restocking it. I was losing interest. Fay was demanding more of my time and I was missing my friends. I suppose over the following weeks, because we were not racing pigeons, I drifted away from the gardens.

The summer holidays ended and I returned to school. The racing season ended and it was only then that I realised I had not seen granda for a few weeks. One Friday night, feeling very guilty, I visited my grandparents. What I found shocked me. The fit old man that I had known wasn't there; a skinny old man who was fighting for every breath had replaced him. He was delighted to see me and told me all about the new pigeons, which he had been given. Granny stood behind him shaking her head.

"The doctor thinks this might be something to do with the dammed pigeons, something to do with the dust and the droppings," she said.

Granda as usual ignored her and we didn't discuss his condition. Later at home, I questioned my father about him.

"We didn't like to tell you son. He is in a bad way. We know how much you think of your granda. We were wrong, we should have warned you," he said.

After that visit I made sure I went to see him every other day. It was heart breaking to see him deteriorating. He still managed to walk to the gardens but it took him ages to get there.

One Saturday morning in December, I visited my grandparent's home and found my granny, standing at the front door, very distressed.

"Just in time son," she said, "I need someone to help me lift granda back into bed. He's been leaning over and fallen out of the bed."

I ran up the stairs to the bedroom and found a skeleton dressed in pyjamas lying alongside the bed. I stared at him in disbelief but his eyes said it all. The eyes that had been so proud and positive now pleaded for help. I bent down and picked him up. I couldn't believe how light he was and I could easily hold him in my arms. Granny fussed around and straightened the sheets and then I laid him on the bed.

"Thanks son," he said, his voice was barely audible.

I pulled a chair alongside the bed and sat beside him. I felt so guilty; I had never seen real illness and I'd had no idea how ill he really was. He fell asleep but I stayed, somehow I knew he wanted me to stay. He didn't sleep for long and when he opened his eyes, he smiled at me.

"I need to tell you something," he said.

What I expected to hear I don't know but his next words surprised me.

"I set fire to Blanco's loft."

Granda spoke the words softly then looked at me as if he expected me to comment. I don't know what he expected me to say but I was shocked. I would never have believed granda capable of carrying out a malicious act against anyone.

"I had to," granda started talking again and I leaned closer to hear. "I had to stop him son, he was a cheat. He had used me and abused my friendship and I knew he had always intended to cheat us. Right from the start, he must have been planning to cheat and he wouldn't have stopped. But I also did it to protect him. Believe me if George Clarke, Tommy Tippins or Malcolm Ash had found out what he was doing they would have really hurt him. Believe me they are hard men, not the type of men you cheat on."

Granda was gasping for air and he closed his eyes.

"You did the right thing granda," I said.

"Remember that night, the night of Pincher's wake." Granda was struggling to speak again. "Well when you were all distracted with the beer and the tripe. I slipped into Blanco's garden; I stuck newspaper under the loft and lit it. I came out and shouted for help then I went back in, opened the loft doors, and let the birds out. The whole thing went up very quickly. I made sure none of his birds were harmed, I hope God will forgive me."

He stopped talking and I could think of nothing to say. Finally, he broke the silence.

"I should never have sent Huwey to that channel race son." The words came out in gasps and he stopped to regain his breath.

"We all thought it was the right thing to do granda. Huwey must have had an accident otherwise he'd have won that race," I said.

It was all I could think of to say. My chest was tight and the lump that was forming in my throat was choking me. However, I knew he wanted to talk.

"Did you call him Huwey after your father?" I asked. Granda's father, my great grandfather, had been called Samuel Hughie Baker and I had always assumed he had used the name as a sign of affection.

Granda smiled, "No I didn't son, one race day your granny was ill and I was late getting to the gardens. It didn't matter because your father was there and he would have timed in."

Once again, he stopped talking and gasped for air then after a while, he continued the story.

"Well, as I was approaching the gardens, the pigeons were just arriving and I could hear all the fanciers shouting to attract their bird's attention. They were all shouting the same thing 'how way, how way' but from a distance, with their Geordie accents, it sounded like Huwey, Huwey. That day I had the idea that if I ever have a good winning pigeon I would call it Huwey. That way everyone on the gardens would be calling for my bird."

He gasped and smiled at me.

"I'll never see the gardens again son," he said.

"You will," I replied.

Then I realised what a stupid thing I had said. I knew he would never see the gardens again. Tears rolling down my cheeks I took his bony hand and held it.

"You'll not forget me son will you?" granda said then he closed his eyes and fell asleep.

When I left, he was still asleep and I never got to say goodbye to him, or to answer his question. He died the next day. His final question had hurt me, how could I ever forget him and how could he ever think I would forget him. Sammy Baker was the greatest man I had ever known and besides I was named after him, my name is also Sammy Baker.

Chapter Forty-Two

I wish I could tell you that Huwey returned home, but he never did. I wish I could tell you that I married Fay and we lived happily ever after, but I did not. Fay eventually married Fatty Turner and they have three children. I wish I could tell you that I got a professional job and pleased my mother but I didn't. Just like my granda and my father, I took up the offer of an apprenticeship and became a joiner and, just like them, I work for the same building company.

Much to my mother's disgust, for six years, my brother continued to work for Malcolm then he opened his own scrap yard. He now has three scrap yards and like a professional man goes to work in a suit. He drives his own car, owns his own house and has a private box at St James Park, Newcastle United's Football ground. Mother still thinks he is a criminal and even refused his offer to build her a new bungalow. I did get married. I married Killer Kilpatrick's daughter. We met at a pigeon club presentation night, not the type granda use to organise. When he died, many things changed. The presentation dinner and dance changed into a disco night and moved from the Co-op to the local workingmens club. Fortunately, my wife also loves the pigeons and often helps father and me. Unlike mother and Fay, she doesn't give me ultimatums about the birds and just like granny, she enjoys the sport. We have two children and my eldest son is called, yes, you guessed it, Sammy Baker.

We never found out who burned down our loft. The police were convinced it was David and unfortunately, he was sent back to the home. There were a number of people who, for various reasons, wanted us to stop racing and breeding. George Clarke, Tommy Tippins and Malcolm Ash's lofts became the most successful on the gardens and in the North East. Their birds were sought after and fanciers came from all over the country to buy from them. Following the burning down of our loft, the three big lofts dominated the racing in the club and the Federation. Then as new fanciers with more money joined the club, their supremacy was diluted and a degree of evenness was re-established.

Within the pigeon club, the Baker family did not take up any more responsible positions. Father was asked by the old timers to stand as secretary but mother put a stop to that. Besides father and I did not have the same commitment as granda. Killer Kilpatrick took over as secretary and still does a good job. Rat Face and his friends have changed their attitude towards us. I believe they no longer see us as figures of authority. We are not friends but the old animosity has gone. The Wednesday league eventually collapsed. It was too much trouble and became too expensive. We never ever re-established our bloodstock or repeated our old successes. However occasionally we do have a winner. Thankfully, there were no more loft burnings and the club has regained a degree of the old charm. However, the old openness has gone. Now all the lofts have security systems installed and the club members still have a fear of being burned out. Only when it has happened to you, when you have seen a life's work go up in smoke can you know the feelings of sheer despair and helplessness that our family felt. I know how badly I felt when the loft was burned down. However, it is only now that I run the loft and have started my own bloodstock can I understand the feelings granda experienced.

We never saw Blanco again. Someone told us he had moved down South and was breeding racing pigeons but I don't know if that's true. I know I never looked for him and I never wanted to see him again. On the gardens, granda was never forgotten. I believe men who knew him still feel privileged to call him a friend. Often the old timers sit in the clubhouse and talk about Sammy, Blanco, Pincher and Huwey. The pigeon club now runs very professionally. The prize money is high and there are some magnificent racing pigeons competing. I suppose the changes that took place on the gardens were inevitable but I do wish that they hadn't been so dramatic. Of course, most importantly as time has passed I have never forgotten my granda, Sammy Baker, how could I?

Certificate Of Active Pigeon Service During The 1914-1918 War

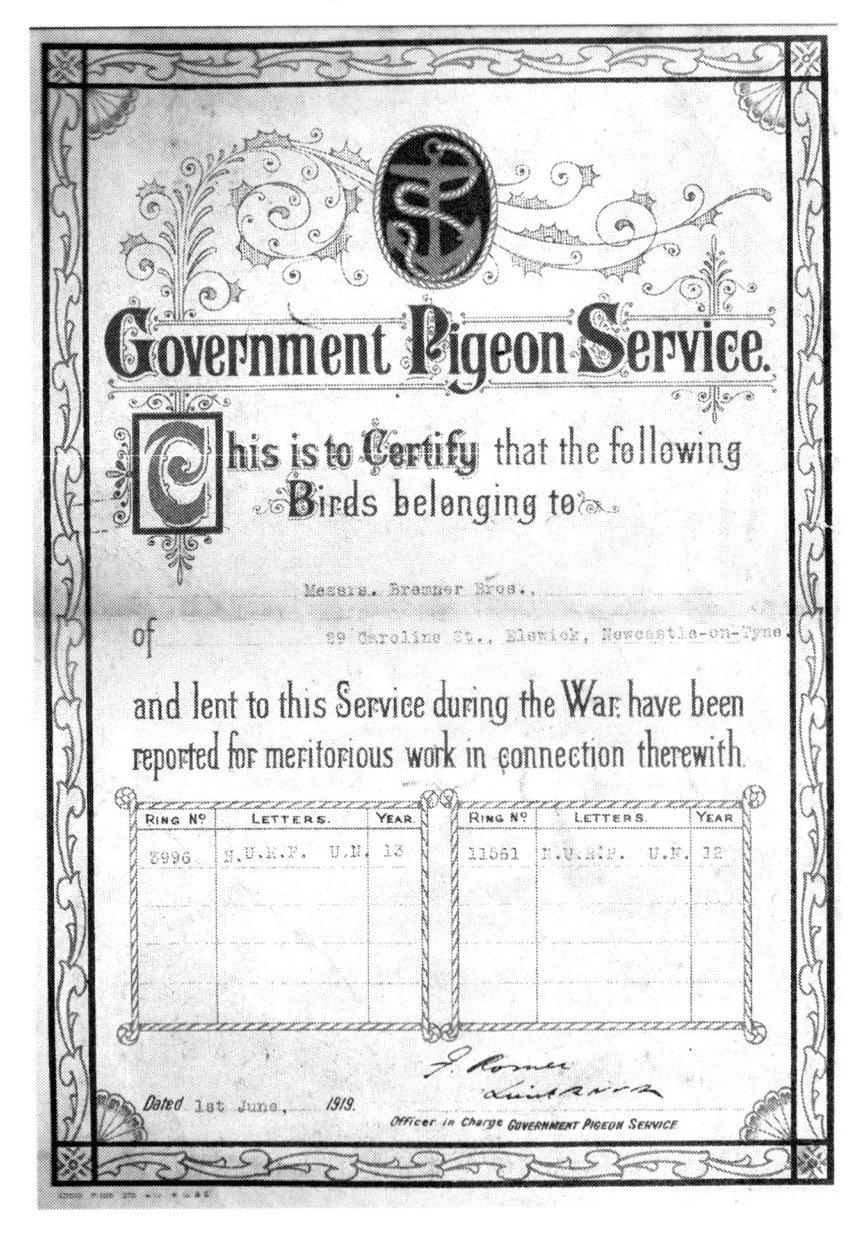

Government Pigeon Service.

This is to Certify that the following Birds belonging to

Messrs. Bremner Bros.,

of 29 Caroline St., Elswick, Newcastle-on-Tyne

and lent to this Service during the War have been reported for meritorious work in connection therewith.

Ring Nº	Letters.	Year	Ring Nº	Letters.	Year
3996	N.U.R.P. U.N.	13	11561	N.U.R.P. U.N.	12

Dated 1st June, 1919.

Officer in Charge GOVERNMENT PIGEON SERVICE